Listening to and Learning from Students

Possibilities for Teaching, Learning, and Curriculum

A volume in
Landscapes of Education
William H. Schubert and Ming Fang He, *Series Editors*

LANDSCAPES OF EDUCATION
William H. Schubert and Ming Fang He , *Series Editors*

_____

Love, Justice, and Education: John Dewey and the Utopians
  By William H. Schubert, University of Illinois at Chicago

*Listening to and Learning from Students: Possibilities for Teaching, Learning,
  and Curriculum*
  Edited by Brian D. Schultz, Northeastern Illinois University

Listening to and Learning from Students

Possibilities for Teaching, Learning, and Curriculum

Edited by

Brian D. Schultz
Northeastern Illinois University

INFORMATION AGE PUBLISHING, INC.
Charlotte, NC • www.infoagepub.com

Library of Congress Cataloging-in-Publication Data

Listening to and learning from students : possibilities for teaching,
learning, and curriculum / edited by Brian D. Schultz.
    p. cm. – (Landscapes of education)
 Includes bibliographical references.
  ISBN 978-1-61735-171-6 (pbk.) – ISBN 978-1-61735-172-3 (hardcover) –
ISBN 978-1-61735-173-0 (e-book)
1. Student-centered learning–United States. 2. Student participation in
curriculum planning–United States. 3. Communication in education–United
States. I. Schultz, Brian D.
 LB1027.23.L57 2010
 371.39–dc22
                                                                2010038055

For Jenn, Addison, and Keegan
And, for the young people who have taught and continue to teach me

CONTENTS

LANDSCAPES OF EDUCATION

William H. Schubert and Ming Fang He

In this book series, we explore panoramic landscapes of education. We invite a wide array of authors from diverse theoretical traditions and geographical locations around the world to ponder deeply and critically undulating and evolving contours of educational experience. We perceive contours of educational experience as landscapes that cultivate and are cultivated by who we were and how we become who we are as individuals and as humanity (Nussbaum, 1997). We engage with complex hills and rift valleys, rocky roads and serene pathways, war torn terrains and flowering gardens, towering trees and wuthering grasses, jagged cliffs and unyielding rocks, flowing rivers and uneven oceans evolving with flows of life that shape our perspectives, modify our ideas, and forge our actions. Building upon John Dewey's (1916) *democratic conception of education* and William Schubert's (2009) *ideals of love, justice, and education*, we perceive landscapes of education not only as schools but also as *gathering places* (Dewey, 1933) for humans to pursue worthwhile living. We honor the poetics of landscapes of education flourishing with divergence, convergence, diversity, and complexity of experience.

We look for authors who can move in new directions. We open dialogue on educational issues and situations of shared concerns. We create a space for educational workers such as public intellectuals, scholars, artists, and practitioners to engage in inquiries into education drawn from multiple

Listening to and Learning from Students, pages xi–xiv
Copyright © 2011 by Information Age Publishing
All rights of reproduction in any form reserved.

perspectives such as art, music, language, literature, philosophy, history, social sciences, and professional studies. We welcome cross-disciplinary, inter-disciplinary, trans-disciplinary, and counter-disciplinary work. We look for possibilities that are fresh and poetic, nuanced and novelistic, theoretical and practical, personal and political, imaginative and improvisational.

We expand parameters of educational inquiry substantively and methodologically. Substantively, books in this series explore multifarious landscapes wherever education occurs. Such explorations provocatively portray education in schools, workplaces, nonschool settings, and relationships. Methodologically, we encourage diverse forms of inquiry drawing on a wide array of research traditions, approaches, methods, and techniques such as ethnomethodology, phenomenology, hermeneutics, feminism, rhizomatics, deconstructionism, grounded theory, case studies, survey studies, interviews, participant observation, action research, teacher research, activist feminist inquiry, self study, life history, teacher lore, autobiography, biography, memoir, documentary studies, art-based inquiry, ethnography/critical ethnography, autoethnography, participatory inquiry, narrative inquiry, fiction, cross-cultural and multicultural narrative inquiry, psychoanalysis, queer inquiry, and personal~passionate~participatory inquiry.

We also feature works that amplify the educational value of mass media such as movies, DVDs, television, the Internet, comics, news comedy, cell phones, My Space and Face Book, videos, videogames, computers, and the World Wide Web. We hope to explore how we learn through such electronic frontiers in vastly new ways with little tutelage. We hope to encourage creative improvising, problem posing, critical inquiring, and joyful learning illuminated in these new ways of learning though electronic frontiers which are often suppressed and repressed in schooling. We hope to acknowledge the power of human beings to learn without lesson plans, manuals, worksheets, standardized tests, acquisitive rewards, or external standards.

We encourage expansions that move beyond Western orthodoxies to embrace landscapes from the Eastern (Asian), Southern (African and Latin American), and Oceanic (islandic) worlds. We especially want to see renditions move into *third spaces* (Gutiérrez, Rymes, & Larson, 1995) and *in-between* (He, 2003, 2010) that push boundaries, shift borders, dissolve barriers, and thrive upon contradictions of life. It is our intention that the works featured in this series reveal more of the world-wide landscapes of cultures, ideas, and practices that transgress dominant Western ideologies and their corporate and colonizing legacies. These works have potential in developing transcendent theories of decolonization (e.g. Tuhiwai Smith, 2001), advocating the liberty of indigenous language, cultural rights, and intellectualism (e.g. Grande, 2004), shattering *monocultures of the mind* (Shiva, 1993), overcoming perils of globalization, and inventing a better human condition for all.

We also highlight activist and social justice oriented research (e.g., Ayers, Quinn, & Stovall, 2009) and personal~passionate~participatory inquiry (e.g., He & Phillion, 2008) that engage participation of all citizens, encourage respect, innovation, interaction, cohesion, justice, and peace, and promote cultural, linguistic, intellectual, and ecological diversity and complexity. We celebrate postcolonial feminist work (e.g., Minh-ha, 1989; Mohanty, 2003/2005; Narayan, 1997) that explores migration, slavery, suppression, resistance, representation, difference, race, gender, place and responses to influential discourses of racism, sexism, classism, and colonialism. We also feature ecofeminist inquiry that explores the intersectionality of repatriarchal historical analysis, spirituality, racism, classism, imperialism, heterosexism, ageism, ableism, anthropocentrism, speciesism, and other forms of oppression (Mies & Shiva, 1993).

Books in this series focus on the what, why, how, when, where, and for whom of relationships, interactions, and transactions that transform human beings to different levels of awareness to build communities and public spaces with shared interests and common goals to strive for equitable, just, and invigorating human conditions. We seek explorations of the educational aspects of relationships (e.g., family, friendship), international, transnational, or intercultural understanding (e.g., exile, diaspora, displacement, indigenous knowledge), and circumstances of living (e.g., poverty, racism, alienation, war, colonization, oppression, and globalization). We want to see how languages, literacies, communities, homes, and families shape images of life's *mysteries and events* (Ulich, 1955), such as love, tradition, birth, death, success or failure, hopes of salvation, or immortality. These educational dimensions of life dynamically influence and are influenced by life in and out of schools (Schubert, 2010) and in-between (He, 2003, 2010). Through engaging in such pursuits, this book series illuminates how human beings improvise lives (Bateson, 1989) and commitments in diverse, complicated, and often contested landscapes of education.

Unlike more definitively crafted book series that explicate inclusions and exclusions with ease and precision, our invitations continuously expand. The depths and breadths of landscapes where we live surpass everyday gaze and complicate static analysis. We showcase books that bring a sense of wonder and surprise, make the strange familiar and the familiar strange, and evoke what we do not expect. We do not narrow or define the topics of this series. Rather, we open doors to new perspectives, diverse paradigms, and creative possibilities. We invite authors to surprise us with their insightful ideas of what has been, what is, and what might be. For this volume, Brian Schultz has surprised us with an inspiring compilation of explorations on what students can teach us about education.

REFERENCES

Ayers, W., Quinn, T., & Stovall, D. (Eds.) (2009). *Handbook of social justice in education.* New York: Routledge.

Bateson, M. C. (1989). *Composing a life.* New York: The Atlantic Monthly Press.

Dewey, J. (1916). *Democracy and education.* New York: Macmillan.

Dewey, J. (1933). Dewey outlines utopian schools. *New York Times*, April 23, p 7. Also in Boydston, J. A. (Ed.), *The later works (1925–1953) of John Dewey,* Volume 9, (pp. 136-140) Carbondale, IL: Southern Illinois University Press, 1989.

Grande, S. (2004). *Red pedagogy: Native American social and political thought.* New York: Rowman & Littlefield.

Gutiérrez, K. D., Rymes, B., & Larson, J. (1995). Script, counterscript, and underlife in the classroom: James Brown versus Brown v. Board of Education. *Harvard Educational Review,* 65(3), 445–471.

He, M. F. (2003). *A river forever flowing: Cross-cultural lives and identities in the multicultural landscape.* Greenwich, CT: Information Age Publishers.

He, M. F. (2010). Exile pedagogy: Teaching in-between. In J. A. Sandlin, B. D. Schultz, & J. Burdick (Eds.), *Handbook of public pedagogy* (pp. 469–482). New York: Routledge.

He, M. F. & Phillion, J. (2008). *Personal~passionate~participatory inquiry into social justice in education.* Charlotte, NC: Information Age Publishing.

Mies, M., & Shiva, S. (1993). *Ecofeminism.* Halifax, Nova Scotia, Canada: Fernwood.

Minh-Ha, T. T. (1989). *Woman, native, other: Writing postcoloniality and feminism* (Midland Books). Bloomington, IN: Indiana University Press.

Mohanty, C. T. (2003/2005). *Feminism without borders: Decolonizing theory, practicing solidarity.* Durham, NC: Duke University Press.

Narayan, U. (1997). *Dislocating cultures: Identities, traditions, and third world feminism.* New York: Routledge.

Nussbaum, M. (1997). *Cultivating humanity: A classical defense of reform in liberal education.* Cambridge, MA: Harvard University Press.

Schubert, W. H. (2009). *Love, justice, and education: John Dewey and the Utopians.* Charlotte, NC: Information Age Publishing.

Schubert, W. H. (2010). Outside curriculum. In C. Kridel (Ed.), *Encyclopedia of curriculum studies* (pp. 624-628). Thousand Oaks, CA: Sage.

Shiva, V. (1993). *Monocultures of the mind: Perspectives on biodiversity and biotechnology.* Atlantic Highlands, NJ: Zed Books.

Tuhiwai Smith, L. (2001). *Decolonizing methodologies: Research and indigenous peoples.* London: Zed Books.

Ulich, R. (1955). Response to Ralph Harper's essay. In N. B. Henry. (Ed.), *Modern philosophies of education,* Fifty-fourth Yearbook (Part I) of the National Society for the Study of Education (pp. 254–257). Chicago: University of Chicago Press.

ACKNOWLEDGEMENTS AND PREFACE

As with any book, there are many people to thank for making words and ideas come to life and appear in print. But, as the old adage goes, to list is to exclude, so this is my best attempt to acknowledge those people who have been especially important in making this project a reality.

Many of the chapters of this edited collection began as a special double issue of *The Sophist's Bane*, a peer-reviewed journal of the Society of Professors of Education that I guest edited. The issue focused on ideas related to youth perspectives on teaching and teacher education, and each author gave me great hope about what education, learning, and curriculum can and ought to be. Thank you: Paris Banks, Tara Brown, Jake Burdick, Cathy Coulter, Shira Eve Epstein, Kevin Galeas, Genell Lewis-Ferrell, Jennifer Ponder, Louie Rodríguez, Michelle Vander Veldt, and Susan Wilcox. I am grateful to the Society of Professors of Education for the opportunity to guest edit the journal, specifically Bob Morris, Bill Wraga, and Peter Hlebowitsh. Further, *The Sophist's Bane* editorial board, outside blind peer-reviewers, and invited reviewers provided tremendous insight on the journal articles that became chapters in this collection. I am greatly appreciative of their comprehensive and developmental feedback. Additionally, I want to thank Voices of Youth in Chicago Education (VOYCE) and Bill Schubert for their provocative contributions. All of these authors' views focus on the hopefulness and the potential of young people; several pieces are even co-written by those very young people they are learning from. Each piece provides me with something to continually strive for in my own teaching and learning.

Also, particular thanks to Rene Antrop-Gonzalez, Bill Ayers, Tom Barone, Raul Botello, Evert Cuesta, Maureen Gillette, Maxine Greene, Dalia Hoffman, Sherick Hughes, Jason Irizarry, Matt Kirsch, Herb Kohl, Pamela Konkol, Jason Lukasik, Pedro Noguera, Erin Mason, Terry Mason, Rachel Oppenheim, Bree Picower, Jenny Sandlin, Mary Lee Smith, Emma Tai, and Cynthia Wheeler for the various support, ideas, critical feedback, virtual introductions, endorsements, and suggestions about this project. Sarah Frank Reichard's excellent copyediting skills have been both helpful and insightful. My wife Jenn's quintessential ability to listen and her willingness to be a sounding board have been paramount in helping make this collection happen. Our two wonderful children, Addison and Keegan, constantly challenge me to find ways to learn from young people and provide great inspiration.

* * *

This book began to emerge after the recent journal issue garnered an enthusiastic response about the prospects of learning from, with, and alongside students. Ming Fang He and Bill Schubert's initial interest in the project for their series, *Landscapes of Education*, was exceptionally encouraging in the early stages. As the book began to take shape and I sought after and deliberated about additional chapters, Ming Fang and Bill's sage advice provided great perspective. Their support, encouragement, as well as friendship made this endeavor particularly worthwhile. Further, Bill's guidance and mentoring is simply amazing, and I sincerely appreciate his willingness to include his piece from *Education and Culture* within this collection.

The prospect of creating a book-length collection of current scholarship that considers in depth how students might approach teaching, learning, and curriculum prompted me to reflect on the theorists who have weighed heavily on my own teaching practices, scholarly endeavors, and inclinations. I felt compelled to reproduce for the reader some of the chapters, articles, and excerpts by critical thinkers that have profoundly affected my own inquiry. The work of Charlie Cobb, John Dewey, Paulo Freire, Tom Hopkins, Caroline Pratt, and Ralph Tyler are provided space in this collection alongside their more contemporary counterparts. In choosing their essays/excerpts, I wanted to find a balance between pieces that some might find readily familiar with texts that are perhaps more obscure but no less important. My intention here is not only to highlight the theorizing of these great thinkers, but also to illuminate the authors' clarifications of misinterpreted ideas, reinforcement of previous statements, and re-articulations of their more widely known work.

While I believe it is imperative to look to such notable figures for curriculum studies' historical precedent and to consider past theorizing as a basis for current interpretations, I believe it is equally important to focus on a new and inspiring generation of artists/activists/authors who contribute novel ideas through public pedagogy and spoken word poetry. In addition to the historical essays included within, there are also poems and stories that should cause us to reflect on how we view both students and ourselves as educators. The provocative prose and in-your-face confrontations of teachers and students kahlil almustafa, Rafael Casal, Kevin Coval, Miracle Graham, and Thomas Lloyd should challenge us all to take notice.

The contemporary scholarship, historical excerpts, and spoken word poetry provide an intertwined tapestry, a weaving of different writings that illustrate, in vastly different ways, what it means to listen and to learn from students in our teaching and curricular practices. As examples, each interlude highlights, echoes, or exemplifies the ideas inherent within the chapters where scholars are working with students to make education and learning more profound and promising. My hope is that the ideas presented, within the weaved fabric of then and now, will encourage you to resist taken-for-granted assumptions, to rethink "commonsense" practices, and to transform worn-out ideas about what it means to reach and respond to your students.

—BDS

FOREWORD

Listen and Learn

Democracy hinges on a precious and yet precarious ideal, the profoundly radical notion that every human being is of incalculable value, that each is unique and distinct and still part of a wildly diverse whole, and that altogether we are each and every one somehow essential in the universe of democracy. In a functional, robust democracy the principles of associative living—community, equality, and liberty—are embraced and brought to life in the public square through practice and participation, and they are sustained through a culture of respect, dialogue, and mutual recognition.

An adequate education for democracy would begin with an acknowledgement of this democratic ideal, and would necessarily nourish and ignite that singular spirit and that common culture. We would, with our students, learn to ask many kinds of essential questions again and again, and then find ways to live within and beyond the answers we receive: What's your story? Who are you in the world? How did you (and I) get this far? What do we know now? What do we have the right to imagine and expect? Where are we going? Who decides? Who's left out? What are the alternatives? Why? In many ways these kinds of questions are themselves the answers, for they lead us into a powerful sense that we can and will make a difference.

In *Listening to and Learning from Students,* Brian Schultz has gathered together a range of classics and contemporaries, a diversity of theorists and practitioners, young and old, of many backgrounds and colors and circumstances in order to ask those questions anew, and at the same time to open

Listening to and Learning from Students, pages xix–xxi
Copyright © 2011 by Information Age Publishing
All rights of reproduction in any form reserved.

up a unique space to re-imagine and re-populate the principles of democracy and education today.

The challenging intellectual work of teaching pivots on our ability to see students as three-dimensional creatures—human beings much like ourselves—with hopes and dreams, aspirations, skills, and capacities; with minds and hearts and spirits; with embodied experiences, histories, and stories to tell of a past and a possible future; with families, neighborhoods, cultural surrounds, and language communities all interacting, dynamic, and entangled. This knotty, complicated challenge requires patience, curiosity, wonder, awe, and more than a small dose of humility. It demands sustained focus, intelligent judgment, inquiry, and investigation. It requires an open heart and an inquiring mind since every judgment is contingent, every view partial, and each conclusion tentative. The student is dynamic, alive, and in motion; nothing is settled, once and for all. No perspective can ever be big enough, no summary ever entirely authoritative. The student grows and changes—yesterday's urgent need is suddenly accomplished and quickly forgotten, today's claims are all-encompassing and brand new. This, then, is an intellectual task of massive proportion.

The challenge involves, as well, an ethical stance and an implied moral contract. The good teacher offers unblinking attention and communicates a deep regard for students' lives, a respect for both their integrity and their vulnerability. An engaged teacher begins with a belief that each student is unique, each the one and only who will ever trod the earth, each worthy of a certain reverence. Regard extends, importantly, to an insistence that students have access to the tools with which to negotiate and perhaps even to transform the world. Love for students just as they are—without any drive or advance toward a future—is false love, enervating and disabling. The teacher must try, in good faith, to do no harm, and then to convince students to reach out, to reinvent, and to seize an education fit for the fullest lives they might hope for.

Another part of the intellectual work of teachers, then, is to see ourselves as in transition, in motion, works in progress. We become students of our students, in part to understand them, in part to know ourselves. A powerful reason to teach has always been to learn ourselves, and no one captures this more beautifully than Paulo Freire (1970/2000):

> Through dialogue the teacher-of-the-students and the students-of-the-teacher cease to exist and a new term emerges: teacher–student and students–teachers. The teacher is no longer merely the-one-who-teaches, but one who is himself taught in dialogue with the students, who in turn while being taught also teach. They become jointly responsible for a process in which all grow. (pp. 79–80)

With eyes wide open and riveted on learners, a further challenge is to stay wide awake to the world, to the concentric circles of context in which we and our students live and work. Teachers must know and care about some aspect of our shared life—our calling, after all, is to shepherd and enable the callings of others. Teachers, then, invite students to become somehow more capable, more thoughtful and powerful in their choices, more engaged in a culture and a civilization, able to participate, to embrace, and, yes, to change all that is before them. How do we warrant that invitation? How do we understand this society and our culture?

Teachers choose—they choose how to see the students before them, how, as well, to see the world, what to embrace and what to reject, whether to support or resist this or that directive. In schools where the insistent illusion that everything has already been settled is heavily promoted, teachers and students alike experience a constricted sense of choice, diminished imaginative space, a feeling of powerlessness regarding the larger purposes of education.

Teaching is harder than learning in one respect: It requires the teacher to listen, to observe, to see, and to *let learn*. The hard work of teaching involves probing, seeking, asking the right questions, creating a context for dialogue, staying engaged with the needs and desires of learners. A teacher who really listens and sees, someone who strives to authentically know her students, can herself learn the world anew.

In *Listening to and Learning from Students,* everyone is clamoring for the mic. Listen to teachers as they listen to students, invite student stories, analyze those stories for common themes and human meaning, and make a plan to act. The discourse communities that the students come from have the wisdom, the talent, and the analytical power to reshape the world. Teachers might find ways to move their classrooms from being sites of invalidation to centers of community organizing.

—William C. Ayers
Chicago, IL

REFERENCE

Freire. P. (2000). *Pedagogy of the oppressed* (30th Anniversary Ed.). New York: Continuum. (Original work published in 1970)

CHAPTER 1

CURRICULAR POSSIBILITIES

Listening to, Hearing, and Learning from Students

Brian D. Schultz
Northeastern Illinois University

Many professors of education waited with bated breath, anticipating how the Obama administration would shape educational policy. Questions abounded about how vague campaign rhetoric regarding change would translate into federal decision making that would affect local schools and their students. In the president's first speech regarding education in March of 2009, he forcefully addressed reform plans, goals, and expectations (Obama, 2009). Among the multitude of lofty ideals and challenges to the American people, President Obama specifically addressed achievement gaps and the need for sensible and dynamic transformation:

> And year after year, a stubborn gap persists between how well white students are doing compared to their African American and Latino classmates. The relative decline of American education is untenable for our economy, unsustainable for our democracy, and unacceptable for our children—and we cannot afford to let it continue. . . . Of course, we have heard all this year after

Listening to and Learning from Students, pages 1–7
Copyright © 2011 by Information Age Publishing
All rights of reproduction in any form reserved.

year after year—and far too little has changed. Not because we are lacking sound ideas or sensible plans—in pockets of excellence across this country, we are seeing what children from all walks of life can and will achieve when we do a good job of preparing them. Rather, it is because politics and ideology have too often trumped our progress.

What kind of progress President Obama and his education team have in mind remains to be seen. Whereas I am hopeful that politics and ideology are pushed aside to create a better education for all as the *No Child Left Behind Act* gets overhauled, reconfigured, and revamped (Dillon, 2010), there persists a troubling mantra that touts the need to raise standards, blame teachers, and hold everyone more accountable for learning outcomes, especially students:

> Of course, no matter how innovative our schools or how effective our teachers, America cannot succeed unless our students take responsibility for their own education. That means showing up for school on time, paying attention in class, seeking out extra tutoring if it's needed, and staying out of trouble. And to any student who's watching, I say this: don't even think about dropping out of school. As I said a couple of weeks ago, dropping out is quitting on yourself, it's quitting on your country, and it is not an option—not anymore. (Obama, 2009)

I fear he may be succumbing to a neoliberal public pedagogy that looks at students from a deficit perspective, as primarily responsible for the situation in which they find themselves. Moreover, this speech and subsequent federal reform movement towards a competitive "Race to the Top" mentality for vital resources (U.S. Department of Education, 2009) blissfully disregards one key way to improve our educational system: valuing the knowledge and ideas our students bring to classrooms.

In the waning moments of the initial speech—what many have said was the most robust articulation on education by a president in decades—President Obama referenced a video in which a group of high school students in California highlighted their concerns about how the economic downturn would affect their lives. In connecting his grandiose educational policy discussion to ordinary citizens, President Obama (2009) proclaimed his attention to students in a compelling and anecdotal way:

> It was heartbreaking that a girl so full of promise was so full of worry that she and her class titled their video, "Is anybody listening?" And so, today, there's something I want to say to Yvonne and her class at Village Academy. I am listening. We are listening. America is listening.

That President Obama indicated that he, we, the people in the United States are (or ought to be) listening to the students is laudable. I am hesitant to believe, however, that this sort of surface-level listening yields the perspectives on teaching and teacher education that can so powerfully galvanize our thinking about school reform. Perhaps, surface-level listening is a starting point. But, I want to challenge President Obama and the "reformers" to think about possibilities for our schools when we not only listen to, but also hear, and learn from our students. Perhaps this can be a beginning to what Mike Rose (2009) calls "in search of a fresh language of schooling" where the American educational system can be a reclaimed space that "inspires" and realizes a vision of "personal dreams" and "democratic aspiration" (p. 25).

*   *   *

Over the years, I have had opportunities to engage with undergraduate and graduate students as they work in small groups to conceptualize, deliberate, and design schools reflective of theories from the progressive era. Throughout semesters, my pre-service and in-service students examine texts highlighting historical, philosophical, cultural, and socio-political tenets related to progressive education. They learn about multiple interpretations of progressive education, particularly varying perspectives related to progressivism as social efficiency and as developmental democracy. In turn, these pre-service and in-service educators are challenged to design contemporary and invigorating schools based on their understanding of theoretical constructs, which emerge as particularly aligned to their views of what a Deweyan democratic school might entail.[1]

As these educators explicitly ground their school designs within progressive theories, they are further challenged with the freedom to develop learning environments that disrupt their common assumptions and imaginations alike. They are eager and passionate as they contemplate how their schools could be experiential, rather than adhering to rote memorization, reflective of society while working to solve social problems, and focus on school structure and curricula related to student interests and needs (Dewey, 1931, 1938; Tozer, Senese, & Violas, 2006).

In efforts to reconcile their own "way out of educational confusion" (Dewey, 1931), I have noticed that the discussions of these cooperative groups are similar in evolution to efforts I have observed over the semesters when my students are engaged with this line of inquiry. Depending on individual experiences and perspectives about the purpose of education and the role of school in society, students often bring an array of views about what should and should not be incorporated into schools. As they focus on specific details about school designs, they debate particular elements and intricacies such as location, scheduling, interdependence on subject matter, and even what it means to be well educated in schools. Initially, when provided with the intellectual space, the opportunity, and the challenge of taking on the responsibility for designing a school, my students tend to surrender to familiar ideas, often related to norms about American schooling. This can be attributed to the years of "on the job training" in their own classrooms as students, where the dominant paradigm is traditional education. But as the weeks progress, my students deliberate more heatedly in class; room for interpretation becomes an integral part of the inquiry. As the discussions gain focus and each group contemplates how to present its ideas to the rest of classes, individuals begin to exert perspectives on how the school ought to be organized. At the same time, groups begin not only to push boundaries about schooling as we know it, but their comfort level also increases as they imagine possibilities, especially in terms of curricular method, design, and deliberation. With unshackled creativity, their conceptions about what could and should be incorporated in ideal schools comes alive. They have created profound, nurturing, student-centered, and provocative places for learning that would provide wondrous opportunities for all.

Interestingly, amidst all of this creativity, their thoughts hit a barrier when deliberating about who would make the "big decisions" in their newly designed schools. Often they look to practices common to school decision makers. Almost consistently, my undergraduate and graduate students name the same governing powers for their schools: administrators, teachers, state boards of education, government bureaucracies, and sometimes, communities and corporations. Inevitably missing from most of their discussions and designs is the notion that students should be able to share authority in powerful ideas related to the structure, function, and delivery of teaching and learning that goes on in their schools. Whereas I am always enamored by the imaginative out-of-the-box thinking of my students and continually get new ideas from intense debates, I am deeply troubled that they usually fail to look to the youth in their schools as potential decision makers. My concern is that pre-service and in-service teachers have become so conditioned by commonplace ways of looking at students. As a result, they miss potentially transforming ways to make schools not only progressive in their approaches but also into places that motivate and engage students and teachers. Even when provoked about such a stance while they are deliberating, seldom do my students theorize about empowering their students in their fictitious classrooms to have such authority.

Although arguments for the involvement of youth and youth perspectives in teaching and learning conclude that such voices are essential for improving school and increasing the participation of its young people (Brown, Wilcox, Schultz, Rodríguez, et al., 2008; Nicholls & Thorkildsen, 1995; see also Section III of Thiessen & Cook-Sather, 2007), as is the case with pre-service and in-service teachers in my classroom, this pedagogical stance is atypical in contemporary school settings. Even with the recent popularity of revolutionizing education through passionate, social justice-oriented, and participatory action research (e.g., Ayers, Hunt, & Quinn, 1998; Cammarota & Fine, 2008; He & Phillion, 2008), current educational policies governed by top-down mandates and prescriptive education make student participation in curriculum development and school decision making a seldom-practiced phenomenon. Students have little control over how they learn or what they learn. They are excluded from discussions of what is worthwhile in and for teaching and learning. Students' insight into and perspectives of the content of classrooms as well as their approaches to teaching and learning seems to be widely disregarded in most schools.

This lack of attention mirrors how students are perceived in many classrooms as mere vessels for deposits of knowledge. The structures associated with schools perpetuate this disconnect, and often, as a result, push children—most notably those from large urban areas—further away from schools. With the belief that students are nothing more than deficits or pathologies, and the inclination that most students do not value their learning, schooling often reinforces cultural reproduction while augmenting stereotypes of urban youth.

Challenging these beliefs are some educators along with their younger counterparts who see the possibility of students having both a stake in and insight into their learning. Such teachers and students show a tremendous will not only to think about but also to act on the challenges and (inequitable) expectations faced in schools. Their stance challenges commonly held assumptions about youth, particularly urban youth, while also leveraging students' insights to teach teachers. A great deal of potential lies in looking to kids *as* teacher educators for insight about what it takes to motivate and engage them. In seeing the power in such ideas, I have been actively working with former elementary students to develop (as well as trouble, complicate, and problematize) line(s) of inquiry related to this profound notion beyond what appears within this book (e.g., Easter & Schultz, 2008; Schultz & Banks, 2009a; Schultz & Banks, 2009b; Schultz et al., 2009). Perhaps this body of scholarship with students, along with other pieces in this volume, can help change the trope of how students are seen, heard, perceived, and valued in and out of school (Schubert, 2010).

What follows in this edited collection is a profound aggregate of related chapters and interludes that advance President Obama's rhetoric of listening toward a radical perspective of hearing and learning from students about what inspires learning. Combining historical excerpts and essays alongside contemporary theory and provocative poetry, the book showcases the kind of unique research, analysis, and insight that ought to be part of the broader educational policy discussions in the United States. Indeed, the potential of listening to, hearing, and learning from students is a powerful idea that scholars and activists featured in this book have come to understand and articulate cogently, and act upon and practice passionately. I sincerely hope that such possibilities for teaching, learning, and curriculum could be embraced as we work with our students to reach the highest potential (Siddle-Walker, 1996) in their lives.

NOTE

1. Special thanks to my colleague and friend Pamela Konkol for the original inspiration and design of this learning activity.

REFERENCES

Ayers, W., Hunt, J. A., & Quinn, T. (Eds.). (1998). *Teaching for social justice: A democracy and education reader*. New York: Teachers College Press.

Brown, T. M., Wilcox, S., Schultz, B. D., & Rodríguez, L. F., et al. (2008). *Youth perspectives on teachers and teaching*. Interactive Symposium conducted at the American Educational Research Association Conference, New York.

Cammarota, J., & Fine, M. (Eds.). (2008). *Revolutionizing education: Youth participatory action research in motion*. New York: Routledge.

Dewey, J. (1931). *The way out of educational confusion*. Cambridge, MA: Harvard University Press.

Dewey, J. (1938). *Experience and education*. New York: Macmillian.

Dillon, S. (2010, March 14). Obama calls for major change in education law. *New York Times*, A1.

Easter, T., & Schultz, B. D. (2008). There are all sorts of possibilities—and take notes. *Journal of Curriculum and Pedagogy 5*(1), 70–74. (Names appear alphabetically; first authorship is shared).

He, M. F., & Phillion, J. (Eds.). (2008). *Personal-passionate-participatory inquiry into social justice in education*. Charlotte, NC: Information Age Publishing.

Nicholls J. G., & Thorkildsen, T. A. (Eds.). (1995). *Reasons for learning: Expanding the conversation on student-teacher collaboration*. New York: Teachers College Press.

Obama, B. (2009, March 10). *Remarks by the President to the Hispanic Chamber of Commerce on a complete and competitive American education*. Washington Marriott Metro Center: Washington, DC. Retrieved March 13, 2009, from http://www.whitehouse.gov/the_press_office/Remarks-of-the-President-to-the-Hispanic-Chamber-of-Commerce

Rose, M. (2009). *Why school? Reclaiming education for all of us*. New York: The New Press.

Schubert, W. H. (2010). Outside curricula and public pedagogy. In J. A. Sandlin, B. D. Schultz, & J. Burdick (Eds.), *Handbook of public pedagogy: Education and learning beyond schooling* (pp. 10–19). New York: Routledge.

Schultz, B. D., & Banks, P. (2009a). A shorty teaching teachers: One kid's perspective about "keepin' it real" in the classroom. *The Sophist's Bane, 5*(1/2), 19–24.

Schultz, B. D., & Banks, P. (2009b). Co-optation, ethical dilemmas, and collective memory in collaborative inquiry: A writing-story. In W. S. Gershon, *The collaborative turn: Working together in qualitative research* (pp. 35–54). Rotterdam, The Netherlands: Sense.

Schultz, B. D., Banks, P., Brewer, L., Davis, S., Easter, T., Pruitt, K., & Thomas, R. (2009). Kids as teacher educators: Looking, listening, and learning from students. In J. Burdick, J. A. Sandlin, & T. Daspit (Eds.), *Complicated conversations and confirmed commitments: Revitalizing education for democracy* (pp. 195–207). Troy, NY: Educator's International Press.

Siddle-Walker, E. V. (1996). *Their highest potential: An African-American school community in the segregated South.* Chapel Hill: University of North Carolina Press.

Thiessen, D., & Cook-Sather, A. (Eds.). (2007). *International handbook of student experience in elementary and secondary school.* London: Springer.

Tozer, S. E., Senese, G., & Violas, P. C. (2006). *School and society: Historical and contemporary perspectives (5th ed.).* Boston: McGraw Hill.

U.S. Department of Education Press Release. (2009, July 24). President Obama, U.S. Secretary of Education Duncan announce national competition to advance school reform: Obama administration starts $4.35 billion "Race to the Top" competition, pledges a total of $10 billion for reforms. Retrieved on December 14, 2009 from http://www2.ed.gov/news/pressreleases/2009/07/07242009.html

CHAPTER 2

INTERLUDE

FROM *PEDAGOGY OF THE OPPRESSED*

Paulo Freire

Unfortunately, those who espouse the cause of liberation are themselves surrounded and influenced by the climate which generates the banking concept, and often do not perceive its true significance or its dehumanizing power. Paradoxically, then, they utilize this same instrument of alienation in what they consider an effort to liberate. Indeed, some "revolutionaries" brand as "innocents," "dreamers," or even "reactionaries" those who would challenge this educational practice. But one does not liberate people by alienating them. Authentic liberation—the process of humanization—is not another deposit to be made in men. Liberation is a praxis: the action and reflection of men and women upon their world in order to transform it. Those truly committed to the cause of liberation can accept neither the mechanistic concept of consciousness as an empty vessel to be filled, nor the use of banking methods of domination (propaganda, slogans—deposits) in the name of liberation.

Listening to and Learning from Students, pages 9–11
Copyright © 2011 by Information Age Publishing
All rights of reproduction in any form reserved.

Those truly committed to liberation must reject the banking concept in its entirety, adopting instead a concept of women and men as conscious beings, and consciousness as consciousness intent upon the world. They must abandon the educational goal of deposit-making and replace it with the posing of the problems of human beings in their relations with the world. "Problem-posing" education, responding to the essence of consciousness—intentionality—rejects communiques and embodies communication. It epitomizes the special characteristic of consciousness: being conscious of not only as intent on objects but as turned in upon itself in a Jasperian "split"—consciousness as consciousness of consciousness.

Liberating education consists in acts of cognition, not transferrals of information. It is a learning situation in which the cognizable object (far from being the end of the cognitive act) intermediates the cognitive actors—teacher on the one hand and students on the other. Accordingly the practice of problem-posing education entails at the outset that the teacher–student contradiction be resolved. Dialogical relations—indispensable to the capacity of cognitive actors to cooperate in perceiving the same cognizable object—are otherwise impossible.

Indeed, problem-posing education, which breaks with the vertical patterns characteristic of banking education, can fulfill its function as the practice of freedom only if it can overcome the above contradiction. Through dialogue, the teacher-of-the-students and the students-of-the-teacher cease to exist and a new term emerges: teacher–student with students–teachers. The teacher is no longer merely the-one-who-teaches, but one who is himself taught in dialogue with the students, who in turn while being taught also teach. They become jointly responsible for a process in which all grow. In this process, arguments based on "authority" are no longer valid; in order to function, authority must be on the side of freedom, not against it. Here, no one teaches another, nor is anyone self-taught. People teach each other, mediated by the world, by the cognizable objects which in banking education are "owned" by the teacher.

The banking concept (with its tendency to dichotomize everything) distinguishes two stages in the action of the educator. During the first he cognizes a cognizable object while he prepares his lessons in his study or his laboratory; during the second, he expounds to his students about that object. The students are not called upon to know, but to memorize the contents narrated by the teacher. Nor do the students practice any act of cognition, since the object towards which that act should be directed is the property of the teacher rather than a medium evoking the critical reflection of both teacher and students. Hence in the name of the "preservation of culture and knowledge" we have a system which achieves neither true knowledge nor true culture.

The problem-posing method does not dichotomize the activity of the teacher-student: she is not "cognitive" at one point and "narrative" at another. She is always "cognitive," whether preparing a project or engaging in dialogue with the students. He does not regard cognizable objects as his private property but as the object of reflection by himself and the students. In this way the problem-posing educator constantly re-forms his reflections in the reflection of the students. The students—no longer docile listeners—are now critical co-investigators in dialogue with the teacher. The teacher presents the material to the students for their consideration, and re-considers her earlier considerations as the students express their own. The role of the problem-posing educator is to create, together with the students, the conditions under which knowledge at the level of the doxa is superseded by true knowledge, at the level of the logos.

Whereas banking education anesthetizes and inhibits creative power, problem-posing education involves a constant unveiling of reality. The former attempts to maintain the submersion of consciousness; the latter strives for the emergence of consciousness and critical intervention in reality.

Students, as they are increasingly posed with problems relating to themselves in the world and with the world, will feel increasingly challenged and obliged to respond to that challenge. Because they apprehend the challenge as interrelated to other problems within a total context, not as a theoretical question, the resulting comprehension tends to be increasingly critical and thus constantly less alienated. Their response to the challenge evokes new challenges, followed by new understandings; and gradually the students come to regard themselves as committed.

Education as the practice of freedom—as opposed to education as the practice of domination—denies that man is abstract, isolated, independent, and unattached to the world; it also denies that the world exists as a reality apart from people. Authentic reflection considers neither abstract man nor the world without people, but pea-pie in their relations with the world. In these relations consciousness and world are simultaneous: consciousness neither precedes the world nor follows it.

CHAPTER 3

CONFRONTING "LIMIT SITUATIONS" IN A YOUTH/ADULT EDUCATIONAL RESEARCH COLLABORATIVE

Tara M. Brown
Brandeis University

Kevin Galeas
Project ARISE Youth Researcher

INTRODUCTION: YOUTH IN SCHOOLING AND RESEARCH

The involvement of youth has been essential to academic educational research since university scholars arose as authorities on K–12 education in the early 20th century (Tyack, 1974). However, youth participation largely has been characterized by a lack of control over inquiry processes and outcomes. Adults (e.g., parents and teachers) have also experienced a relative lack of power in university-based research. However, the silencing and objectification of youth has been particularly severe for reasons linked to hierarchical power relations in schools and society and embedded cultural beliefs about children and adolescents.

Listening to and Learning from Students, pages 13–26
Copyright © 2011 by Information Age Publishing
All rights of reproduction in any form reserved.

Buckingham (2000) points out that young people are "defined in terms of their [assumed] lack of rationality, social understanding or self-control" (p. 14) and "denied the right to self-determination" (p. 13). This reflects widely shared cultural perceptions that youth cannot discern their own needs and how they should be addressed and that (responsible) adults must act on their behalf. These perceptions are often deeply manifest in schools serving poor, Latino/a and Black, "low-achieving" children, especially those identified as having learning, emotional and/or behavioral disabilities. In these school settings, young people's activities are often highly regimented, regulated, and configured in ways over which they have little control. Given assumptions about their intellectual inadequacies, it is not surprising that they are afforded little or no power over the terms of or investigations into their schooling conditions. This also reflects a longstanding belief, within the academy, "that naming the world [and people's experiences within it] is the task of an elite" (Freire, 1970, p. 90), based on a false dichotomization of the revered "expert" knowledge of academic researchers and the devalued "experiential" knowledge of local people (Gaventa, 1993). This, in combination with diminished perceptions about young people's intellectual capacity creates a "double jeopardy" that is intensified for educationally and socio-politically marginalized youth who have been unduly scrutinized, problematized, and disempowered in academic research processes (Cammarota & Fine, 2008).

University-based, educational research directly impacts the daily lives of youth through its influence on school policy and practice. Denying them control over this research violates a basic democratic obligation to afford people "the opportunity to speak [their] mind, be heard and counted by others, and...to have an influence on outcomes" (Cook-Sather, 2006, p. 363) in matters related to their lives. This is not, however, merely a matter of ethics. Young people hold valuable insights into schooling, from which university researchers are largely distanced (by virtue of age, race/ethnicity, class, everyday experience, etc.). Further, youth have tremendous capacity to discern, analyze, and respond to the challenges they face, as demonstrated in the *Opportunity Gap Research Project* (Fine et al., 2005) in which youth researchers were able to "identify cracks in the opportunity structure...and to develop their own intellectual and organizing capacities" for addressing educational inequities (p. 523). Thus, we delimit young people's role in educational research at the expense of the quality and applicability of scholarly knowledge and the interventions they inform.

In speaking about social transformation, Freire (1970) asks, "Who are better prepared than the oppressed to understand the terrible significance of an oppressive society? [and] Who can better understand the necessity of liberation?" (p. 44). This speaks to the significance of investment in change. Noguera (2003) points out that in public education, failures to significantly ameliorate educational inequities reflect a lack of "will and conviction [among those in control] to make it happen" (p. 157). Many researchers and policy makers build successful careers investigating and responding to inequitable schooling conditions and outcomes that do not directly and negatively impact their everyday lives and opportunities for success. However, educationally marginalized youth suffer directly from these inequities. They have the most to gain from their transformation and, therefore, are particularly promising agents of change. Thus, we ask: Who better to help us understand and address the ways in which schooling has not worked than those for whom school has not worked?

However, although educationally marginalized youth are profoundly negatively impacted by schooling inequities, their conscious investment in change—in understanding and action—requires a process of (re)education through which they must confront, critically analyze, and overcome "the situations which limit them" (Freire, 1970, p. 99). Therefore, in addition to methodological considerations, scholarly research projects on educational equity and justice that engage marginalized youth in meaningful ways must also be pedagogical processes dedicated to their intellectual, social, and political growth and development.

In this chapter, we examine such a project—a participatory action research (PAR) project involving high school students and university researchers that investigated educational issues. Throughout the implementation of the research we encountered "limit situations" (Freire, 1970, p. 104) that posed significant challenges. Following, we describe the project and examine three limit situations facing the youth researchers—(1) being labeled as deficient by schools and society, (2) assimilating to subordination within a hierarchy of power relations, and (3) having insufficient academic preparation—that the research team had to confront so that it could successfully carry out the work and meet the goals of the project. We conduct this examination using poems composed by the youth researcher and second author, Kevin Galeas (KG), drawn from his personal experience and project data, and connecting them conceptually and by example to the implementation of the project through the more conventional academic writing of the principle investigator (Tara).

THE ARISE STUDY

Theoretical Context

The study described in this chapter, Action Research into School Exclusion (ARISE), was a two-year participatory action research (PAR) project. PAR is a methodological approach in which those directly affected by the issue under investigation actively engage in all stages of the research. PAR has the explicit goal of "action" or intervening into the problem under investigation in a meaningful way. PAR draws on the work of critical theorists like Antonio Gramsci and Paulo Freire, who posit that controlling knowledge is a primary means through which dominant groups exercise their power over subjugated groups (Córdova, 2004; Gaventa, 1993). PAR projects customarily focus on aspects of social inequality and are designed to assist oppressed peoples in better understanding and transforming the conditions of oppression.

PAR is grounded in the assumption that effective understandings of and interventions into social problems require the knowledge of those affected by those problems—local informants—and that an essential component of validity is that the ways in which problems are conceptualized, investigated, and represented be authentic to local informants. This reflects the epistemological orientation of PAR work, which holds that local people are experts in their own experiences.

Study Setting and Participants

The setting of the study, from which the ARISE youth researchers were drawn, was an independent, urban, alternative special education school. All students were court-appointed to the school through social services or the juvenile justice system and were identified as having a physical, behavioral, emotional, and/or learning disability. All were Black or Latina/o and many had been expelled from area public schools. Over the course of the study, twelve 11th and 12th graders participated as researchers—four boys and four girls were African American, three girls and one boy were Latina/o. A core group of nine participated consistently. The research team included Tara Brown and two doctoral graduate assistants (GAs). Consistent with PAR methodology, the study was driven by the concerns and interests of the youth researchers who collaborated in study design, data collection and analysis, and the use and representation of study findings. To train and support the young people in the work of the project, the adult researchers taught a for-credit *Research and Action Seminar* twice a week at the school.

Project Description and Methodology

The goals of ARISE were (1) to better understand the schooling experiences of adolescents excluded from mainstream public schools, (2) to build on the strengths and address the challenges of students at risk for exclusion, and (3) to develop an action plan to improve the schooling experiences of excluded students. The research team conducted interviews with students and teachers at the school. Interviews were videotaped, transcribed, and analyzed. We also analyzed local and national statistics related to school disciplinary policies and procedures. As action, the team designed and conducted four workshops for pre-service teachers at a local, major research university and presented our research at three national research conferences. At these events, work products like PowerPoint presentations, artwork, reflective writings, videos, and other multimedia projects, which the team created to represent study findings, were used for presentational and educational purposes, and represented additional data points for this study.

CONFRONTING "LIMIT SITUATIONS"

Deficiency Labels: Un-Truth in Advertising

As previously noted, all of the youth researchers were labeled as having a learning, emotional, and/or behavioral "disability" or "disorder." These labels and the assumptions they engender were both salient and extremely painful for many of the youth researchers and participants. For example, Tanisha, a student participant who was interviewed for the study, said, "I understand that they [teachers] feel that we're special needs students and that we're not gonna amount to much, that we're not gonna learn much in life. . . ." As with Tanisha, there was a prevailing belief among the youth researchers that labels like "special education," "behavioral problem," and "learning disabled" signaled to others that they were deficient in some way. Being removed from the general school population fortified this belief. KG captures the challenges and doubts that accompany being labeled as deficient, particularly with regards to one's ability to learn.

Purpose

A connection rang
It followed me as it sang
Telling me what I am
flowed out like a water dam
People knowing what I have become
Still ponder if I'm the special one
What are my needs
Education is ready to be feed
Wanting it so much
Just my luck
strikes to punch
I ask do you really care
this is what I have finally shared

—KG

KG describes how a person's way of being gets connected to schooling. Specifically, if how one learns does not match expectations in school, it can result in official declarations or deficiency labels that follow a young person throughout his or her formal education. As KG infers, these labels are socially constructed and ascribed by others. While some see special education identification as a process of *finding out what's wrong with a person*, KG characterizes it as a process of *making what's with a person wrong* in a public way. This is evident in how he characterizes "learning disabled" not as something he is, but as something "I have become" through a process over which he had no control.

The youth researchers resisted the labels ascribed to them, sometimes in ways that challenged the work and goals of the project. For example, in our first university workshop I suggested that we invite interviewees to attend the presentation. The youth researchers agreed with one caveat—most did not want to invite Tanisha because they felt she resembled the stereotypic image of a special education student. She wore glasses, had one eye that strayed outward, and as one researcher stated, "says some crazy stuff." The prospect of being seen as the same "kind" of person as Tanisha was distressing, causing another researcher to say, very sadly, "I never thought I'd be in a school with someone like her." Of course, excluding Tanisha went against our core principles, which were anti-exclusionary and strove to honor everyone's contributions and ways of being. I was adamant that we invite all or none of the interviewees. The research team opted to invite none, much to my disappointment. However, this incident, which occurred early in the project, helped us to build vital understandings about each other and about working as a team.

When I, as the adult and seminar instructor, made the case for Tanisha, the youth researcher most opposed assumed a foregone conclusion. He grew despondent, saying, "Go ahead, bring her. I don't care." The deliberations that ensued, which eventually led to the consensual decision not to invite any of the interviewees, demonstrated to the youth researchers that I meant to seriously consider their perspectives and was committed to collaborative decision making. This incident impressed upon me, as one never ascribed a deficiency label, the incredible depth of personal pain and stigma these labels cause and their potential for raising doubts about one's own capacities and self-worth.

KG addresses this, "still ponder[ing] if I'm the special one." The youth were clear about what being labeled "special" in the school context meant to others, but were in a constant process of figuring out what it meant to them, particularly as learners. As low-income, Black and Latina/o, special and alternative education students, schooling had too often "come[s] with a punch." That is, schools and the processes of schooling exacerbated their troubles through low expectations and menial curriculum, lack of adult caring, gendered and racialized stereotypes, and administrative disorganization (Brown, 2007; Dance, 2002; Ferguson, 2000; Grant, 1994; Lopez, 2003; Nieto, 1999; Noguera, 2008; Oakes, 1985; Valenzuela, 1999). The youth researchers struggled to reconcile the messages from such prior schooling experiences with what they knew about their own promise.

The youth researchers accomplished many things (e.g., conducting academic research, designing and implementing teacher trainings, and presenting at conferences) that exploded perceptions about the intellectual capacity of students labeled as deficient. One way that I encouraged them to think about and use the deficiency labels ascribed to them was as evidence of their lack of "truth in advertising," which was a major finding of the study. This required that they publicly acknowledge the labels, which proved to be painfully difficult. Before each workshop and presentation, the youth deliberated over whether to take the personal risk of acknowledging their ascribed labels in order to make the vital point about the true intellectual potential of youth labeled as deficient. That this had to be continually renegotiated shows their profound desire to begin with a clean slate and to just be "normal." Each time, they arrived at a consensus to acknowledge the labels, which speaks to their dedication to confronting and overcoming this limit situation in service of project goals.

Reconstituting Power

Virtually all public schools have a clear power hierarchy in which students are the least powerful constituency. In schools serving relatively large numbers of "at risk" youth, particularly those with academic or disciplinary troubles, the press to control students is often intensified and the power structure can be especially rigid (Akom, 2001; Fine, 1991; Haberman, 1994; Noguera, 2003). Facing highly structured and controlled curriculum and harsh and inflexible disciplinary policies, many of these young people grow accustomed to capitulating to the power of school adults even when it is not used in their best interest.

In the following poem, KG describes how school adults' power over youth can be both destructive and replete.

Truth with a Stare

People don't care
Damage your life that you can't even spare
You keep going but things aren't fair
The reality that you can't bare
Take the time to listen to be aware
Why do these people even dare?

Why can't people be there?
Split the life of student until it tears
Let them breathe, give them air
Life damages until you declare
People are ready to share
But life seems so cold with a stare
Things just come with a blare—[Loud harsh noise]
Life comes with a harsh glare
Truth comes with a scare

—KG

"Truth with a Stare" conveys the sense of powerlessness among some youth to protect lives that they "can't even spare" from the devastation of uncaring school adults. In the poem, KG questions their motives and beseeches them to understand their impact on students and to change their behaviors. For him, the power of school adults to "split the life of student until it tears," juxtaposed to his lack of power as a student, has been a difficult reality to lay bare.

Because there are few institutionally sanctioned ways that students can effectively challenge school practices, resistance often takes punishable forms like disruption, disrespect, and insubordination (Brown & Rodriguez, 2008; Fine, 1991). All of the ARISE youth researchers had engaged in punishable resistance in school which, for most, was the primary reason for their exclusion from mainstream public schools. Yet, they remained invested in traditional school roles in which control is taken by adults and relinquished by youth. This posed challenges to creating a genuinely collaborative research process and proved to be a "limit situation" that the research team had to confront, as reflected in the following two examples.

Over the first semester of the project, the team lost four youth researchers (two dropped out, one left school, and one was incarcerated), and I wanted to replace them. I posed this to the remaining five, and four rejected the idea. I asked them to give it more consideration, promising to revisit the conversation the following week. At the next discussion I decided not to risk disturbing the group dynamic and cohesion by adding new members. However, I soon changed my mind again after further thought about my own needs as a tenure-track assistant professor and the heavy workload of the project. I raised the issue again and some of the young people were clearly exasperated. One said, "First you say we're not adding people [to the research team] and then we are. Just make a decision!"

In the second instance, the research team was reviewing a draft of a questionnaire we were designing. I asked the youth researchers for feedback on a particular question to ensure it was worded in a way that would evoke an honest response. One researcher hastily offered a suggestion, which I asked him to repeat, so I could write it down. He repeated the question in an exasperated tone saying, "It's simple. *You're* supposed to be the doctor!" Rather than helping me with the questionnaire, the youth researchers spent next five minutes trying to convince me why I should not have needed their help.

In both instances, the young people pressed me to be the "expert" decision maker who directed their actions. They were likely comfortable with this arrangement, which is prevalent in high-poverty urban schools like those they had attended (Haberman, 1994; Lipman, 2004) and is easier than grappling with difficult decisions. It was clear to me that some of the youth researchers had never been expected to exercise control over the terms of their learning or to collaborate with adults in the ways I expected. They were clearly uneasy with my indecisiveness, my admitted lack of expertise, and my reliance on their knowledge. This was likely also connected to one of the study findings: students' confidence in teachers rests, in part, on their ability to "control the classroom," as one interviewee said.

Assimilation to the traditional teacher/student power hierarchy—by the young people and by myself and the GAs, as former classroom teachers— was a limit situation that we all had to confront and overcome in order to achieve genuine collaboration and shared decision making, which are key components of PAR. This required a continual process of conscious resocialization that, through the regularization of things like consensus building, collaborative teaching and learning, and leadership development, became easier for us all over time.

Academic Preparation: Meet Where I Am and Take Me Where I Need to Go

Most of the youth researchers had attended high-minority, high-poverty, urban public schools for most of their lives. As research shows, these schools are often fraught with troubles that stunt students' academic development. Inadequate funding, low expectations, lack of teacher training and menial curriculum are among the longstanding problems (Ferguson, 2000; Grant, 1994; Oakes, 1985; Rist, 1973; Skiba, Knesting, & Bush, 2002; Valenzuela, 1999). This was evident in the academic skill levels of the ARISE youth researchers. For example, KG, who was the class valedictorian, was required to take remedial classes at the community college to which he was provisionally accepted. This reflects the relatively shoddy academic preparation that many young people receive in urban public schools.

Students struggling academically are often denied and perceived as incapable of mastering rigorous curriculum and challenging ideas. Project ARISE explicitly worked against common assumptions about students with histories of school failure and disengagement. Thus, there was no academic prerequisite for youth researchers. However, I realized early on that many of the research tasks would be extremely challenging for most youth researchers. Due to time constraints, not every youth researcher was thoroughly trained in every aspect of research. However, the GAs and I used strategies to assist in the development of academic skills and to ensure that everyone could participate in all phases of the research.

For example, conceptually situating our research required critically analyzing scholarly texts. As some of the youth researchers read at an elementary school level, we had to find strategies to make these texts accessible. We took turns reading texts out loud, paragraph by paragraph, and each young person highlighted unfamiliar words on their copy. We ascertained the meanings of individual words and sentences. Then we re-read the paragraph and identified the main idea(s). This was a very time-consuming process, but deconstructing texts in this way helped the young people to build vocabulary and comprehension skills. We also used many non-textual resources like related documentaries and radio segments (many from National Public Radio).

The youth researchers were also challenged by traditional methods of data analysis. One way we addressed this was by conducting a workshop on calculating percentages, which was vital to understanding existing data on disciplinary exclusion. Coding interview transcripts also proved difficult, particularly for those with underdeveloped reading skills. As all interviews were videotaped, we addressed this by adding a video analysis component. All researchers reviewed the footage of each interview, making note of key words and phrases and non-verbal cues. As a group, we discussed and compared our notes and identified significant patterns and themes using deductive and inductive approaches to make sense of the data.

Each research task or some aspect of it was adapted and/or scaffolded to meet the youth researchers where they were—academically and intellectually—and to push them, with adequate support, beyond their preexisting abilities. In these ways, we were able to make all stages of the research process accessible and provide means for all researchers to contribute in a meaningful way. This enhanced the validity and rigor of the study, which could not be compromised. Following, KG writes about how Project ARISE and participation in it was experienced, particularly by the youth researchers.

Rose up, No illusion

How a project came with a high level
Students & teachers listen as we trembled
Poetry Meet ARISE
ARISE brought nothing but time
Helped us open our minds about our self
Thinking how we can help
Knowledge, background, and strength came from within

Leader spoke out with no pretend
Action Research Into School Exclusion
This team delivered the final conclusion
There is no confusion
ARISE was not a delusion

—KG

Here, KG writes about the rigor of the study and how the youth summoned their background knowledge and experience and inner strength to meet the challenge. In doing so, they became outspoken leaders and activists in the educational community, teaching and informing university and K–12 faculty and administrators through workshops and conferences.

Their successes also reflect the project goal to capitalize on their interests and strengths, which included music, art, videotaping, editing, and various forms of writing. One example of this is the present chapter, which in its writing, took us through a challenging process. As a component of PAR (the use and representation of findings), it was imperative that KG contribute to this paper in a meaningful way. However, he is not yet able to write at the academic level expected for a scholarly publication. I provided multiple writing prompts and we engaged in collaborative editing that, most often, compromised the authenticity of KG's original texts. Ironically, it was months before I truly understood the aforementioned project goal. Capturing human experience through poetry is one of KG's strengths that we incorporated throughout the project, as reflected in the line, "Poetry Meet ARISE." It was not until KG and I decided to unite the forms of writing that we each do well that this paper came together.

The project tasks were very often at levels of intellectual and academic rigor at which deficiency-labeled and excluded low-income Black and Latina/o adolescents are expected to fail. For most of the youth researchers, their lack of academic preparation posed a limit situation over which they were able to prevail in many ways, with the support of the research team. As KG writes, how he now perceives his ability to take on challenging work like that of the project, and how he developed personally and academically through that work "was not a delusion." That is, these are not false beliefs held in spite of the contradictory evidence, namely, the vestiges of inadequate schools and common assumptions about young people like him. About that, he writes, "there is no confusion."

CONCLUSION

At the outset of this chapter, we made the strong case for university researchers to engage young people in social science research focused on issues that affect their everyday lives, and we have found PAR to be an extremely effective methodology through which to do this. Using this methodology can enhance the quality and validity of research and scholarly knowledge and the interventions they inform, and it can help young people to develop competencies they will need to "build political structures that can challenge the status quo" (Giroux, 2001, p. 203). This is particularly vital for marginalized youth who have the most to lose if the current structures are not transformed.

As we have shown, despite diminished perceptions about the intellectual capacities of youth, specifically low-income, Black and Latina/o, excluded, and deficiency-labeled youth, they are quite capable of rigorous intellectual work regardless of their existing academic skills and school histories. However, having experienced the social and intellectual traumas associated with urban public schools, many of these young people are likely to be initially unprepared for the rigors of academic research. This speaks to the general issue of preparing local informants—particularly, educationally, economically, and sociopolitically marginalized youth and adults—to conduct scholarly research and generate knowledge that they can actually use to work against the ways in which they have been pathologized and disenfranchised.

We found that in truly collaborative research any limit situation facing an individual researcher became a limit situation facing the research team that had to be confronted collectively in order to accomplish the tasks and goals of the project. With few existing resources, we dealt with our limit situations largely through trial and error. In justice-oriented, participatory action research, we would like to see the dissemination of more information on the theoretical and methodological preparation and development of local researchers. This would contribute significantly to the capacity of university-based researchers to plan and implement and increase the rigor and validity of PAR—a methodology that we see as vital in (re)constructing academic research as an instrument for real and realized social transformation and justice.

REFERENCES

Akom, A. A. (2001). Racial profiling at school: The politics of race and discipline at Berkeley High. In R. J. Skiba, & G. G. Noam (Eds.), *Zero tolerance: Can suspension and expulsion keep schools safe?* (pp. 51–63). San Francisco: Jossey-Bass.

Brown, T. M. (2007). Lost and turned out: Academic, social and emotional experiences of students excluded from school. *Urban Education, 42*(5), 432–455.

Brown, T. M, & Rodríguez, L.F. (2008). School and the co-construction of dropout. *International Journal of Qualitative Studies in Education, 21*(1), 1–21.

Buckingham, D. (2000). *After the death of childhood: Growing up in the age of electronic media.* Malden, MA: Blackwell Publishing.

Cammarota, J., & Fine, M. (Eds.). (2008). *Revolutionizing education: Youth participatory action research.* New York: Routledge.

Cook-Sather, A. (2006). Sound, presence, and power: "Student voice" in educational research and reform. *Curriculum Inquiry, 36*(4), 359–390.

Córdova, T. (2004). Plugging the brain drain: Bringing our education back home. In J. Mora & D. R. Diaz (Eds.), *Latino social policy: A participatory research model* (pp. 25–53). New York: The Haworth Press.

Dance, L. J. (2002). *Tough fronts: The impact of street culture on schooling.* New York: RoutledgeFalmer.

Ferguson, A. A. (2000). *Bad boys: Public schools in the making of black masculinity.* Ann Arbor: The University of Michigan Press.

Fine, M. (1991). *Framing dropouts: Notes on the politics of an urban public high school.* Albany: State University of New York Press.

Fine, M., Bloom, J., Burns, A., Chajet, L., Guishard, M., Payne, Y., Perkins-Munn, T., & Torre, M. (2005). Dear Zora: A letter to Zora Neale Hurston 15 years after Brown. *Teachers College Record, 107*(3), 496–528.

Freire, P. (1970). *Pedagogy of the oppressed.* New York: Seabury.

Gaventa, J. (1993). The powerful, the powerless, and the experts: Knowledge struggles in an information age. In P. Park, M. Brydon-Miller, B. Hall, & T. Jackson (Eds.), *Voices of change* (pp. 21–40). Westport, CT: Greenwood Publishing.

Giroux, H. A. (2001). *Theory and resistance in education: Towards a pedagogy for the opposition.* Westport, CT: Bergin & Garvey.

Grant, C. A. (1994). Urban teachers: Their new colleagues and curriculum. In J. Kretovics & E. J. Nussell (Eds.), *Transforming urban education* (pp. 315–326). Boston: Allyn and Bacon.

Haberman, M. (1994). The pedagogy of poverty versus good teaching. In J. Kretovics & E. J. Nussell (Eds.), *Transforming urban education* (pp. 305–314). Boston: Allyn and Bacon.

Lipman, P. (2004). *High stakes education: Inequality, globalization, and urban school reform.* New York: RoutledgeFalmer.

Lopez, N. (2003). *Hopeful girls, troubled boys: Race and gender disparity in urban education.* New York: Routledge.

Nieto, S. (1999). *The light in their eyes: Creating multicultural learning communities.* New York: Teachers College Press.

Noguera, P. (2003). *City schools and the American dream: Reclaiming the promise of public education.* New York: Teachers College Press.

Noguera, P. (2008). *The trouble with black boys and other reflections on race, equity, and the future of public education.* San Francisco: Jossey-Bass.

Oakes, J. (1985). *Keeping track: How schools structure inequality.* New Haven, CT: Yale University Press.

Rist, R. C. (1973). *The urban school: A factory for failure: A study of education in American society.* Cambridge, MA: MIT Press.

Skiba, R. J., Knesting, K., & Bush, L. D. (2002). Culturally competent assessment: More than nonbiased tests. *Journal of Child and Family Studies, 11*(1), 61–78.

Tyack, D. B. (1974). *The one best system: A history of American urban education.* Cambridge, MA: Harvard University Press.

Valenzuela, A. (1999). *Subtractive schooling: U.S.–Mexican youth and the politics of caring.* Albany: State University of New York Press.

CHAPTER 4

INTERLUDE

---

from the mouths of babes

for Dawn Walker

Kevin Coval
Louder Than A Bomb

---

it's a deep guilt thing white folks suffer—
afraid . . . we will do to you and your fathers
what you and your people have done to us

—Minister Farrakan on Phil Donahue

at the end of a long day i like to go home and kill white people / on paper
it's one of my favorite aspects of writing /one of the things hip-hop taught me
actual rage enacted metaphorically

i tell students

at a school straddling the northern border of Chicago
who get the kind of integration Brown v. Board of Education
prophesied 50 years ago / the kind where white kids take AP classes
latinos take ESL classes and black boys are BD to the bone

Listening to and Learning from Students, pages 27–28
Copyright © 2011 by Information Age Publishing

their 5th senile substitute this week can't get them to read
Robert Frost / cuz they way too cool
an aging hippy turned teacher raises the question
do you mean all white people because my family is irish-catholic
and when we arrived here were considered the nig...
blaaaaaaaaaaaaaacks of america and...

and i want to fill the blanks with every kike dago polack such&such
and ask this mick on the verge of tears about all the batons in Bridgeport
wielded her countrymen's hands

before i do a hand from the back row
attached to a young woman in a fuzzy pink jogging suit
skin like heavily creamed coffee says

i'm haitian
but when cops pull me over
all they see is
                                black

CHAPTER 5

LEARNING TO WALK QUIETLY

Cathy Coulter
University of Alaska Anchorage

The sentence starter was: "The first week of school my teacher taught me. . . . " In the blank, the child had written, "how to walk quietly."

VICKI: KINDERGARTEN

The little girl hovers at the door of the small room. Ms. Stryk looks up from the clipboard she has in her hand. "Vicki Mendez? Finally! You're late." She looks back down at the clipboard, tapping her pen against it as she reads. Vicki peeks around the doorframe but stays where she is. Ms. Stryk looks up again and forces a breath out. "What are you waiting for?" She pats the chair next to her. "Sit down." Vicki sidles in. She has to push up against both arms and turn to sit, and her legs don't quite touch the floor. Large brown eyes peek around a curtain of brown hair as she quickly looks around the room and then down at her hands in her lap.

Ms. Stryk puts a paper in front of her. "I'm going to read you some instructions and I want you to follow them as I read. Understand?" Vicki looks up at her and back down at her hands. She focuses on the *esclava* around her wrist. The gold chain is as familiar to her as her own arm. It has been on

Listening to and Learning from Students, pages 29–38

her wrist since she was days old, a gift from her grandmother. What isn't as familiar is the dark brown of her skin, the tan that deepened all summer as she played with her cousins in the Mexican sun. The warmth changed her very skin. She imagines this room is making her lighter by the minute. Cold takes many forms. The teacher seems angry. Vicki wishes she could understand what *la maestra* wants. The *esclava* isn't the only piece of home she has with her: Vicki has been taught to respect her elders. No matter what. Not so easy when you don't understand a word they're saying.

Ms. Stryk exhales through her mouth in an irritated breath, taps the paper in front of Vicki, and slaps a sharpened pencil down on top of it. Vicki looks up at Ms. Stryk and reaches for the pencil. She looks at the paper in front of her. There is a picture of a little green man with antennae sticking up out of his head. He is standing next to a farm.

"Okay. Ready?" Vicki looks at Ms. Stryk, pencil in hand. Ms. Stryk reads from the instructions: "An alien has landed on Earth and is visiting a farm. Draw a line to show which farm animals the alien visited. First, he visited the cows. Point to the cows."

Vicki looks at her, pencil still in hand. What is she saying? What does she want?

"Point to the cows!" Ms. Stryk says again.

Vicki looks at her, pencil still in hand. Her small hand tightens a bit around the pencil, but otherwise doesn't move. She's supposed to write something, but what?

Ms. Stryk's lips tighten into a hard line. "The cows! Start with the cows!" she says, thumping the picture of the cows with her finger. Vicki moves her pencil to the cows and points. "Yes, yes! Start with the cows!" Ms. Stryk reaches for Vicki's hand. Vicki flinches away, but doesn't protest as Ms. Stryk puts her hand over Vicki's and moves her hand for her, forcing her to draw a mark next to the cows. Even Ms. Stryk's large, white hand feels cold.

"Okay. Now, listen again to the instructions: 'Draw a line to show which farm animals the alien visited. First he visited the cows. Next, he went to the pigs. Then, he went to see the hens. . . .'" She looks down at Vicki, who is looking down at her hands, which are once again folded in her lap. The pencil lay on the paper. "Why aren't you listening? Vicki, draw a line from the cows to where he went next. Where did he go next?" She grabs the pencil and holds it out to Vicki again. Vicki takes the pencil again. She looks at the paper and back at Ms. Stryk, unsure. Ms. Stryk takes Vicki's small hand in hers again and draws a line from the cows to the pigs. "Like that, Vicki. Do you get it?" Vicki looks at Ms. Stryk then back at the paper. Her words don't make sense, and Vicki can't figure out what she wants her to do. She takes a wild guess. Her hand tightens around the pencil and she draws a line from the pigs to the sheep.

"No, no! I haven't read you the instructions yet!" Ms. Stryk says. She yanks the pencil from Vicki's hand and, pushing down hard on the eraser, fusses away the line. She brushes the eraser bits away with angry movements. "Listen first!" she says. She hands Vicki the pencil again. Vicki doesn't look at Ms. Stryk, but takes the pencil in her hand. The teacher is angry with her, but she doesn't understand what she wants. Tears begin to well up in her eyes and her legs start moving back and forth in small movements. "Stop crying! Now listen: 'Then, he went to see the hens.' Okay? So draw a line to the hens. Hold still!" She places her hand on the girl's legs to stop them from moving. Vicki freezes. Two tears drop down on her lap.

"Draw a line to the hens!" Ms. Stryk repeats, slamming the pencil down on the paper again. Vicki reaches for the pencil in a stiff motion. She gets a grip on the pencil and draws a line from the cows to the sheep.

Ms. Stryk grabs the pencil from Vicki again. "No, no no!" She erases the mark. "From the pigs to the hens, Vicki! The alien went from the cows to the pigs to the hens!" Vicki doesn't reach for the pencil again. She keeps her blurred gaze on her *esclava* as the tears move quietly down her cheeks.

VICKI: THIRD GRADE

Ms. Cripe's class is standing against the wall, waiting in line to use the restroom when Mrs. Lawton's class walks by. Mrs. Lawton was Vicki's second grade teacher. Vicki sees her coming and bends down to tie her shoes. This conversation is as predictable as the bell schedule.

"How's it going with her?" Mrs. Lawton says.

"Oh, you know. The usual." Ms. Cripe thinks she's disguising her words. Like they aren't bouncing off the decorated bulletin boards and spilling into the open ears of Vicki's classmates.

Mrs. Lawton chuckles. "Yeah, well, good luck trying to get her parents to come to any parent–teacher conferences."

"Even if they did, they wouldn't understand a word." They both laugh as Mrs. Lawton leads her class away.

Vicki stands and smiles at her classmates as though she hasn't heard a thing.

VICKI: SOPHOMORE YEAR

Mr. Hatfield, my Earth Science teacher, shouldn't have been allowed to teach at all. One day in class, we are all doing the usual end-of-the-chapter questions. I'm bored out of my mind. I look around the room at all the other high school droids. Their books are open and they are writing in their spiral notebooks, same as me. Well, all except the front row of football players, who are chatting with Mr. Hatfield. They'll copy the homework from their girlfriends later.

I'm doing the end-of-the-chapter questions just like everyone else, but there's something different about them. I know it already, but I can't quite put my finger on it. I'm going through the motions, just like them. But I'm only doing it to honor my father's dream: for me to graduate from Northwest High School. I know already that it won't happen. I just know it. I'm just biding time, pretending. Their answers will get them that golden diploma. Mine won't.

I finish the first question, skip a line, and write a number two on my paper. I read number two. "Describe a cirque glacier. What does the presence of a cirque glacier indicate about the mountain range of which it is a part?" I'm turning the pages of my book back to the part about cirque glaciers when Mr. Hatfield interrupts.

"Class, listen up!" he says. We all look up toward him. "I have a point to prove," he continues. "The gentlemen up front and I have been discussing things of a biological nature. Darryl Shabazz, come up here." Darryl looks up at Mr. Hatfield. He hesitates, then stands and walks toward the front of the room.

"Class, observe," he says. He leans down toward Darryl's leg. Darryl backs away.

"Wait a minute, Darryl. It's okay." Mr. Hatfield says. He leans down again and pulls up the leg of Darryl's jeans. "Observe the physique of the African American male." I look at Darryl's calf. His muscle stands out. He is clearly very strong. "And that, my friends, is why Black men are better athletes than White men. The physique of the African-American male is stronger and more defined. Case closed," he says to the boys at the front of the room.

The boys laugh. Darryl goes back to his seat.

Mr. Hatfield is still chatting away at the boys in front. I look at Darryl again. His head is on his arms. From the front of the room it must look like he is doing his homework. But I see his face. His mouth is set, and his eyes are focused on the desk, not his textbook.

Mr. Hatfield sits in his teacher's chair with his legs propped up on the desk. There's a speck of spit in the corner of his mouth.

I look around the room at my droid classmates. Does everyone think this is okay? I look back at my homework, but I can no longer focus on it. Who cares about cirque glaciers, anyway?

VICKI: SENIOR YEAR, FIRST SEMESTER

Mr. Hatfield, of all people, gets an administrative internship at Northwest my senior year. He is exactly the right choice to carry on the Northwest High tradition of catch-and-release. Certain kinds of fish at this school are simply not acceptable.

His first week as an intern he makes a point of calling me to his office.

"So, Vicki. Do you have any idea how many truancies you have?" he asks. He pulls his radio from his belt clip and puts it directly on the desk in front of him. I can imagine him taking it home with him after his first day as an intern and playing with it. There is a stack of files on the side of his desk. He pulls one out and opens it. I see my name written neatly on the label. The top page inside the file is a spreadsheet, and notes are written in each square. I recognize his handwriting from the assignments he used to list on the board in science, "Read chapter 8. Do questions 1–35 on page 134." That was the extent of his teaching. It seems he takes more of an interest in this job.

"Hello to you, Mr. Sunshine," I say, and sit in an empty chair in front of his desk. I pick up a framed picture of him standing next to a smiling brunette with sunglasses. They're leaning on ski poles, wearing matching red REI jackets. "Funny . . . I took you as a blond guy."

He shuts the file in his hand. The noise doesn't seem to gratify him, so he slams it down on the desk and snatches the photo from me. "This is serious business, Vicki."

"Lighten up, Sunshine. So....just how many felonies do I have?"

"According to my records, you have nine tardies. Three tardies equal one truancy, you know."

"Whoa. That's gotta be like, twenty to life, right?"

Mr. Hatfield puts the photo back on his desk, and squints at me for a moment, which is all his attention span can hold.

"When you work at McDonald's, do you think they'll tolerate you being late to work every day? Two minutes, twenty minutes, no difference. A tardy is a tardy, and three tardies is a truancy. Four truancies and you're out."

He looks at me with his brand-new principal stare. I imagine he practices it at home in the mirror. I look at him for a moment. His eyebrows are bushy, and there are a few hairs growing on the bridge of his nose. I want to tell him he ought to pluck a few. There are a few key hairs growing out of his nostrils, too. I look down because those hairs bother me. More, he seems flat, unreal. He is the villain in a play that is simply too predictable. He'll find a way to kick me out. It is inevitable. I'm the protagonist, but I don't deserve to be. I'm neither hero nor victim. Just the lead, the chosen actor. So we play out this scene as the script instructs, he with zeal, and me with casual indifference. In the end, though, he'll put away my file and go on to the next.

But I won't make it easy for him.

Mr. Hatfield stands and holsters his radio. "Probably just doing you a favor. Why waste your time? You're dismissed, McDonalds."

I exit stage left.

VICKI: SENIOR YEAR, 2ND SEMESTER

It's a cold day at Northwest High School. I'm in second period. Pottery class. When the office aide comes into the room with the white slip, I know it's for me.

Ms. Traspy is sitting at her desk, grading our last quiz. Even when she looks down, I can see her rouge, smeared in a straight pink line across her face. Her fluffy hair moves together, big curls in orchestrated movements. I can imagine her pulling out each curler carefully, then spraying for about 20 seconds so it'll all stay in place.

When the office aide comes in with the white slip, Ms. Traspy looks up at the door, and then back at me.

"Good morning, Amber," she says to the aide.

"Hi, Ms. Traspy," Amber says. She hands Ms. Traspy the white slip. Amber looks at me while Ms. Traspy makes a show of looking at the white slip. She takes too long pretending to read my name at the top of the slip.

"Vicki," she says, like it's some great surprise or something.

It's like everyone else knows it, too. Everyone looks at me while I stand up and walk toward Ms. Traspy, toward the white slip and my future. My chair scrapes loudly on the floor, and I drop my pencil.

I leave it.

It seems like it takes forever to walk to Ms. Traspy. She's holding the white slip up for me, her thickly made-up face frozen in a pose that she must think looks innocent. But looking up like that, how she looks is triumphant.

A simple act, handing me a slip to report to the office. A simple act, me walking up to get it. But we all know it's more than that. It's a moment I will carry with me for the rest of my life. For Ms. Traspy, though, it's a moment to revel in, one she'll remember for the whole week. She may even mention it in the teachers' lounge. "Yeah, I finally got rid of that little brat," she'll say.

It's only seconds later, but it feels like years. It's only seconds later that I finally get close enough for her to hand me the white slip with a little flourish. Her curls bounce once in insistence. I will my hand to take it from her. The sooner I take it and go, the sooner it will be over. But it's irrevocable, this little slip. I hear a little cough behind me. I reach up and take it. I turn away and leave the classroom. I know I won't be back. I wonder for a moment what will happen after I leave. Will they all cheer? Will they just get back to their worksheet on texture? Was I even a blip on their radar?

The hall is empty as I walk toward the office. My shoes squeak on the freshly waxed floor. It's a long walk. It's part of my punishment, this long walk of shame. My chance to think about my behavior.

But all I think about is my father.

VICKI: IN-BETWEEN

It was there all along. I always knew it. I wasn't welcome. I was a pest, and they had pest-bombed the school. The fact that my parents didn't know that didn't lessen their disappointment. Or my shame. I carry it with me still.

But I left with a strong sense of self. I would make it. My own way.

VICKI: TEACHING ASSISTANT

It's lunchtime and I'm out on the playground, avoiding the teachers' lounge as usual. I don't have lunch duty, but I like it better out here. At least here I don't have to hear crotchety old Ms. Bithy complain about the kids. She longs for the good ole days when her students were all working-class white. Bitter and pissed that demographics have changed, all she does is complain about the dirty, brown, lice-infected kids with the parents who don't care and don't bother to learn English. She's just waiting for her paycheck to come. Twenty-two more paychecks until retirement.

I'm standing in the shade against the wall, watching the kids. A handful of third-grade girls have taken over the swings. Nereyda and Monica, inseparable as always, are waiting for their turn, talking quietly in Spanish. Just then, the P.E. teacher, Ms. Montana, pulls into the parking lot in her red VW Bug. Her school ID dangles as she reaches into her car for her purse and a tray of Starbucks. She clip-clops into the teachers' lounge without so much as a glance at the kids. Nereyda and Monica look up and stop talking. They watch as Ms. Montana walks past them and into the teachers' lounge. Whatever has riveted their attention, the red car, the name badge, the tray of Starbucks, some glimpse of grandeur they will never belong to, whatever it is won't be here next year. Ms. Montana has already accepted a position in Santa Barbara. She'll pack up her Chapman University degree and clipboard in a box that she can carry to a program where she can teach pilates. Away from what she sees: the ghetto, lice-infected children and crotchety old Ms. Bithy.

The bell rings and I watch as the girls turn and walk quietly back to class. That's when I make them the silent promise: I'll be there next year. I'll be there with my name badge, I'll be there bilingual, and I may even bring Starbucks. In my box, I'll be bringing our shared history of oppression, of substandard education, of silencing, of hanging our heads.

I won't be teaching them to walk quietly.

AFTERWORD

This chapter resulted from a follow-up to a study of the experiences of English learners in a comprehensive high school that I conducted several years ago (Coulter & Smith, 2006; Coulter, 2003). It includes data from both the original study and newly collected sources, including interviews with Vicki and some classmates, school artifacts (including an ethnographic autobiography recently written by Vicki in her teacher preparation program), field notes, and my own teacher journals that I kept as Vicki's teacher (high school ESL) as well as research journals I've kept over the course of my ongoing research.

Data were analyzed narratively (Barone, 2000, 2007; Clandinin & Connelly, 2000; Connelly & Clandinin, 1990; Ecker, 1966; Freeman, 2007; Polkinghorne, 1995) as I read and reread the corpus of data and searched for a unifying theme or metaphor (Barone, 2000; Ecker, 1966). Analysis of the data revealed that Vicki's changing perceptions of teachers and teacher preparation were deeply based in experience (and less so in the intellectual impact of readings and instruction in her teacher preparation program). Thus, the best way to reveal Vicki's perceptions were through narrative constructions (Barone, 2007) that came from creative redescriptions (Freeman, 2007) of Vicki's lived experiences.

Narrative research is an heuristic, interpretive form of research. As the reader transacts with the narratives, she will construct her own, unique meanings. The bones of Vicki's stories will uphold the various transactions readers will have with the text: Vicki is the protagonist whose experiences often filled her with shame. She always felt like an outsider who was barely tolerated. In high school she was blatantly pushed out of school (Coulter, 2003). Later, as a teacher assistant and today as an intern and pre-service teacher, she witnesses the ways in which urban school children are marginalized through oppressive social and economic forces similar to what she experienced, even though she attended schools in predominantly white, upper-middle-class areas. Literary elements in these narratives provide further interpretive context. A full discussion of these would be repetitive to the narratives themselves, but I offer one of the more obvious: The point of view changes from Vicki's kindergarten experience (in third person omniscient perspective) to limited third person in her 3rd grade experience to first person in the scenes following, symbolizing Vicki's growing sense of agency. (The reader is asked to suspend judgment on the fact that the narratives, though written in first person from Vicki's perspective, are actually written by me. Collaboration is key in narrative research studies, and Vicki read and made suggestions on ongoing drafts as our understandings developed and evolved. Though the actual text is written by me, it is co-constructed through the research process.)

This is where I'm supposed to frame the study and tell you what the implications are. If these aren't clear from the narratives, then they aren't well written. Suffice it to say that when Vicki and I discussed it, she recommended that we follow the culturally relevant pedagogy recommended by many educational researchers: Paulo Friere and Gloria Ladson-Billings, Guadalupe Valdes, Tamara Lucas, bell hooks, and many others who show us ways to change schools into transformative, emancipatory communities. Schooling communities that promote in all children the chance to become what Barone [based on Harold Bloom, 1974)] calls "Strong Poets":

> A strong poet is someone who refuses to accept as useful the descriptions of her life as written by others. Instead, the strong poet is a strong storyteller, continuously revising her life story in the light of her own experience and imagination. The strong poet constantly redescribes her past interactions with the world around her, constantly reinvents her self, so that she may act in the future with ever greater integrity and coherence. The strong poet plots her life story toward her own emergent ends and purposes...an individual contributes to communal growth whenever she successfully redefines herself; and conversely, an individual is fulfilled only through enlarging the community's sense of what is possible. (2000, p. 125)

Strong poets do not walk quietly.

There are no new answers in this study. Perhaps, though, there is a new imperative in the question: What can we do?

REFERENCES

Barone, T. (2000). *Aesthetics, politics, and educational inquiry: Essays and examples.* New York: Peter Lang.

Barone, T. (2007). A return to the gold standard? Questioning the future of narrative construction as educational research. *Qualitative Inquiry, 13*(4), 454–470.

Clandinin, D. J., & Connelly, M. F. (2000). *Narrative inquiry.* San Francisco: Jossey-Bass.

Connelly, F. M., & Clandinin, D. J. (1990). Stories of experience and narrative inquiry. *Educational Researcher, 19*(5), 2–14.

Coulter, C. (2003). *Snow White, revolutions, the American dream and other fairy tales: Growing up immigrant in an American high school.* Unpublished doctoral dissertation, Arizona State University.

Coulter, C. & Smith, M. L. (2006). English language learners in a comprehensive high school. *Bilingual Research Journal, 30*(2), 309–335.

Ecker, D. (1966). The artistic process as qualitative problem-solving. In E. Eisner & D. Ecker (Eds.), *Readings in art education* (pp. 57–68). Waltham, MA: Blaidsdell.

Freeman, M. (2007). Autobiographical understanding and narrative inquiry. In D. J. Clandinin (Ed.), *Handbook of narrative inquiry: Mapping a methodology* (pp. 120–145). Thousand Oaks, CA: Sage Publications.

Polkinghorne, D. E. (1995). Narrative configuration in qualitative analysis. In J. A. Hatch & R. Wisniewski (Eds.), *Life History and Narrative* (pp. 5–24). London: The Falmer Press.

CHAPTER 6

INTERLUDE

MY FIRST VOYAGE

L. Thomas Hopkins
Teachers College, Columbia University

Since this was my first voyage in education for pupil self-development, I must tell you a few facts about me as a self, not as an educator, as to why and how I undertook it.

First: I was reared in self-development by Mother who taught me how to make, accept, evaluate, and improve my own decisions. If I made a judgment with adverse consequences to me and others, Mother *never reprimanded me*. She always said, "Let's sit down and talk this over." And we did. Thus I learned how to locate and develop the *hidden* factors which I had *overlooked* but were the essentials for self-development. So I came to know, and use a normal biological process of learning called in these days horse sense, or stable thinking.

Second: At Tufts the professors taught subject matter from books so I gave them what they wanted and the College gave me Magna Cum Laude and Phi Beta Kappa. Only *three* professors during these years understood me, realized why I was different and helped me continue my growth. I left in 1911

Listening to and Learning from Students, pages 39–44
Copyright © 2011 by Information Age Publishing

with a MA degree in History, with all courses taken at Harvard. I accepted a position as Principal of Brewster, Massachusetts, High School, which was one large and one small room above the elementary school. The Assistant and I were new to teaching. Each selected the desired courses, but I kept U.S. History, required by law of all Juniors for high school diploma.

This is the background; now I will tell you *why* I undertook this research in pupil self-development, *how* the experiment was conducted, and *what* were the results.

My first year 1911–1912, I taught U.S history as the Harvard professors had taught it to me, even though at the time I rebelled internally against it. At the end of this first class, I realized I must make a radical change but was not sure of how to do it. So I decided to wait until I could obtain the judgment and cooperation of the pupils.

In the fall of 1912, I began the class as usual, with the same ineffective results. The day before Thanksgiving recess, I opened the period by saying, "I am not happy with the way we are working in this class, and neither are you. I suggest that you think about it over the holidays and return next Monday to discuss *what is wrong* here and how *we* can remedy it." I emphasized the *WE*, and all caught the meaning as they were chatting about it when they left.

On Monday I asked for suggestions for improvement, but no person wanted to talk, so we chatted during the period. I knew they were testing me to make sure I meant what I said last Wednesday. On Tuesday I opened the original question of what is *wrong* here and how can *we* remedy it. I received some very cautious replies, most of which were related to the very uninteresting material in the textbook (required by law) which they must study. I thanked them for this helpful information but suggested that they look for other reasons to share tomorrow. I emphasized WRONG since I knew this was a common word in their vocabulary.

On Wednesday everyone seemed excited and alert, so I expected an early, pointed discussion but received more than I anticipated. Shortly, the oldest boy in the class (he was a year older than I) who had been fishing all summer and entered six weeks late, said, "Do you want to know what is wrong here?" "I certainly do." "Do you *really* want to know?" When he emphasized the word really, I knew he meant what he would say. "Yes," I replied. "Then I will tell you. The trouble here is that *you are a rotten teacher.*" He said this slowly and emphasized each word.

I took a deep breath, regained my composure and replied, "I do not want to be a rotten teacher as I expect to teach all of my life. Since you know what makes a rotten teacher, why don't you make me over into the good teacher that you would like to have and that I wish to become." There was silence.

I walked to the blackboard and wrote down two column headings. The first was "Rotten Teacher," the second was "Good Teacher." I then asked,

"What shall I put down under Rotten Teacher?" The replies were rapid. All dealt with subject matter as uninteresting, useless, no value to them, no reason for studying it. After a short pause, an older girl who had been a maid for a summer family and had come in a month late held up the textbook and said, "You never can be a good teacher if you have to teach this STUFF (heavily emphasized)." Quickly a great protest against studying history followed.

When all was again quiet, I asked, "What about the history that is inside of you?" A chorus of responses—"There isn't any. We won't study it." Immediately, I knew they believed history occurred ONLY in the textbook. When all was calm again, I asked the boy who had called me a rotten teacher, "Leland (*not his right name*), how old are you?" "Twenty-three," he answered. "Then you have twenty-three years of history inside (*with emphasis*) of you." I asked the girl who had been a maid, her age. "Nineteen," she answered. Then I responded, "You have nineteen years of history inside of you." And so I went around the group, selecting pupils of all ages and making the same statement.

When I finished, a girl asked immediately, "How did the history get inside of us if we will not learn it?" "A good question," I replied. "You learned it by living with people—family, other children, friends—in this environment which is the town of Brewster. Each of you is his history. Your history is YOU, yourself, and who you are."

The questions now came rapidly. Does each person have a different history than anyone else? Why are the children in our family NOT alike? Do people who live in other parts of the country have a different history inside them than we do? Do those who live in other countries have a different history also? Is it true that the Indians who lived here originally had a different history inside them than the settlers?

I jotted down most of the questions and suggested that they discuss them with other people. Jokingly, I said, "With both friends and enemies since frequently they know more about you than your friends. We will begin tomorrow with what history is inside of us and how did it get there."

For the first time, each was interested and chatting with others as he left the classroom.

The next day a girl opened with this question to which I saw many heads nodding in agreement. "You said that each of us has a different history inside than anyone else. This history is who we are. It is ourselves. How did we get it?"

"Each of us has a different history inside for many reasons. First we are born with different possibilities for growth which we cannot change but are our own great assets; second, we are reared in a different environment. Every child grows by taking in something from the environment. We all know he takes in food for physical growth. He also takes in feelings, attitudes, behavior of others toward him, whether they be other children or parents. You know that no two children in a home feel they are treated the same by anyone. From all of this each child takes in what he accepts to become a part of himself or his history. Third, each baby inherits a way or what is called a process of growing or learning, which he cannot change so he must understand and use it. The same is true of any living thing—a tree, shrub, hay in a meadow, lilies in a pond, a kitten, puppy, calf, chicken—they use their way of growing by instinct, which means they do not have to think about it. We can't do that. We must think about our way or process of growing in order to use it for our best self-development.

"Let us look again at these three reasons why we are all different selves. First, we are born with different capacities for growing; second, we are not treated the same by people wherever we live; third, nobody helps us to understand and use our inherited way of growing. Can you give some examples of how you have observed this in your lifetime? Forget my big words. Tell them as you see them."

For many succeeding days, we discussed why and how all people everywhere were different, in parts of the United States, in other countries. Suddenly, a girl said, "I see now why we have a textbook. It has in it the history that was inside of George Washington, Thomas Jefferson." And so she went on, "I can now see why their history, and not my ancestors', was written down." Now came a review of ancestors, what they had accomplished, and why their work was too localized to be in national history books ("You must do something which benefits ALL of the people in the United States").

As the discussion slowed, a boy asserted that the material in the history book is NOT what was inside the people; it is only what the writers think was inside of them. So now the argument ranged around "How can you tell the difference whether it was or not?" They jockeyed around on this, concluding it was not, but they did not know why or what difference it made.

I told them the difference was great and pointed out my experiences in college, the professors who judged me, put on record their estimate of my achievement by what they thought was inside of me, which was certainly not so. I had taken it in to pass their examinations and thrown it out as soon as I received a grade in the course. What remained inside of me was their lack of understanding of people. "I showed this same lack of understanding of you when I began teaching U.S. History last fall."

I went on to explain the differences in viewpoint of a person who is living through any problem trying to reach a reasonable conclusion, and that of a person on the outside watching his behavior. "Only under the most favorable conditions will a person reveal how he really feels or what he thinks on the inside." Whereupon a few pupils replied, "Yes, we know, we feel the change in this class." I smiled and said, "I begin to feel different myself." A pupil now suggested that an outsider could write about what was inside of another only when he had left a diary telling how he felt or thought, but the writer must interpret it HIS way according to his self, so, much could be lost depending upon the writer. I agreed and pointed out how it usually was reinterpreted.

By now, December, January, and February had passed. I pointed out that all life situations included some requirements, demands, restrictions within which we must work. We live in a society, or civilization, which has some rules and regulations or laws which everyone must follow. Massachusetts State law says you must study this required textbook to pass. If you fail U.S. History, your high school diploma is endangered. The law does not say what you must KNOW; it only says you must STUDY, so each can self-select what is valuable to him. Now how do you wish to meet this requirement? They asked for time to think about this over the weekend. I made the further suggestion that they obtain other U.S History books to compare material on the same topic. We had no school library, only a bookcase with titles of little value. They assured me they could find other books.

On Monday, everyone had so much to say that it took nearly half a period to locate a central topic. A boy found it when he said, "I feel different about history now than when we began. I know it is inside of me and how it got there. I must live with it and use it every day. I shall be happy to learn about the history which was inside the people who did so much for our country."

Immediately, the class selected these topics. First, *The Revolution*, the events leading up to it, how the Founding Fathers agreed on so many important things to do, why they guaranteed *freedom* in the Constitution and what it all meant. Here I asked, "And how does it operate today?" Second, *The Civil War*, with causes and effects. The third was where are we now, and where are we going? When they selected this one, one pupil laughed and said, "You said we used the history inside of us to make our future so we could use the history of the United States to us what is the future for our country." I complimented him on his insight and assured him that this was entirely possible but might take more time than we had available. And so we began the LEGAL study of U.S. History after six months of the year had passed. But what a difference these six months had made.

The pupils researched every book available, read more than any teacher would dare to require. The discussions were focused, thoughtful, sincere. For the final examination, required by law, I asked them to write about the values they *now* saw in history and how they would use them for better self-growth in the future. The two final periods were informal chats which enlightened me on how better to work with other classes in the future. They thanked me for helping them see the value of the history inside of them, and unanimously gave me the accolade of being a Good Teacher. End of teaching–learning episode. The teacher as counselor had not yet entered the educational arena.

Now some after-effects. The first question usually asked me is, "Where did you learn to teach this way?" Immediately I reply, "Not from any course in methods of teaching or psychology of learning, as I never had either. Yet I was the only person at that time who knew how and had the courage to work this way." Where did I learn this? In my childhood years before I went to college. I was taught that each growing person MAKES the decisions which determine how he will grow. The real question is how does he make them, on what evidence, and with what deliberation? I was also taught that growth is always UP. The only direction for a growing boy to go was UP. In those years I learned through firsthand experience the direction and deliberative process of growing UP. After the Brewster experience, I researched both the life purpose and the process so as to convince open-minded learners, educators, or laymen.

That summer, 1913, I went to Hyannis Normal School to obtain credits in methods of teaching, to obtain a license to become Superintendent of Schools in Massachusetts. The Principal, "Billy" Baldwin, suggested I read Dewey's *The Child and the Curriculum*, published in 1902. Here I learned that we had independently reached the same conclusion. The purpose of education was self-realization, as he called it. He gave little indication how to apply this in schools. He told me later at Teachers College, he had tried it with the traditional teachers in the University School of the University of Chicago where he was Professor of Philosophy but that it was an "impossible task," so he came to Columbia to specialize in Philosophical Theory, a more "possible task."

In the fall of 1913, I became Superintendent of Schools in Union District #20, which was Brewster, Dennis, Yarmouth on Cape Cod, followed by Marblehead and Amesbury, before entering Harvard for my Ed.D. degree. In each position I tried every reasonable way to introduce education for self-realization, even demonstrating how to do it on invitation from interested classroom teachers.

My next classroom teaching began in the fall of 1922 as an Associate Professor of Education at the University of Colorado. There I continued to use and advocate to others—colleagues, school teachers, and parents—student self-development by his normal biological process of learning as the purpose of education. My life work had been to help children, pupils, college students, adults of all ages activate their growth process so as to overcome the arrested development which the traditional family and school impose on everyone from childhood through the college years.

CHAPTER 7

A SHORTY TEACHING TEACHERS

Student Insight and Perspective on "Keepin' It Real" in the Classroom[1]

Brian D. Schultz
Northeastern Illinois University

Paris Banks
Chicago Public Schools

In Pedro Noguera's (2008) critically acclaimed book, *The Trouble with Black Boys... And Other Reflections on Race, Equity, and the Future of Public Education*, readers are challenged to boldly look to students for perspective on how to improve schools, teaching, and learning (pp. 61–71). Noguera contends that possible solutions to issues related to achievement gaps, school safety and discipline, as well as student motivation might be remedied by looking to actual children in classrooms. There is deep potential to transform education since, as he argues, "students may very well have ideas and insights adults are not privy to [which] could prove to be very helpful to improving schools if adults were willing to listen" (p. 69). Whereas Noguera makes

Listening to and Learning from Students, pages 45–57
Copyright © 2011 by Information Age Publishing
All rights of reproduction in any form reserved.

a convincing argument, much of the current literature in teacher education and practice in schools falls short of his thesis. If his contention were something new, radical, or even controversial, it might be understandable, but the premise of looking to students for what is worthwhile has a rich, yet often ignored, history in American public education.

Why is it that with such theoretical guidance over the century in curriculum history (Kliebard, 2004; Schubert, 1997) and the history of public education in the United States, we cannot find it in ourselves to leverage the insight, imaginations, and creativity of our students? Certainly, one can easily look to John Dewey's (e.g., 1897, 1909, 1916, 1938) detailed notions of involving learners in designing curricula and overall schooling experiences. Likewise, L. Thomas Hopkins' (1954) questioning of what makes the curriculum—where he purports that classroom content was always developed by adults outside the classroom to (their own) unsatisfactory results—could be a starting point not only to rhetorically value student input in curriculum making, but also to embrace the possibilities. A rereading of Joseph Schwab's (1971) argument about curricular commonplaces could shed light on the value and necessity of students' interplay on teaching and learning. And, certainly looking to Freire's (1970) insistence on people's critical reading of their worlds could be paralleled to this plea for listening to students as well as learning from, with, and alongside them.

Using the constructs from the rich history of curriculum studies outlined by the theorists noted above, it becomes evident that involving youth and tapping into their perspectives in teaching and learning has great potential for improving education and increasing young people's participation in school (see Brown, Wilcox, Schultz, Rodríguez, et al., 2008). Unfortunately, given current educational policy, top-down mandates, and prescriptive education, student participation in curriculum development is seldom practiced or even seen as a possibility (Au, 2009; Schultz, 2008). Students typically have very little control over how they learn and what they learn, and they are largely left out of discussions about what is considered to be worthwhile within teaching and learning (Schubert, 1997). This disregard for students' insights or perspectives regarding content taught and approaches to classroom dynamics is closely related to how many students are viewed in urban schools—merely as empty vessels for (someone else's) knowledge to be deposited (Freire, 1970). As Lipman (2003) and others argue, the structures associated with schools further this disconnect, and often as a result, either silence or push children—especially historically marginalized groups from urban areas—further away from the classroom (Au, 2009; Fine & Weis, 2003; Noguera, 2008). Given the common belief that urban students are nothing more than deficits and pathologies (Ayers, 2004) coupled with the (inaccurate) inclinations that the majority of this particular group of students do not value their learning, schooling reinforces the notions of cultural reproduction (Apple,

1995). Challenging these beliefs are youth who have a stake in their learning and a tremendous will not only to think about, but also to act on the challenges of (inequitable) expectations they face in schools. Looking to students for insight about what it takes to motivate and engage them has tremendous possibilities in transforming our schools. It rejects commonly held assumptions about urban youth, while it also has the potential of leveraging students' insights in "constructing a rigorous, practical, culturally and socio-economically sensitive, just, and engaging urban education" (Kincheloe, 2006, p. 3).

This chapter is an attempt to capture one student's perspective and insight about teaching and learning in the hopes that others can begin to listen to and learn from youth perspectives about teaching and teacher education. In this chapter, a former classroom teacher and his student from five years earlier reflect on what is meaningful, striking, and pertinent about the student's learning experiences—then and now. Together, the co-authors embrace the idea that students not only have perspectives about what good teaching is and what good teaching looks like, but also have the capacity to affect change for how both future and practicing educators perceive, connect, and engage with their students. Inherent in the insight and emergent storytelling should be a challenge to the common assumptions and stereotypes about city kids. Through this discussion, the authors believe they are beginning to heed Noguera's (2008) call to listen to students for help with solving the dire problems our urban schools face.

NARRATIVE CONSTRUCTION, STUDENT LORE, AND PERSPECTIVES OF STUDENTING

The following narrative inquiry emerges as co-written text, storytelling, and reflection (Easter & Schultz, 2008). Although a singular essay is told through the narrative construction (Barone, 2007), the reflections are based on the two authors' synthesis of ideas, telling, and "retelling and reliving of stories" (Clandinin, Pushor, & Orr, 2007, p. 33). Together the authors worked to keep the student's (second author) voice (and that of his peers) prominent and authentic, while also working to be accurate to his language and form. For the purpose of this chapter, the accuracy referred to is meant to be reflective of the narrator's point of view, perspective, and language usage in an effort to capture the essence of his student voice as narrator, student, and teacher. The student voice, constructed by both authors, isn't in conventional, standard-written English, but attempts to capture more "truth" and wisdom because of the forms of expression that name ideas and concepts particularly and precisely.

The construction focuses on *studenting* (Fenstermacher, 1986; Gershon, 2008; Hughes & Wiggins, 2008; Schultz, Baricovich, & McSurley, 2009). According to Hughes and Wiggins (2008), studenting "involves a struggle to gain new and difficult concepts," with specific insight to "learning for the sake of learning," and where "an intrinsic motivation . . . to reaching one's highest potential are inherent and unquestioned" (p. 58). In the process of being and doing in school, studenting perspectives take on ideas related to teacher and student lore. Lore is a form of educational inquiry that is an interpretive, artistic practice both teachers and students engage in as they actively seek to learn from their own experiences in classrooms (Schubert, 1991; Schubert & Ayers, 1999). Constructing and analyzing lore affords readers an opportunity to gain insight through the "practical research and inquiry" that the student conducted "through daily practice" (Schubert, 1989, p. 282) within both formal schooling and informal learning experiences. Related to Connelly and Clandinin's (1988) ideas of "personal practical knowledge," the co-written text becomes the "nexus of the theoretical, the practical, the objective, and the subjective" (Clandinin, 1985, p. 361), helping to seek meaning about a particular phenomenon.

A multiplicity of data were used to inform the storytelling, including informal conversations in out-of-school learning contexts (Schubert, 1981); semi-structured, emergent interviews; dialogue between the authors; presentation scripts from the American Educational Research Association (2008) annual meeting and the Center for Civic Education (2004); and classroom dialogue drawn from a previous inquiry in which both authors were involved (Schultz, 2008). We present the data in the form of a narrative split text (Blumenfeld-Jones & Barone, 1997; Lather & Smithies, 1997; Oyler, 2001; Schultz & Oyler, 2006). The narratives in outlined text boxes followed by analysis emerge as student lore. Some of this lore is drawn from primary documentation as cited, while other stories and analysis are co-written. Several approaches produced these constructions including: the second author dictating to the first author; the first author drafting suggestions and having the second author provide feedback, responses, and changes; the first author prompting the second author based on ideas from their ongoing and collaborative experiences together; or, a synthesis of conversations between the authors. This effort at writing together constructs the student's voice in a way so as to keep language and ideas in a spirit of authenticity through the use of words and form representative of the second author while the first author assembled the text for presentation here. This sometimes smooth, sometimes clumsy effort is our attempt at "keepin' it real", and the rough edges apparent here are at the heart of our back and forth dialogue.[2]

"KEEPIN' IT REAL": AN INTRODUCTION

Teachers have got to make school exciting for students; they need to "keep it real" in the classroom. Keepin' it real means that school connects with the students and teachers put effort into the work their students do. It also means that school is related to the students' lives. When school connects and relates to the kids, it shows what is on the students' minds in every way. When this happens, kids want to be in school and are motivated by what happens in the classroom. Unfortunately, too often school is not the place that kids want to be because there is a big disconnect with what goes on in school with students' lives. It is no wonder that kids drop out, skip, or sleep through school. There are many reasons school does not seem right for a lot of city kids. Some of the reasons that kids stop caring about school is because of their teachers' approaches, the content teachers actually teach their students, how teachers relate to the kids' parents and neighborhoods, and how they see the kids. Based on my experiences, teachers can do things differently in their classrooms. There are ways teachers can make school a place that gets students excited or as we call it, "geeked up." Now this is where you, the reader of my writing, probably ask, "How can a teacher create this sort of interest for students in school?" That's the question. Well, it is not something that is simple, but it starts with some things that are simple. Let me explain.

LETTING THE KIDS ASK THE QUESTIONS, AND JUST DOING THINGS

I was more than excited. I was on my first-ever airplane ride. Me and my old classmates headed to St. Louis with our old teacher to present to a bunch of adults about the last school year when my classroom fought for a new school building for our neighborhood. At the time I was in the sixth grade and at a different school, but the Center for Civic Education people wanted us to tell a whole group of grown-ups about our experiences the year before in identifying a problem in our neighborhood of Cabrini Green and coming up with a solution. Before we got to St. Louis, believe it or not, I was just plain old excited, not nervous at all. I presented so many times about this stuff for over a year by then that I figured it would be the same old–same old. . . .

What was nice about the trip was that it was not all planned out for us in advance by some old folks. We got to do some planning, just like we had done all the time the year before. It really felt like a reward for all the work we were doing to help ourselves and it reminded me about all the activities we had done during our fight for a better school. This is important because we DID things during that year. We petitioned, surveyed, produced documentaries, and all types of other things during that year of school instead of just hearing about others doing it or reading about it in books. . . .

After we walked around the city, ate some good food, and played in a big, nice hotel, we went to our presentation. We got a proper-style intro by the head person from the Center for Civic Education while we were on center stage in front of over 600 people. Me and my old classmates dusted off some speeches about our fight for what was right and our push in the 'hood of trying to get a better place to learn. Even though I thought it was going to be the same old talk, it was so different to me. I had never been in front of so many people. Y'know kids that age can be shy in front of adults and I did not want to let my classmates down. Good thing we had practiced with the technology and our speeches because we could've really messed it up. As we told them our story, we showed them some movies, a PowerPoint presentation and took them to our website. . . .

While the last one of my classmates showed off that website, I stayed busy taking some notes. I knew that once we finished our bang-up presenting job, there were going to be some important folk that wanted to question us all about our project. Not only did I need to be prepared, I had some things on my own mind that I figured I would ask the audience—only fair, right? As the MC got up to the mic to thank us and start allowing all them questions, I shortstopped her and got her to listen to what I had in mind. I whispered in her ear and convinced her to let me take the mic before all them questions were fired at us from the audience. After she heard what I had to say, she did get back up to the podium but I think her message was a little different. She said, "instead of having questions from the legislators and all of you, Paris would like to address you all again."

As I think about how this went down, I laughed at myself. I was all pimped out—pinstripes and exclusive shoes—not sure I would ever dress that way again! I was a real shorty back then, too, barely able to see over the podium. I cleared my throat before I began speaking to the crowd again and said, "Before you ask us any questions, I have a few questions for all of you!"

The audience snickered and laughed at what I was saying. But, y'know, I think that kids should be able to ask the questions that are important to them. So, I repeated the same thing again and then started to read off some of my notes that I took while my classmates were presenting. The audience responded with some props when I asked if they liked what we had done. But to be honest, I don't think that crowd understood what we was all about. As they continued their applause, I talked over them. This quieted them down real fast. I wanted them to get our point. I said,

"It is fine and good that y'all think we did good work, cause I agree, we did. Thank you. But, how you gonna help us? You know it costs a lot of money to get a new school, and kids can't go to schools like our bootleg, old one. I am not saying we want your money now, but when you leave out of here, I bet there are schools just like ours in y'all cities. What are you going to do to make a difference for them kids and them schools? You can't just think we did good, clap a lot—which I like by the way—and then not do something in your communities. Think about it."

—Paris Banks, Keynote Address, Center for Civic Education National Conference on Project Citizen, St. Louis, Missouri, 2004

First off, how teachers teach is real important. The best experiences I have had in school were when the class was based on doing activities. When I got to actually do things rather than just hear the teach talk about them, the learning was much more interesting to me. In classrooms where kids got to experiment, I was always involved. But, if I had to sit still, with my hands folded on my desk, and (supposedly) listen, I did not pay any attention to that teacher. This should be of no surprise to teachers, but some still need to hear it out loud because most of my teachers talk at kids instead of with them. And, most don't listen to them neither. Everyone knows it is boring and makes you sleepy to have someone lecture to you for hours on end.

To build on this idea, I think one of the biggest problems is that so many teachers think that kids don't know what they are talking about and don't know anything. This is the farthest from the real deal. My friends and I know a lot, but almost all my teachers treat me as if I am an idiot. I know that many of my teachers judge me before I even have the chance to speak in the classroom. They draw conclusions by how I dress, or the friends that I hang out with in the halls—I can hear them mumbling under their breaths that I must be some drug-dealing gangbanger. It amazes me about what they do not know. This is bogus 'cause I know I am smart, but you would never know it from the way the teacher approaches learning or treats me in the classroom. This is one of the worst things about schools. It seems like most teachers are always jumping to conclusions about their students. And, when a teacher makes a mistake and the kids try and correct it, they don't want to hear about it.

Since I have been a little kid, I have wondered why school is like this. It seems that school is all about memorizing stuff rather than really trying to learn things. Just 'cause someone can memorize something does not mean they know it—you know I can remember stuff, just ask me that same old question us kids always be hearing: How you can learn all them hip hop lyrics, but you can't learn my history and my math?

My idea is to make the school all about the kids. Asking the students in your classroom what they think is important can make it fun for everyone. Let the kids do things. Let them make things. Let them build and even break things. Kids will pick challenging ideas if they are given opportunities because they know that they will never get better by just picking something easy. Kids got a lot of great ideas, but it always feels like no one wants to hear about them. When kids get to choose what they want to learn about, they can be as creative as they can be. If they are focused on something that is important to them, they want to represent well. This means that not only will they put in a lot of effort, they will work hard at it to make sure they understand it from all directions. They will make it look cool with technology and art because they know that it will help them in understanding what they are studying.

Bottom line: School is usually all about what the teacher wants to teach, or at least, what they are supposed to teach. But what if this little thing was different? Kids have lots of questions that are important to them, just like I was ready with questions after our presentation. What if teachers let the kids ask the questions in school instead of always being the ones asking the questions? What if they did activities that were relevant to the kids' lives instead of just reading or hearing about them? While I have been in schools for what seems like forever—actually shuffled around from various high schools and alternative schools recently—I have had some experiences where kids were asking questions that changed the way I think about learning and school.

COMMUNITY, PARENTS, AND GETTING TO KNOW THE STUDENTS

Ann[3] was straight up about kids and education and . . . demonstrat(ed) that classrooms do not have to be only in school but can be part of the community just as the community should be part of them. . . .

Growing up in a place like Cabrini Green there weren't many people that cared about us kids other than family. The Greens, as we called our housing project, was a rough, ghetto neighborhood where you really got to be careful in every part you go. When I met Ann, I came to realize that there were people outside in the world besides family that care about kids. She did not care about where we were from, how bad our neighborhood was, or anything else, she just cared about what we were doing to get a better place to learn. Our classroom ended up being not just our teacher and us, but we got other people involved. These other people, like Ann, gave us some wonderful ideas that we would never have thought of doing. For me, this made school different than ever because people with fresh ideas and experiences showed them to us fifth graders. This made our subjects in school much more exciting because it was not just using books and dictionaries, but getting other people's thoughts. To further describe, Ann's involvement in our classroom showed me that there are different ways everyday folks can get involved in schools without even having to come to them.

—Tywon Easter, *Journal of Curriculum & Pedagogy* (Easter & Schultz, 2008, pp. 70–73); Interactive Symposium, American Educational Research Association Annual Meeting, 2008

Just like Tywon said how it is really important to get the community involved in urban classrooms and to get classrooms involved in the community, I am here to tell you about how important it is to get parents involved in the classrooms. Getting our parents involved in school is so important. My teacher used to call my house every week! At the time, I thought it was too much—Mr. Schultz is calling again—but he was not calling to tell bad news and it was really a good thing.

I think most teachers only call kids' mommas when their kids are in trouble. This is not good. If teachers call parents regularly and tell what is happening in the classroom, the parents can support the teacher. They want to support the teacher. Parents should be involved all the time, and in our case it was good because most of the parents really got involved in our cause. I think too many teachers think that city kids' parents don't care about their kids' education. This is just plain wrong.

My momma really cares about what I am learning, why I am learning it, and what she can do to support help me. Without my teacher inviting her to get involved, she could not help out. An example of this was when my mom took off work to travel with us to present a conference out of town.... And now here in New York is another one of our mommas... So the bottom line—make sure you find ways to get the parents involved. They do care! They can help!

—Kaprice Pruitt, Interactive Symposium, American Educational Research Association Annual Meeting, 2008

Getting to know the kids in your classroom is extremely important. Really, it is all about respect and seeing the kids as having something to offer. In all the years that I have been in school, the teachers seemed never to care about learning what the kids are all about or what interests them. Teachers never understood my friends or me, they only talked to my parents when there was trouble, and they really did not want to come to my neighborhood. They even thought my parents were trouble! There are a lot of different ways that a teacher can do better by the kids in front of them.

If teachers got to know the kids' interests and learned about them, I think school could be a better a place. Most of my teachers really never knew me. Most don't have a clue and did not try to find out what was important to us kids. To them, I was just another Black face in the class. To them, we all blended together. No distinctions by attitude or behavior or smarts. This makes for a bad situation. A teacher ought to want to know about his or her students. Teachers and students need to have a connection, but this won't happen if they don't even try to know each other. Stated differently, if the teacher gets to learning about the students in his or her classroom, he or she can make the kids want to be in school much easier. For instance, when I get to know my teacher and have a personal relationship with him or her, believe it or not, I actually want to be in school. Just check my attendance record; it shows which teachers made that effort and which teachers did not. With a connection, I actually want to be around in school. Unfortunately, most of the time I really don't care to stay in school cause my teachers have no idea what I am all about.

I think part of it is that teachers see themselves as different than the kids in their classrooms. This is especially true in terms of the teachers working with the students' parents. It always seemed weird to me that the teachers might be the same age as the kids' parents. They don't want to build relationships with the parents. And, what I see almost every single day is that teachers are always putting it on the parents when some kid gives them a problem in the classroom. I just gotta ask all the teachers: What are you doing to make the parents feel welcome, like they can be a part of what's happening in the school or the classroom?

Learning about the neighborhoods that the kids come from is something that might help teachers in getting to know kids in their classrooms. So many of my teachers think that the kids are bad because they come from a bad neighborhood—or should I say, a supposedly bad neighborhood. Most of my teachers did not grow up in the ghetto. Not only that, most had never set foot in one before. For this reason, I think that teachers see themselves as different or even better than us kids. They think the ghetto is so terrible. They see it as dangerous. They are scared of it. All this makes some of them believe that us kids are terrible, dangerous, and scary. I am not saying everything is fine in the hood, cause it's not, but there is distance between many teachers and me cause they see me as different. It just goes to show that most teachers know so little about what the projects and the kids in their classrooms from the projects are all about.

Teachers need to understand that because bad things are happening in a neighborhood does not mean that everything in that neighborhood is bad. To tell you the truth, everybody that is from the projects where I grew up in is like a big family. We all have each others' backs and really do care about each other a lot. My advice is that teachers should sometimes go into our hood with their students so they can begin to learn about us through our neighborhood. I am not saying that they should come in all the time, but if they even visited a little, they would get to see what our lives are really like—not just what the inner city is like on TV. If teachers got this kind of first-hand experience, I think they would see us as people just like them, people that have to put up with a lot. From this sort of experience, they may begin to understand their students and the neighborhoods where they teach better.

To be honest, I believe that kids really can teach their teachers—a lot. If you have gotten this far in reading what I have to say, my hope is that maybe, just maybe, you will try some of the things I've been thinking about here. I bet school could be a better place for everyone—students, teachers, parents—if kids got to ask the questions; if kids got to have real-life experiences in schools; if kids were not immediately looked down upon because of their skin color or how they dressed or what crew they hung with. I cannot encourage you enough to listen to the young folk in your classrooms. Let them ask questions. Go to their all communities. Spend some time with their parents. Not only will you learn something, maybe you will make that connection to them by letting them teach you. Maybe you could keep it real.

NOTES

1. This chapter is a modified version of the article: Schultz, B. D., & Banks, P. (2009a). A shorty teaching teachers: One kid's perspective about 'keepin' it real' in the classroom. *The Sophist's Bane,* 5(1/2), 19–24.

2. As the first author, former teacher, and educational researcher, I wrestle with the complexity and resultant ethical dilemmas from our work together. There are obvious power dynamics at play while an adult and his former student write together. Paris and I discuss this at length and elsewhere we have written into this complexity, focusing on such ethical dilemmas and the fine line of co-optation in terms of our collaboration and collective memory (see Schultz & Banks, 2009b). Even with this conscientiousness and reflexivity about such influences, I believe it is necessary to continue to problematize this work together.

3. This extended quote comes from the Perspectives section of an issue of *Journal of Curriculum & Pedagogy* (2008) titled: "Collective Memory, Curriculum Studies, and a Scoffing Dragon: Celebrating the Life, Love, and Legacy of Ann Lynn Lopez Schubert." Tywon refers to the ongoing relationship he and his class had with the outside community and in particular, Ann Lopez Schubert, during a previous school year.

REFERENCES

Apple, M. W. (1995). *Education and power.* New York: Routledge.

Au, W. (2009). *Unequal by design: High-stakes testing and the standardization of inequality.* New York: Routledge.

Ayers, W. C. (2004). *Teaching towards freedom: Moral commitment and ethical action in the classroom.* Boston: Beacon Press.

Barone, T. (2007). A return to the gold standard? Questioning the future of narrative construction as educational research. *Qualitative Inquiry, 13*(4), 454–470.

Blumenfeld-Jones, D. S., & Barone, T. E. (1997). Interrupting the sign: The aesthetics of research texts. In J. A. Jipson & N. Paley (Eds.), *Daredevil research: Re-creating analytic practice* (pp. 83–107). New York: Peter Lang.

Brown, T. M., Wilcox, S., Schultz, B. D., & Rodríguez, L., et al. (2008). *Youth perspectives on teachers and teaching.* Interactive Symposium presented at the American Educational Research Association Conference, New York.

Clandinin, D. J. (1985). Personal practical knowledge: A study of teachers' classroom images. *Curriculum Inquiry, 15*(4), 361–385.

Clandinin, D. J., Pushor, D., & Orr, A. M. (2007). Navigating sites for narrative inquiry. *Journal of Teacher Education, 58*(1), 21–35.

Connelly, F. M., & Clandinin, D. J. (1988). *Teachers as curriculum planners: Narratives of experience.* New York: Teachers College Press.

Dewey, J. (1897). *My pedagogic creed.* New York: E. L. Kellogg & Co.

Dewey, J. (1909). Moral principles in education. New York: Houghton Mifflin Company. Retrieved July 21, 2009, from http://www.gutenberg.org/files/25172/25172-h/25172-h.htm

Dewey, J. (1916). *Democracy and education.* New York: Free Press.

Dewey, J. (1938). *Experience and education.* New York: Macmillan.

Easter, T., & Schultz, B. D. (2008). There are all sorts of possibilities—and take notes. *Journal of Curriculum and Pedagogy 5*(1), 70–74. Note: Names are alphabetically; first authorship is shared.

Fenstermacher, G. D. (1986). Philosophy of research on teaching. In M. O. Wittrock (Ed.), *Handbook of research on teaching* (3rd ed.) (pp. 37–49). New York: Macmillan.

Fine, M., & Weis, L. (2003). *Silenced voices and extraordinary conversations: Re-imagining schools.* New York: Teachers College Press.

Freire, P. (1970). *Pedagogy of the oppressed.* New York: Seabury.

Gershon, W. (2008). Intent and expression: Complexity, ethnography and lines of power in classrooms. *Journal of the Canadian Association for Curriculum Studies, 6*(1), 45–71.

Hopkins, L. T. (1954). *The emerging self in school and home.* New York: Harper and Brothers.

Hughes, S., & Wiggins, A. (2008). Learning to reframe academic inequity: Revisiting the "structuralist" vs. "culturalist" dichotomy in educational research. *The Sophist's Bane, 4*(1/2), 51–62.

Kincheloe, J. (2006). Introducing metropedagogy: Sorry, no short cuts in urban education. In J. Kincheloe & k. hayes (Eds.), *Metropedagogy: Power, justice and the urban classroom* (pp. 3–39). Rotterdam: Sense Publishers.

Kliebard, H. (2004). *The Struggle for the American Curriculum, 1893–1958* (3rd ed.). New York: Routledge.

Lather, P., & Smithies, C. (1997). *Troubling the angels: Women living with HIV/AIDS.* Boulder, CO: Westview Press.

Lipman, P. (2003). *High stakes education: Inequality, globalization, and urban school reform.* New York: RoutledgeFalmer.

Noguera, P. (2008). *The trouble with black boys…and other reflections on race, equity, and the future of public education.* San Francisco: Jossey-Bass.

Oyler, C. (2001). Extending narrative inquiry. *Curriculum Inquiry, 31*(1), 77–88.

Schubert, W. H. (1981). Knowledge about out-of-school curriculum. *Educational Forum 45*(2), 185–199.

Schubert, W. H. (1989). On the practical value of practical inquiry for teachers and students. *Journal of Thought, 24*(1), 41–74.

Schubert, W. H. (1991). Teacher lore: A basis for understanding praxis. In C. Witherall & N. Noddings (Eds.), *Stories lives tell: Narrative and dialogue in education* (pp. 207–233). New York, Teachers College Press.

Schubert, W. H. (1997). *Curriculum: Perspective, paradigm, and possibility.* Upper Saddle River, NJ: Prentice Hall.

Schubert, W. H., & Ayers, W. (Eds.). (1999). *Teacher lore: Learning from our own experience.* Troy, NY: Educator's International Press.

Schultz, B. D. (2008). *Spectacular things happen along the way: Lessons from an urban classroom.* New York: Teachers College Press.

Schultz, B. D., & Banks, P. (2009a). A shorty teaching teachers: One kid's perspective about 'keepin' it real' in the classroom. *The Sophist's Bane, 5*(1/2), 19–24.

Schultz, B. D., & Banks, P. (2009b). Co-optation, ethical dilemmas, and collective memory in collaborative inquiry: A writing-story. In W. S. Gershon, *The collaborative turn: Working together in qualitative research* (pp. 35–54). Rotterdam, The Netherlands: Sense.

Schultz, B. D., & Oyler, C. (2006). We make this road as we walk together: Sharing teacher authority in a social action curriculum project. *Curriculum Inquiry, 36*(4), 423–451.

Schultz, B. D., Baricovich, J., & McSurley, J. (2009). Beyond these tired walls: Social action curriculum project induction as public pedagogy. In J. A. Sandlin, B. D. Schultz, & J. Burdick (Eds.), *Handbook of public pedagogy: Education and learning beyond schooling* (pp. 368–380). New York: Routledge.

Schwab, J. J. (1971). The practical: Arts of eclectic. *School Review, 79*, 493–542.

CHAPTER 8

INTERLUDE

WHAT IS A SCHOOL?

From *I Learn From Children*

Caroline Pratt
City and Country School, New York

Often during my three decades in the City and Country School I have thought we should have a doctor on hand at all times. Not for the children (we took care of that) but for innocent visitors to our classrooms. Sometimes, emerging from a morning of observation, they have seemed visibly to be suffering from shock!

This was not likely to be true of mothers—a mother more often came away from her first visit with a look of bewildered pleasure. She had watched a group of happy children without always knowing what they were happy about, but for the moment it was enough that they were happy.

Occasionally a father looked jolted, worried; how, in that turmoil, would his son ever get ready for Harvard?

But the sharpest reaction could be counted on to come from the good teacher whose entire life had been spent in a traditional classroom.

Listening to and Learning from Students, pages 59–66
Copyright © 2011 by Information Age Publishing
All rights of reproduction in any form reserved.

"Do you call this a school?" She would ask the question in terms more or less politely veiled depending on how far her principles had been outraged. And I could sympathize with her, having served my time in the kind of classroom where each child sits on a bench nailed to the floor, at a desk as firmly fixed in its place, incommunicado as far as all the other children are concerned—and the teacher at the front of the room sternly bound to maintain the discipline without which, it is assumed, the work will not get done.

I have put such a teacher among, say, our sixth-graders, the Elevens, to share a part of their full and busy day. By contrast to the nailed-down dependability of her own classroom, here nothing was fixed, nothing stayed put, not even the furniture; above all, not the children!

Some would be in the print room, turning out a job. There they were anchored at least to the presses; yet through the wide doorway there would be a constant movement of active young bodies round and round among type cases and stock shelves, with a chatter of voices as continuous as the hum and clatter of the presses. Orders, comments, criticisms, a shouted question to the teacher from the foreman-of-the-week: "We finished the Sevens' reading work—shall we start on the library card order or the Parents' Association letterheads?"

Within the classroom itself there would be no stillness, either visual or auditory. Treble howls of disagreement might be rising from the corner where the editorial committee of the Elevens' magazine, soon going to press, debated the literary merits of a nine-year-old's story—or a Thirteen's, the more sharply criticized because of the author's advanced age. A pigtailed Eight bounded into the room, her small face solemnly on duty bent, a canvas mail pouch hanging from her shoulders; postman from the Eights' post-office, she carried a Special Delivery letter, an invitation to the Elevens from the Tens to attend a performance of their play in the Gym the next morning. Two Elevens returned, laden with packages of paper, pencils, notebooks, jars of bright paints, supplies bought for the group at the school store run by the Nines. A tall Twelve, splotches of mimeographing ink competing with the freckles on his nose, carried in a stack of copies of *The Yardbird*, weekly newspaper published by his group, to be sold later at 1¢ apiece. (The price, I understand, has recently risen to 3¢—another case of rising costs of production.)

Half a dozen Elevens might now bang in from work in the science room, the clay room, the shop, and you could tell which, for the marks of their labors would be plain on their worn and stained dungarees. With the new arrivals there would be a shifting of tables and chairs, a foraging in lockers to get out an arithmetic book which needed correcting, a linoleum cut to be finished, a topic—Astronomy in the Middle Ages—to be written up in a notebook. The teacher might be asked, "How much time before Yard?" but rarely, "What shall we do now?" Each child apparently knew what unfinished work he had on hand and promptly applied himself to it. From the class treasurer of the week, pushing a lock of brown hair behind an ear while she worked on her accounts there might come a piteous wail—"We'll have to stop losing pencils! If we have to buy pencils again this week we can't afford the trip to Chinatown!"

And swirling around the visitor's head, beating against her unaccustomed ears, there was *noise*, until the walls the room must bulge with it. Of twenty souls in the room, only one was quiet—the teacher.

Of course the visitor was right in her complaint: this did not look or sound like any schoolroom. But it was very much like something else. It was like a segment of grown-up activity, an office, a small factory, or perhaps office and factory combined. Nor did these children look like school children, starched and clean-faced, the boys in white shirts, the girls in crisp frocks. These children wore work-clothes, or overalls, boys and girls alike (occasionally a dress, the exercise of individual prerogative), and they and their work-clothes bore the evidences of their work. "Do they to have to get so dirty?" mothers have been asking for thirty years. But was there ever a printer without ink on his trousers and his cheek, a cook without flour on her elbows and aprons?

This classroom was a place where work was done. The workers could not be fastened down; they had to come and go about their various jobs, fetch supplies, seek advice, examine, compare, discuss. The work got done, not in proportion to the silence in the room, but in proportion to the responsibility of each worker to his job and to the group. Some were more able, more responsible workers than others—as among adults. And, as among adults, there was a supervisor (not a boss, however) directing, counseling, channeling the abundant energies of these young workers, keeping balance among personalities, keeping the schedule of the day's program and its constantly varying tasks, checking accomplishment of both group and individual.

No wonder the visitor was confounded. The movement bewildered her; the noise came between her and the work. But she was the only one in the room who was bewildered. She could not see the pattern, so unlike the traditional one with which she was familiar, so much more complex. Yet it was an obvious and familiar pattern, seen everywhere except in the traditional schoolroom. It was the traditional pattern, rather than this one, which was strange and unfamiliar. This one was the normal pattern of human activity, adult or child. Because these were children, noise was louder, the movement more explosive. And because these were children, the task of the teacher and her student-teacher assistant was so much more than merely that of a shop foreman or a supervisor in an adult project that here, in truth, the analogy breaks down. This teacher had a task so subtle, so exacting, that a traditionally trained teacher could scarcely hope to comprehend it at a glance.

And when she asked us, as in one way or another she always did, is this a school?—we could ask in our turn, *what is a school?*

To answer that a school is place of learning is no answer at all, only another way of stating the question. A place of learning what? A place of learning, *how?*

I was seventeen when I taught my first class—a one-room school in the country—and I had had none of the benefits of normal school, teacher training, nor even, possibly, had ever heard the word *pedagogy*. What I did have was a deep conviction, unspoken, indeed unconscious until much later, that a desire to learn was as natural and inevitable in children as the desire to walk in babies.

How could anyone doubt that it was? Once beyond the eating–sleeping stage, every day, every hour of a young child's waking life is devoted to adventure, exploration, discovery of the world around him. His fiercest struggles are to learn—to turn over, to sit up, to walk, to climb; later, to grasp a toy, to shake a rattle, to roll and recapture a ball; still later, to investigate the working light switches, telephones, clocks. ("Why must he be so *destructive?*" protests the dismayed mother; our forefathers had to see their houses burned down before they knew how fire worked.) His greatest frustrations, aside from his own limitations, are the restrictions placed upon him by the adult world in his effort to touch, to feel, to see and smell and taste. And his method of learning? The first and best one, the one used by Neanderthal man and by the atomic scientist—trial and error.

No one who has watched a baby return to his lessons day after day—and persist in them despite bumps and bruises—can doubt the drive of the young human being to learn. And indeed if man did not have this compulsion to explore, to understand, and to conquer or at least come to terms with the world in which he lives, including his own person, he must surely have disappeared from the earth ages ago, along with the millions of other forms of life which have vanished, even the mighty dinosaur.

But something happens, alas, to this great driving force. All but a very few men and women in the world, a few unique beings touched with some kind of genius, have lost the urge to learn.

They lost it, in fact, long before they were grown. They lost it while they were still little children, while they were still spending their days in the place of learning, the school—perhaps that was where they lost it!

A visitor from out of town—not an educator, merely a perceptive and sensitive mother—told me something once which I have never forgotten. She had spent an hour or two in the school, and sat down with me afterward to talk about her own boys, who were pupils at a fine traditional private school.

"When they were six they were so busy, so active, so alive!" she said. "They had so many interests, wanted to do so many things—and did them!

Now they are eleven and nine, and it's all gone. They have no interest, no curiosity, no initiative or imagination or individuality. They might have been turned out in a factory." I remember that there were tears in her eyes.

Maybe because circumstances had made me a teacher, and maybe because I was a teacher before I learned the accepted ways to teach—whatever the reason, I was in my twenties when I began to look for the child's lost desire to learn. It seemed to me that if we could keep this desire alive through childhood and into adult life, we would release a force more precious and powerful for good than any physical force the scientists ever discovered for mankind's use.

At least, I reasoned it, would make the years learning, the school years, meaningful. The child would learn in such a way that his knowledge would actually go with him from the schoolroom into the world; his knowledge would become part of him, as the knowledge the infant gains by his own trial and error method becomes part of him.

I had seen fifteen-year-old boys who had been faithfully taught their three R's in the public school struck dumb and helpless when they needed to divide a fifteen-inch board into two halves in the shop. It was only one evidence—but how revealing—of what I had seen again and again, that our teaching had failed to teach, that it had only crammed knowledge like excelsior into unreceptive little heads, knowledge that was unused because it was unusable as we had given it, unrelated, undigested. Most dreadful of all, unwanted.

I once asked a cooking teacher why she did not let the children experiment with the flour and yeast, to see whether they could make bread. She said in a shocked voice, "But that would be so wasteful!"

She was no more shocked by my question than I by her answer. That materials used in education should be considered wasted! Ours must be a strange educational system, I thought. And, of course, the more I studied it, the more convinced I became that it was very strange indeed. It was saving of materials, ah yes—but how wasteful of children!

Once in our school I watched a little girl take sheets of good drawing paper, one by one, from a pile—I counted up to fifty. She made a little mark on each one with a crayon, and threw it away. Fifty sheets of paper wasted, and nobody said, "Don't!" On the contrary, when she stopped and looked fearfully at the teacher, she got a smile and an encouraging, "Try another one." That little girl was in school for the first time, and terrified. She could not speak at all, could not look at the teacher without shriveling. Those fifty sheets of paper were a beginning for her; she drew, then played with blocks, then answered the child who played beside her on the floor, and in a few weeks she had begun to find her way through the jungle of her own terrors and was learning to be a happy, busy, little school girl.

Yes, no doubt we are wasteful of paper and paints and clay and wood and few pounds of flour and few cents' worth of yeast. But we try not to waste the child, or his energies, or his time. I have seen time wasted in the traditional classroom, where out of forty children one is reciting, while thirty-nine sit with empty hands, empty faces—and empty heads. I have seen a little boy with his chin in his hand and his eyes on the door, doing nothing, thinking nothing, waiting with dreadful resignation for the moment when the bell would ring and the door would open, and he could get out of school.

But the child, unhampered, does not waste time. Not a minute of it. He is driven constantly by that little fire burning inside him, to do, to see, to learn. You will not find a child anywhere who will sit still and idle unless he is sick—or in a traditional classroom.

How this unnatural treatment of children came about was not my concern. I would not, even if I could, go into the history of education, a course in which I was an unhappy failure at Teachers College so many years ago. My own education was given me, not in teacher-training courses, not by professors of pedagogy, but by children themselves.

A child playing on his nursery floor, constructing an entire railroad system out of blocks and odd boxes he had salvaged from the wastepaper basket, taught me that the play impulse in children is really a work impulse. Childhood's work is learning, and it is in his play—before he ever gets into the hands of teachers in organized education—that the child works at his job. No child ever lavished on a history book the energy poured into a game of cowboys and Indians. But cowboys and Indians are a part of the history of our country which he must learn. What is wrong with learning history by playing it?

Surely the school was at fault, not the child. Was it unreasonable to try to fit the school to the child, rather than—as we were doing with indifferent success—fitting the child to the school?

I sometimes thought, in my rebellious twenties, that the educators had never seen a child. It is one thing to have a child handed you, as the traditional teacher is handed her young charges, at the age of five or six—and then to proceed with him according to the curriculum. But that is not to *see* a child, any more than looking at a lion in a zoo is to see a lion.

To see a child means seeing him in terms of his own horizons, and almost from the day he is born. You see then how the circle of his interest widens outward, like the circles made by a stone thrown into a pond. First he is concerned with his own person—his hands and feet, the motion of his body. Then his mother's face, his crib, his nursery floor, the house in which he lives and the people in it, the milkman and the grocer's boy who deliver his food, the street and the park in which he plays.

Children "play house," and how ill we understand the word "play." They are working in deadly earnest at the job of preparing to be adults, with the most serious of adult responsibilities, that of parenthood. A little girl pinned into a big apron stirs the batter for a cake—a favorite magazine advertisement in full color, favorite because it is quaint. Instead of cooing over her quaintness, we should treat her with respect. She is learning to be a mother in her own kitchen some day, learning to cook with loving care for the health and enjoyment of her own family.

Again and again in my life of learning from children I have remembered my own childhood, and that eager desire to help grown-ups in grown-up work—only to be given the lowliest and least interesting chores to do. How happily I would have washed the pots and pans, if I had had a hand in the cooking that was done in them! But that would have been wasteful; I might have spilled or spoiled good food. Perhaps it would be wasteful in the home when a limited budget must actually feed the family (although even of this I am not convinced). But a school is a place of learning; what economy have we served if we have wasted the urge to learn?

Children have their own meaning for the word *play*. To them it does not, as it does to adults, carry the ideas of idleness, purposelessness, relaxation from work. When we began our school we had named it a "play school," as a telegraphic way of saying that in our way of teaching, the children learned by playing. It was the children who made us, early in the school's history, delete the word from the school's name. To them it was not a "play school" but a school, and they were working hard at their schooling.

How hard they work, only we who have watched them really know. They do not waste one precious moment. They are going about their jobs all the time. No father in his office or mother in her home works at such a pace. For a long time I was principally afraid that they would exhaust themselves in this strenuous new kind of school.

Every step of the way, I was learning too. I had set myself the task of learning where, in our teaching of children, we were letting the precious desire to learn dribble wastefully away. I was going to find the leak in the dike and put my finger in it. Often it seemed to me that there were too many leaks, that the ponderous system we had erected for bringing children up both in school and in the home resembled more a sieve than a dike. I found myself going back toward the beginning, earlier and earlier in the child's life.

I followed the urge to learn through some of its many aspects. I saw it as the urge to play: at the moment that we scorned this impulse and set it aside, and treated it as something apart from serious work, at that moment we were beginning to waste the child.

I saw the urge to see, touch, experience everything at first hand. At the moment that we interpose second-hand knowledge—from the teacher instead of from the world itself, from books rather than from life—again we have begun to waste the child. True, there comes a time in a child's learning about his constantly expanding world when he can no longer go out and see for himself. For the far-away and long-ago he must turn to books and museums. But the moment when he must begin to do his learning from second-hand sources is a critical one. If we thrust him toward it too soon, before he has learned to gather his facts and relate them for himself, to ask his own questions and find his own answers, then we have opened another breach through which the desire to learn can be lost.

And I saw, too, the urge to learn with a purpose that is immediate, practical, and within the scope of a child to understand. It is as much good to a child to know his three R's by rote, to have been poured full of knowledge of skills without the ability to use them, as it is to a man to know the principles of swimming and not be able to save himself from drowning.

It has taken me a lifetime of learning from children to begin to know these things: how to stop the waste, how to channel the precious forces of children.

CHAPTER 9

NINTH-GRADE STUDENT VOICES IN A SOCIAL ACTION PROJECT

"They Went for Us, They Cared"

Shira Eve Epstein
The City College of New York (CUNY)

In the spring of 2006, a class of ninth graders worked with facilitators of a community-based organization to plan and run a safe-sex health fair in their urban high school, The Leadership Academy.[1] The social action project was based around the students' questions and concerns, and the youth had the opportunity to feel that their voices mattered. I explore this form of student involvement with the aim of providing a vision for how teachers can share authority with their students and create relevant learning opportunities. The chapter begins with a broad discussion of student voice in curriculum and the merit of social action projects. I then detail various curricular events and student responses to the social action project in The Leadership Academy, concluding with recommendations for educators.

Listening to and Learning from Students, pages 67–77
Copyright © 2011 by Information Age Publishing
All rights of reproduction in any form reserved.

SOCIAL ACTION VS. THE GRAMMAR OF SCHOOLING

Students and teachers in American schools often experience the hard "fact of unequal power," as teachers commonly work with enhanced authority and students are asked to passively follow instructions (Jackson, 1990, p. 28). Such an allocation of power is part of the "basic grammar of schooling" that has stabilized the roles of teachers and students for decades (Tyack & Cuban, 1995, p. 85). Educators utilizing traditional, teacher-centered curriculum and pedagogical methods can ignore the voices and experiences of students. This silencing of students protects hierarchies structured around class, race, gender, and sexual orientation and can lead schools to disregard unwanted perspectives and privilege of normative perspectives (Fine & Weis, 2003, p. 7). While some teachers abide by the grammar of schooling and bank desired bits of knowledge in students positioned as "depositories," others take a dialogic and interactive approach, where both teachers and students co-create knowledge (Freire, 1970, p. 72). Instead of silencing student voices, teachers can uplift them and place them at the heart of the curriculum.

Teachers wishing to include student voices in this way may find it a struggle in the present era of accountability. Teachers must contend with various forms of monitoring and surveillance geared toward ensuring that they enforce the status quo through testing and scripted curriculum (Lipman, 2007). As current policies emphasize accountability to standards and tests, students receive limited opportunities to develop critical thinking skills that can help them challenge the inequities that pervade our society. Furthermore, textbooks and perceptions of what constitutes "official knowledge" work heavily to silence student views, particularly those that are marginalized (Apple, 2000). School leaders can stress dominant forms of knowledge when responding to the expectations of the standards movement that enforces the vision of students as containers to be filled with specific pieces of information (Sleeter, 2005). The impact of No Child Left Behind is representative of and exacerbates these trends, as the reform narrows the scope of the curriculum, limiting room for teachers to consider the social and emotional needs and interests of students, let alone integrate them into the curriculum (Cochran-Smith & Lytle, 2006). Overall, teachers face pressures that may lead them to emphasize rote learning over critical thinking and focus on testing more than holistic teaching and assessment methods.

Within this context, the importance of curricula that validate student voices, integrate relevant subject matter, and scaffold opportunities for students to act with agency is clear. If we wish to motivate students and address their social, emotional, political, and artistic intelligences, providing opportunities for such student-centered learning becomes crucial. This chapter is meant to support teachers who seek to challenge entrenched systems that limit student empowerment and aid them in considering ways for students to play an active role in curriculum enactment.

Incorporating social action projects into the traditional school day can serve this purpose. Social action projects are associated with a social reconstructionist curriculum orientation, which argues that curricula can be established around the goal of teaching students about the possibilities of building a better world (Eisner, 1985). When students get involved in social action projects, they are asked to take action in response to social problems by participating in the community and providing needed services. While taking action in this way, social action projects offer students opportunities to critically reflect on the problems, recognize their complexity, and ultimately question the status quo (Wade, 1997; Wade & Saxe, 1996).

For example, Darts (2006) discusses the work of high school students who identified social problems of concern, conducted research on these problems, taught their classmates about them, and designed artistic action projects to raise awareness or advocate for social change. One action entailed a street theater-type performance that began with students yelling discriminatory phrases at each other during a school assembly. Once the student actors revealed their intent—to stand against hate and violence—they led small group discussions on related topics, including bullying, and later created multimedia artwork on these themes to display around the school.

Students may choose to base social action projects around various issues including racism, gang violence, or the war in Iraq. To address these problems, they have been seen to write newspaper editorials, form discussion groups, or film documentaries. These and many other action steps can be linked to academic skills and standards, as a project may ask students to research and critically assess a social problem, create written and visual aids to raise awareness about it, and work with numerical statistics to present its impact. In speaking specifically about their own lives, students can engage in the intellectual and activist work of liberation or praxis, gaining awareness of their situations and taking critical, empowered steps in reference to this awareness (Freire, 1970). Such learning activities can foster students' political, academic, social, personal/moral, and vocational development (Furco, 1994).

Clearly, through social action projects, students can practice a potent form of agency and learn to use their voices in powerful ways—countering traditional power schemas in classrooms. While teachers might integrate student voice and share authority during many curricular experiences, questions around authority are highlighted during social action projects, as the critical and social intent of the projects allow students to negotiate entry into real-life political contexts (Schultz & Oyler, 2006). When teachers mediate their own voice and power so as to allow for this entry, they give students the opportunity to determine what to do about identified social problems. Even elementary-aged children have designed sophisticated projects yielding their own self-empowerment and community betterment (Schultz, 2008). This vision places the expectation on teachers to ask students about the issues that occupy their attention and structure a process in which the students do something about them. This yields a sharing of authority in which sometimes the teacher leads, sometimes the students lead, and all ultimately gain in power (Oyler, 1996). Such sharing of authority was observed in a ninth-grade classroom in The Leadership Academy. The following sections detail the program at work and the students' views of this experience.

UNDERSTANDING THE URBAN YOUTH PROGRAM

The social action project in The Leadership Academy was enacted in cooperation with an organization called Urban Youth that employed facilitators to visit urban high schools on a weekly basis and enact a curriculum based around the themes of student empowerment and social action. The Urban Youth program aims to equip adolescents with authentic life skills, prepare them for adulthood, and give them opportunities to participate in an action project to effect change in their communities. The lessons during the opening months of the program focus on the developing of leadership skills including public speaking and goal setting. In the latter half of the year, the program revolves around the creation and execution of social action projects. Each Urban Youth classroom designs a different action project arising from the students' combined interests. The social action project in the Leadership Academy evolved out of the students' concern that they were not being taught how to make healthy and safe decisions about sex. It culminated with a safe-sex health fair in which the entire ninth grade had the opportunity to learn about safe-sex practices.

Two ninth-grade advisory classes within The Leadership Academy came together once a week for the Urban Youth program, yielding a class size of thirty students. The two advisory teachers cooperated in the enactment of Urban Youth curriculum. The students participating in the program during the time of observation were exclusively students of color and they all lived in urban neighborhoods surrounding the school. They worked with three Urban Youth staff, including Tanisha Maguire, who played a key leadership role.

The Urban Youth facilitators believed that as non-teachers, free from responsibilities around content-area knowledge or academic skills, they could enact a student-centered curriculum and create what Tanisha called "a more free flowing environment." Another Urban Youth facilitator noted, "There is more freedom in this versus being a regular teacher where you are mandated to do 'x', 'y', and 'z,' and you have to report to all these different people." They felt able to focus on the students' social and emotional leadership development and avoid the possibly oppressive expectations implied within academic standards or standardized tests. I raise this point to illustrate the way a "regular teacher" may feel constrained around curricular mandates. Indeed, when projects that aim to uplift student voice are funded, staffed, and planned outside of the school system, the leaders of the project can focus on their visions of social change and youth empowerment in a sustained way, often unlike teachers working within schools (Mitra, 2006). This finding reflects the Urban Youth facilitators' belief that in enacting a program developed by a community-based organization, as opposed to a board of education or a corporate-curriculum company focused on standards and test results, they gained a distance from the norms that can silence students.

However, classroom teachers can learn from and apply the principles that drive the Urban Youth curriculum and question the limits that they may experience in reference to norms of accountability. I challenge the belief that curricular mandates must stifle student voices and wish to instigate discussions of how teachers in traditional content areas implement instruction that is student-centered and promotes social action. The teachers in The Leadership Academy supported the Urban Youth facilitators in the social action curriculum enactment, showing the possibility for content-area teachers to engage in this work. With the necessary vision and tools, K–12 teachers can enact social action curriculum during the traditional school day. This process may revitalize teachers who feel drained and limited by the pressures of standards and standardized testing. The following description of the Urban Youth program, and the students' positive views of it, can inform K–12 teachers about an approach to consider for their classrooms, allowing them to integrate student voice.

Data on the Urban Youth program were collected during a four-month observation period in The Leadership Academy. During this time, I observed the weekly sessions, recorded field notes, and interviewed students, teachers, and Urban Youth employees. This qualitative study, including the methodology, is grounded in critical theory. Critical theory suggests that power orientations and political implications of all roles should be considered. In turn, I worked to recognize and mediate my own power in the research process by establishing dialectical relationships with the participants. Furthermore, the following discussion analyzes the ways the facilitators and the students held power within the curriculum enactment. The views of Jason and Mona, two ninth-graders interviewed separately, are highlighted, as they illustrate student views of the Urban Youth facilitators' efforts to share authority and the emergent social action project.

VALUING STUDENT VOICES
IN A SOCIAL ACTION PROJECT

The Urban Youth facilitators' commitment to student expression was observed at the very start of the social action project when they asked the students to determine the topic that would guide their work. The ninth graders subsequently brainstormed multiple problems in the community. Once the board was filled with ideas, they identified how many of the issues were linked to either drugs or sexual health. A teacher suggested that they vote between the two and the majority selected sexual health. Class votes may not be fully participatory in that they do not always encourage the expression of student voice or allow for deliberation. However, such a pedagogic move can be placed on a spectrum of democratic activities and illustrate teachers' intent to value students' views. The discussion around this vote revealed the students' belief that their peers did not know enough about safe sex health practices, and the students subsequently decided to create a safe-sex health fair to share information that would help their peers make sound decisions.

The student-centered decision-making process grew more sophisticated in the following sessions, as the students debated which aspects of sexual health and sexual relationships they would address. In one active discussion, the students disagreed on whether they should talk about rape, as a female student determined that she would not attend class if the project focused on rape. They ultimately chose not to highlight this topic. An advisory teacher explained that in engaging with this student, the other students learned that "we have to be very sensitive to how we bring things up because you may not know if a person . . . has had a negative experience." In expressing her opinion in the classroom, that student helped the others recognize the delicacy of the topic.

The students looked fondly upon their active role in the development and enactment of the fair in general. They often spoke about their ownership of the project. Days after the fair occurred, Mona reported: "We had to make the idea" and in the running of the fair "everybody had a part . . . everybody did something." This view was further reinforced in an exchange with Jason and his classmate, Paula:

> **Jason:** We felt in charge when we did the health fair.
> **SEE:** Let's talk about that for one minute because you mentioned that to me in class a few weeks ago. Why did you feel like you were in charge of the project?
> **Paula:** 'Cause we made the decisions about what, when. And we did it.
> **Jason:** Exactly.

SEE: Give me an example.

Jason: Like if we would have never voted for sex, the category itself, they wouldn't have had a health fair. I think if we had voted for police assault, we would have never had a health fair. We would have done a project or something on it or made videos or something like that.

SEE: Got it.

Jason: Like, the ideas in the health fair were from us.

The students felt that were it not for their ideas, the health fair would have never evolved. These sentiments illustrate the students' feelings of ownership and engagement within the project.

The facilitators did not simply show this interest in student voice during the social action project, as they prioritized active student engagement throughout the year. At the start of each session, the classroom desks were pushed out of the way and the chairs were placed in a circle. Then, the students were asked to "check in." During these informal preliminary discussions, the ninth graders responded to prompts ranging in style from "When people see you, what do they see?" to "What is your favorite cartoon character?" The check-ins served to provoke student expression and help the students grow as a community.

The facilitators also implemented team-building activities that fostered student participation. For example, the "magic path" game sent the message that each student was needed and important. The goal of the game was for the students to silently find a path through a grid of squares constructed on the floor with masking tape. The facilitator made a buzzing sound with her voice if a student stepped in squares that were off limits. When the first student finished the maze, the remaining students supported each other by pointing out the correct squares. One teacher commented, "I think every single student participated and that had never happened. That was the biggest turning point for the whole year." The Urban Youth facilitators' approach instigated a unique form of student engagement that had been previously absent within the classroom. Also, the teacher's perception of this moment as a significant turning point shows that she valued the Urban Youth focus on activities that would prompt student agency and involvement. The facilitators designed multiple opportunities for students to speak and act, laying the groundwork for the students to play an active role in the social action project.

Within the context of these efforts, the students in The Leadership Academy identified the facilitators as friendly and trustworthy. Mona, a student, explained how the students developed a familiarity with the facilitators. She said:

We started talking to them. They started talking to us. We got to see how they was and we felt comfortable. After a while we started knowing them more and more. So, it was like a family in a classroom. . . . They got nice, so I started liking it.

Jason described Tanisha by saying, "She would come and be like a friend. She would talk to you. How was your day? This and that. She would talk to you. Mad cool and stuff." The students were happy with all the "talking" that they did with the facilitators and the way that the facilitators seemed to listen to the students as friends would. Tanisha used similar language when she explained that through this process, the students "learned that teachers and adults are their friends." The advisory teachers confirmed the students' attraction to Tanisha, explaining how much they appreciated her approach. When viewing the project and the Urban Youth curriculum overall it is clear that Tanisha and the other Urban Youth facilitators did much more than act in a friendly way to build these relationships. They encouraged the students' active participation in class activities, enlisted the ninth graders to speak about their authentic concerns, even sensitive and personal ones, and in turn allowed them to play an active role in shaping the curriculum.

Jason's experience with his regular teachers spoke to their difficulties connecting to the students in this way. He repeatedly noted that teachers are "doing it to get paid," citing examples of teachers ignoring the individuality and needs of the students. He explained:

When I was in junior high school I had teachers that would just write the assignment on the board and they wouldn't even help you. . . . Every time a student would talk and stuff they would sit there, being "Well, I don't care, it's not my experience, it is your education."

He viewed his teachers as avoiding direct contact with the students and adhering to the traditional grammar of schooling in which they had authority and students were asked to passively follow directions. His account also speaks of the teachers' frustrations with classroom management and possible inability to proactively address students who may have been "speaking out of turn." Another student even described advisory class, which is intended to be student centered, as "boring" when the Urban Youth facilitators were not there. She said such "boring" classes make her want to be "non-attending."

Jason did not see all his teachers in this negative light and appreciated teachers who validated student experiences. For example, he noted that some teachers were "really focusing on me . . . they went for us, they cared." If Jason's experience is typical, we may conclude that students are attracted to teachers who listen to them and seriously consider their interests and questions. This explains the ninth graders' interest and involvement in the

Urban Youth social action project. K–12 teachers as well as supplemental program facilitators can learn from these student views and consider how to craft their practice so to elicit and integrate student voices in the curriculum.

THOUGHTS FOR EDUCATORS

The case of the safe-sex health fair in The Leadership Academy illustrates how teachers can share authority with students. The students selected the topic of the project and the facilitators elicited their active participation throughout the year. In this context, the students' expressed their interest in and ownership of the project. This process stands in contrast to the teaching approaches often associated with punitive and limiting aspects of testing and standards, which can frustrate learners.

Given my praise of this approach, it should be noted that social action projects are not uniformly developed in reference to the students' voices. Teachers can involve students in projects based on contemporary social issues, yet simultaneously limit the integration of student voice. Teachers may privilege their own opinions, instead of allowing for the sharing of multiple viewpoints, and work to ensure that their students value a particular perspective on a social issue. Even if a range of perspectives is welcome into the classroom discussion, teachers may heavily exercise their authority when determining the nature of the action component. This was seen in the enactment of the health fair in The Leadership Academy. In the weeks leading up to the fair, the facilitators arranged for a keynote speaker, assigned student roles, and gained outside corporate funding—all without contribution from the students. Furthermore, students will not always show an interest in participating in activities, even if the curricula reflect their interests. There were incidents when students in The Leadership Academy expressed negativity about the fair and wanted to sit out from activities leading up to this action.

Nevertheless, through the social action project, the ninth graders had an opportunity to feel that their experiences and opinions mattered. The facilitators identified their stories as important, in contrast to the traditional role of teacher as silencing banker of information. In addition, by allowing the students to express their authority at the beginning of the project, the facilitators gained the students' trust to act on their behalf so to plan the more logistical aspects of the health fair. This example supports the argument that when teachers share authority with students, their own authority can be extended (Oyler, 1996).

Teachers interested in applying this approach should consider the following questions: How can I share authority with students? In what ways can I integrate student voices into the curriculum? More specifically, teachers may want to use the story of the Urban Youth facilitators as a guide for integrating student-centered social action projects into their classrooms. The facilitators modeled various teacher practices that could be adopted in K–12 classrooms. They introduced games and check-ins to help students feel wanted and comfortable with their own voices. They then elicited the students' stories at the start of the project and subsequently identified a topic for their project in reference to these stories. As a result, the students' social concerns were at the heart of the project and they were able to see in a very specific way that they could have agency within the school and in their lives. Teachers may choose to enact a social action project based around students' concerns, yet make certain decisions that compare to those of the Urban Youth facilitators. For example, they may choose to address traditional subject-oriented standards through the project or incorporate student voice to a greater extent during the action component of the project. Of course, teachers should make these decisions based on the context-specific nuances of their classrooms.

Within the dynamic decision-making processes that teachers experience, the value of student voice and authority should be recognized so to interrupt the pernicious silencing of students and involve them in their schooling. Students can come to feel that school is a place where they matter when their voices are at the center of the curriculum.

NOTE

1. The names of all people, schools, and organizations are pseudonyms so to protect the participants' identities.

REFERENCES

Apple, M. W. (2000). *Official knowledge: Democratic education in a conservative age.* New York: Routledge.

Cochran-Smith, M., & Lytle, S. L. (2006). Troubling images of teaching in No Child Left Behind. *Harvard Educational Review, 76*(4), 668–697.

Darts, D. (2006). Art education for a change: Contemporary issues and the visual arts. *Art Education, 59*(5), 6–12.

Eisner, E. W. (1985). *The educational imagination: On the design and evaluation of school programs.* New York: Macmillan.

Fine, M., & Weis, L. (2003). Silenced voices and extraordinary conversations. In M. Fine & L. Weis (Eds.), *Silenced voices and extraordinary conversations . . . Reimagining schools* (pp. 1–8). New York: Teachers College Press.

Freire, P. (1970). *Pedagogy of the oppressed.* New York: The Continuum International Publishing Group.

Furco, A. (1994). A conceptual framework for the institutionalization of youth service programs in primary and secondary education. *Journal of Adolescence, 17,* 395–409.

Jackson, P. W. (1990). *Life in classrooms.* New York: Teachers College Press.

Lipman, P. (2007). *High stakes education Inequality, globalization, and urban school reform.* New York: RoutledgeFalmer.

Mitra, D. L. (2006). Student voice from the inside and the outside: The positioning of challengers. *International Journal of Leadership in Education, 9*(4), 315–328.

Oyler, C. (1996). *Making room for students: Sharing authority in Room 104.* New York: Teachers College Press.

Schultz, B. D. (2008). *Spectacular things happen along the way: Lessons from an urban classroom.* New York: Teacher College Press.

Schultz, B. D., & Oyler, C. (2006). We make this road as we walk together: Sharing teacher authority in a social action curriculum project. *Curriculum Inquiry, 36*(4), 423–451.

Sleeter, C. E. (2005). *Un-standardizing curriculum: Multicultural teaching in the standards-based classroom.* New York: Teachers College Press.

Tyack, D., & Cuban, L. (1995). *Tinkering toward utopia: A century of public school reform.* Cambridge: Harvard University Press.

Wade, R. (1997). Community service learning and the social studies curriculum: Challenges to effective practice. *The Social Studies, 88,* 197–202.

Wade, R., & Saxe, D. W. (1996). Community service-learning in the social studies: Historical roots, empirical evidence, critical issues. *Theory and Research in Social Education, 24*(4), 331–359.

CHAPTER 10

INTERLUDE

HI(STORY) & HOPE

How the Stories of Our Individual and Collective Pasts Determine What We Believe is Possible

kahlil almustafa
Urban Word NYC

Almost everything I was ever told was a lie.
—Immortal Technique—*Revolutionary Volume II*

Yes, it matters! This is what I want to say to the young women and men I visit in New York City public schools to facilitate poetry workshops. I wish someone said these words to me when I was their age. I want to rip the earphones out of their ears, push back the fitted caps shadowing their faces so their eyes could meet my own, and scream directly into their souls, "Yes, you matter!" Sometimes I say these actual words but it is but a faint voice straining to make it through a wall of stories built before their grandparents' grandparents were born. I tell them, "Forget what the world thinks. You matter!" But when they look around, their evidence says different.

I see myself in the faces of the young, brown students I teach. They are hopeless, not only for themselves, but usually for the entire human race. How did they get so hopeless, so young? In my case, it was the stories about my life and about the world, none of which had happy endings.

As a young Black man growing up in the eighties, my future was clear. A poem I wrote during my teenage years captured my outlook, "This place is a hallway with two doors on either side. One door leads to my grave, the other to a cage." During my formative years, I believed I would end up dead or in jail. Statistics, images, and ideas of the endangered Black man permeated the air, and the stench of it was strongest at the funeral homes and curbside memorials I visited.

My stories about the world were as hopeless as the ones I believed about myself. If you asked me about humanity, I would probably have said, "People are selfish and mean individuals; always have been, always will be." If you asked me about Black people, I would probably tell you we were a failure as a race and no matter how hard we tried, this fact was unlikely to change. It is stories like these that made me believe "it didn't matter" because "I didn't matter" and it seemed "nothing truly mattered to anyone else." It is these stories that I see in my students' eyes and in the bodies they drag into their classrooms. They wear these stories like a heavy second skin.

My stories about Black people came from my lived experiences. Everywhere the narrative was the same, white people are good and Black people are bad. In this race called the human race, white people were winning at everything that's good and Black people were winning at everything that's bad. In obtaining money, graduating from college, life expectancy, becoming Hollywood stars, and dad-to-family ratio, white people were winning. In going to prison, dying from AIDS, being poor, teenage pregnancy and teenage funerals, baby mamma drama and prideful ignorance—Black people were gold medalists; so sometimes I hated being on the black team.

As much as this narrative was based in what I observed and what I experienced, it was also rooted in an historical narrative I learned in school and in church, often with the support of media. In school, I learned that all of the founding fathers were white, the heroes that founded this country were white, the president and all other important members of society were white, and the foundation of all knowledge came from ancient, white Greek society. In church, my white pastor led me in prayer to a white-faced Jesus, the son of a white god who created everything in the universe, including me. This whitewashed version of history had me hating my black skin.

According to the narrative of third-grade textbooks, Black people entered the human story as slaves in chained bondage, brought to the "land of the free and home of the brave from the Dark Continent of Africa." Our history began as savages, less than human, less than white people. We were lost and killing ourselves until we were saved by white Europeans who invited us to become part of civilization. We were slaves until another great white man named Abraham Lincoln set us free. The only Black man I remember contributing to the founding of this country was Crispus Attucks, and the only thing I remember him doing was being a Black man who was the first person to die in the Revolutionary War. This is the narrative I learned in school. This is the history I carried with me that had me believing I did not matter because within this history there was no hope for my future.

I did not begin to have hope for my future until I began to learn about the injustices Black people have faced throughout the history of the United States. Black people were not inherently inferior, but were navigating a violent and hostile racist society. I was able to see Black people, and myself, as a dignified people struggling to maintain their humanity in the face of white supremacy. This sent me on a search of finding out about these injustices with the belief that if I exposed them, they would somehow complete me. Paulo Freire (1970/2000) speaks about this process in *Pedagogy of the Oppressed:*

> Hope is rooted in men's incompletion, from which they move out in constant search—a search which can only be carried out in communion with others. Hopelessness is a form of silence, of denying the world and fleeing from it. The dehumanization resulting from an unjust order is not a cause for despair, but for hope, leading to the incessant pursuit of the humanity denied by injustice. Hope, however, does not consist in crossing one's arms and waiting. As long as I fight, I am moved by hope; and I fight with hope, then I can wait. (pp. 91–92)

I had hope because I had a reason to fight, "incessant pursuit of the humanity denied by injustice." I waged this battle, not just for myself, but for my family, my ancestors, for Black people and for all humanity.

History and hope have an intimate relationship. What one believes about the past, both personal and political, usually determines what they believe about what is possible and probable in the(ir) future. What a person believes about the future directly impacts their behavior.

What exactly am I speaking of when I say history? I am not speaking of history as an objective and unchanging record of past events as we learn in seventh-grade Social Studies. Objectivity in history is one of the first myths we learn in our educational system. All historical narratives reflect the philosophy, assumptions, and opinions of the history-teller. History is not simply an accurate re-telling of the past. History telling is about capturing the imagination of people in the present moment. Historian and author Gerda Lerner (1986) notes in *The Creation of Patriarchy,*

> History gives meaning to human life and connects each life to immortality, but history has yet another function. In preserving the collective past and

reinterpreting it to the present, human beings define their potential and explore the limits of their possibilities. (p. 6)

What makes history valuable is not its accuracy, but whether or not it resonates with other people, and how this historical narrative impacts their idea about their possibilities and therefore their actions.

The essential part of history is the story. These stories are learned as scholarly narratives found in books, but they are also gained through stories passed down from great-grandparents, religious texts, poetry and music, cultural traditions, and today more than ever from visual media. These stories make up the narrative through which we live our lives.

In *Why History Matters*, Gerda Lerner (1997) shows how history shapes our definitions of ourselves and impacts our outlook on our futures:

> Our self-representation, the way we define who we are, also takes the shape of the life story we tell. What we remember, what we stress as significant, and what we omit of our past defines our present. And since the boundaries of our self-definition also delimit our hopes and aspirations, this personal history affects our future. If we see ourselves as victimized, as powerless and overwhelmed by forces we cannot understand or control, we will choose to live cautiously, avoid conflict, and evade pain. If we see ourselves as loved, grounded, powerful, we will embrace the future, live courageously, and accept challenges with confidence. (p. 199)

It is this self-representation that I attempt to help my students transform through their poetry. Through poetry, I transformed the narrative of my life from "a young Black man trying not to become a statistic," into "a survivor, warrior-poet, historian, scholar, social engineer, and humanitarian-in-action." It was through reading from a vast library of Black scholarly works, mining for the stories within my own family heritage, listening to the storytelling of elders, and using poetry to rewrite the narrative of my life that I transformed my story. It is this new story that makes it possible for me to teach in New York City public schools because when I see these young women and men, I see myself, I see possibility, I see hope.

REFERENCES

Freire, P. (1970/2000). *Pedagogy of the oppressed* (30th Anniversary ed.). New York: Continuum.

Lerner, G. (1986). *The creation of patriarchy (women and history)*. New York: Oxford University Press.

Lerner, G. (1998). *Why history matters: Life and thought*. New York: Oxford University Press.

THEY THINK KIDS HAVE NOTHING TO SAY

Lloyd Thomas
*Urban Word NYC In-School Residency
and New York City Schools*

They think Kids have nothing to say.
Who are they?
They are our leaders, the CEOs,
anyone bigger than us.
But, from this pen from which I write,
the truth will be revealed before it is
too late.
We Kids created the world.
We made the past and will
make the future.
From Joan of Arc to us today
Kids have made a difference.
Sure we never went to space or
made a brand new drug,
but those people who did
were Kids once.
They had hopes and dreams.
Their dreams became ideas and
their ideas became reality.
We are pawns in a game of chess,
a sacrifice much taken.
But we can become the powerful queen
if guided by the caring player
saving every piece.
When let free, we bloom, we blossom
into a rose, a blend of beauty and power.
But as we grow, the frost of the world
nips at us, we lose our innocence
we lie, we cheat.
And so our petals fall off one by one
by one until a stick with thorns remains

no hope, no love.
Some people lose their petals faster than others.
Some may keep their petals forever
But today, they, our leaders fill the world
with thorns, choking any roses which emerge.
So today Kids must speak out
past the doubt and past the hate
to shed light on the world once more
before it is too late.
For now more than ever
Kids have lots to say.

LISTEN

Miracle Graham
*Urban Word NYC In-School Residency
and New York City Schools*

My pen is my instrument.
Its abilities are somewhat creative.
But then again, it's not, because it depends on the person who's using it.
Me, yeah, me.

And I know when I be writing those things at times in the form of poetry
What the Lord blessed me with the time.
And I shall write and speak freely
Because my pen and my words is my instrument.
The key to this element is to listen.
My words are expressed through universal dimensions,
critical thinking, decisions, diverse opinions, and . . .
All I ask of you is to listen, 'cause my words is my instrument.

Right now you may not be taking in what I'm saying,
But I'm not surprised 'cause you're nothing
But a trial and tribulation,
And I am today's generation,
Meaning that I have the right to have the urge to speak
'Cause my voices deserve to be heard.

And my voice shall be released out my soul by my ink to hit my sheet.
Because my voice is the effect of the course of corruption.
Corruption. Course of corruption
That you create in your lies or reluctance to speak the truth.

You, you, you must consider the youth.
You, you, you and your stable mind of judgment,
Causing a heart of hate,
Not realizing that those who do a good job of selling weed and drugs will
do a good job of real estate.

Gravity and attention, like those who run the streets and know the streets,
Making them to be easy to be great spokesmens in the politics.
And following. I am the next sun rising.

Me, me, me. Wait.
We, we, we. We, we, we.

We are today's generation.
We are the change and the difference.
We have the urge.
We are the angels that the Lord has sent, and our words deserve to be heard
Because our, Because our
Because our words is our instruments.

And hopefully
And hopefully someone will stop to listen.
Because our words is our instruments.

CHAPTER 11

CHALLENGING TEST-PREP PEDAGOGY

Urban High School Students Educate Pre-Service Teachers Using Liberatory Pedagogy

Louie F. Rodríguez
California State University, San Bernardino

INTRODUCTION

Low-income schools and communities are under tremendous pressure to meet state and federal mandates, in part because of the Bush administration's No Child Left Behind Act of 2001 (Noguera, 2005). This pressure has caused considerable distress for district- and school-level educators, particularly in historically low-performing areas by encouraging and, in many ways, forcing them to shape local polices and practices that revolve largely around raising standardized test scores. For instance, many chronically low-performing schools have reduced the entire school day to what I call a "Test-Prep Pedagogy" in which the relationship between teaching

Listening to and Learning from Students, pages 87–100

and learning, teachers and students, and the overall intellectual experience is reduced to raising test scores. In schools that practice Test-Prep Pedagogy, teaching and learning is reduced to test review, such as repetitively reviewing test questions. In such schools, teachers and students are given very few, if any, opportunities to build community (Meier & Wood, 2004) or establish respectful and personalized relationships (Conchas & Rodríguez, 2007; Rodríguez, 2005), and they are often blocked in imagining what is possible (Nieto, 1994), especially in light of research that shows such processes are critical to the success of low-income students of color in U.S. schools (Valenzuela, 1999). Equally troubling, Test-Prep Pedagogy has in many ways stifled the creativity of teachers and students, both limiting the ways in which knowledge is produced and restricting any chances of realizing liberatory practice, particularly in urban schools that can serve as social spaces of activism and resistance (Lauria & Mirón, 2005). Liberatory practice, as defined by Freire, involves pedagogies driven by dialogue, reciprocity, and transformation—processes that are in direct contradiction with Test-Prep Pedagogy.

As a professor in a college of education, I have observed that while many university-level educators may be aware of the challenges associated with urban education, the pedagogies used to engage pre-service teachers do not veer too far from the traditional technical methods and skills that historically have driven teacher development (Bartolomé, 1994; Trueba, 1999). Namely, pre-service teachers are still encouraged to create perfect lesson plans, apply the best behavioral management techniques, take courses that rely on tests that require memorization of facts rather than understanding (only to find themselves forgetting what they memorized), and are religiously encouraged to employ the latest "best practices" without a critical consideration of the social context. While pre-service teachers are trained to be good instructors, a significant percentage of low-income Black and Latina/o children in urban communities face concentrated poverty, community violence, under-resourced schools, little or no access to health care, and political disenfranchisement. The incongruence between the realities facing urban education and the ways in which pre-service teachers are engaged in teacher education programs requires a new type of pedagogy—one that is relevant, courageous, and liberatory.

This chapter describes the outcome of a dialogue between pre-service teachers and urban high school students. First, I provide the theoretical perspectives and principles that drive the pedagogy used in this project, followed by the teacher and student context in which this work is conducted. Then, I discuss the various components of the program followed by an analysis of the impact that this initiative had on the dispositions of pre-service teachers.

CONCEPTUAL CONTEXT

As this initiative developed, it was clear from the beginning that as a university-level professor, my role as a politician would surface as I would be denouncing what Freire called domesticating practices and advocating for liberatory pedagogy through dialogue (Shor, 1993). Whereas Test-Prep Pedagogy mirrors the "banking method" as described by Freire (1970), where teachers deposit information into the so-called empty vessels of students' minds, liberatory pedagogy is driven by principles of love, hope, and justice (Freire, 1970).

One way that dialogical pedagogy is practiced is through Freire's problem-posing method (Rodríguez, 2004; Solórzano, 1989). Problem posing is driven in part by the experiences and realities of the people involved in the educational endeavor (Freire, 1970)—in this case, urban high school students and pre-service teachers. This pedagogical approach avoids doing education *to* or *for* people and rather focuses on students and teachers doing education *with* one another. This dynamic also positions students and teachers as co-producers of knowledge versus the conventional situation where teachers should be all-knowing experts. Thus, dialogical pedagogy attempts to create conditions where students and pre-service teachers dialogue with one another in order to conquer and transform the world. Freire states:

> Because dialogue is an encounter among women and men who name the world, it must not be a situation where some name on behalf of others. It is an act of creation; it must not serve as a crafty instrument for the domination of one person by another. The domination itself implicit in dialogue is that of the world by the dialoguers; it is conquest of the world for the liberation of humankind. (Freire, 1970, p. 70)

Thus, within the context of this initiative, the goal was to create a space wherein urban high school students and pre-service teachers engage in critical dialogue where historically marginalized youth are transformed from students into teachers.

METHODOLOGY AND DESIGN

The Participants

During the summer of 2007, I taught a Research Seminar to a group of high school students as part of a six-week summer institute at a large, comprehensive urban university in the southeastern part of the U.S. The students in the seminar were participants in a project aimed to improve the personal, political, and intellectual dimensions of students' lives. These high school students attended one of most notorious high schools in the city known for chronic academic failure, high rates of violence, and an inescapable social context of high poverty. All the students were either Black or Latina/o and nearly all of the students qualified for free or reduced lunch. Over the course of the summer, the high school student researchers were provided a space to discuss educational inequality and were exposed to various theories and methodologies associated with participatory action research (Cordova, 2004; Fine et al., 2005). The end product was a series of presentations focused on topics researched and analyzed by the student researchers.

During the same summer, I also taught an undergraduate, upper-division foundations course to pre-service teachers. This required course aimed to engage pre-service teachers in critical issues facing urban education. Forty-one of the 45 students enrolled in the course were female. A majority of the students were born and raised in the city in which they attended college, were primarily middle-class, and of Hispanic/Latina/o background (i.e., Caribbean or South American).

The Dialogue

Given that pre-service teachers are rarely provided opportunities to meaningfully engage with urban high school students prior to entering the classroom, a series of dialogues were organized in three ways: (1) High School Students as Researchers, (2) High School Students as Experts, and (3) Open Dialogues between High School Students and Pre-Service Teachers. The first dialogue structure was created as a forum so that the high school student researchers could share their research findings with pre-service teachers. The purpose was to demonstrate how a group of urban high school students could engage in high-quality, rigorous, and intellectual work driven by their experiences and life knowledge. The second dialogue structure was meant for pre-service teachers to ask questions and seek advice from the high school students. This is particularly enlightening since adults are typically used to talking to students, rather than listening. This unique space positioned the students in the role of teacher or expert in an academic setting. Prior to the session, the pre-service teachers read and discussed varying perspectives on youth, particularly in research, the media, and in the general public discourse. Rather than viewing low-income youth of color as being "at-risk" (Flores, Cousin, & Diaz, 1991) and through a deficit perspective (Solorzano & Yosso, 2001; Valencia & Solorzano, 1997), the pre-service teachers were encouraged to recognize historically marginalized communities as intellectually and culturally wealthy, capitalizing on the strengths that low-income youth of color bring to classrooms, schools, and communities (Yosso, 2005). Finally, the third dialogue structure was open dialogues that were organically driven, revolving around student–teacher relationships, creativity in the classroom, and student dropouts. The data below evolves out of these dialogues.

The Data

The data from the dialogues were collected in two parts during the summer of 2007. The dialogues occurred across two sessions lasting two to three hours each. The first dialogue began with the student research presentations. The second dialogue was a continuation of the first. Both dialogues were video/audio recorded, reviewed, and transcribed verbatim. The pre-service teachers also submitted written reflections, questions, and comments. These reflections were particularly meaningful in the context of the video footage and transcripts. For example, among the pre-service teachers who participated verbally during the dialogues, their participation was compared and contrasted to their written reflections. Using grounded theory, the data were coded and analyzed through an examination of pre-service teachers' responses to and experiences with the youth during the dialogues (Strauss & Corbin, 1998). Finally, fieldnotes were recorded and analyzed to capture observations made during and after the dialogues (Emerson, Fretz, & Shaw, 1995). All three data sources served as the primary data set for this chapter.

FINDINGS

Three core themes emerged from the data and will be analyzed as such: (1) the ways in which pre-service teachers reacted to the physical presence and content of the student researcher presentations, (2) the role that respect played during the dialogues, and (3) the impact that the dialogues had on the overall dispositions of pre-service urban teachers.

Presence and Reception

Upon completing a presentation on the relationship between low expectations and the culture of power (Delpit, 1996) in their own school, the high school student researchers provided a series of recommendations that were primarily directed toward school administrators and the school board. To illustrate this idea, Kiki, a Haitian female and student researcher stated, "Our recommendation...is...to quit hiring unqualified teachers. We need the greatest teachers in the world....The smarter the teachers that the principal hires, the better it is for our school to gain the knowledge we desire." The high school researchers presented compelling interview data collected from other high school students addressing the issue of teacher discrimination. Kiki, like many of her peers, associated unqualified teachers with those who were more likely to discriminate against students. Students found that many Black students felt discriminated against by Hispanic/Latina/o and White teachers.

Most of the pre-service teachers were impressed by the rigor, depth, and organization of the youth presentations. Many of the pre-service teachers were able to recognize the courage it took to present in a college classroom and most agreed that these students were dynamic and passionate about the veracity of discrimination in their school. For instance, Lorena, a Latina pre-service teacher, told the student researchers after their presentation:

> I want to praise you and I want to congratulate you for being strong and actually taking the steps toward changing it [discrimination] and finding out what is wrong with your school. I think you are very courageous...so, you guys are awesome.

Other words of praise emanated from the pre-service teachers. Amanda, a Haitian pre-service teacher, who shared many of her personal experiences of discrimination and racism throughout the course, said:

> I think it takes a lot of strength and courage for students to speak out, and that's a problem, that nobody is speaking out and that's why we still have this discrimination...going on in the schools because the kids aren't acting out....I think this is great.

The written reflections described above were positive, but were not necessarily the norm. Interestingly, I found that the pre-service teachers who provided positive verbal feedback also displayed evidence of a critical consciousness (Freire, 1973) of themselves and the world in which they live, attributable in part to their admitted struggles in their own lives (Bartolomé, 2002; Bartolomé & Balderrama, 2001). For example, both Lorena and Amanda were women of color and identified as such. Over the course of the semester, they both shared critical insights about their own struggles as young people, particularly related to issues of race, gender, culture, and language differences.

Unfortunately, however, Lorena and Amanda were an anomaly as many of the pre-service teachers had a difficult time receiving the presentations. Not only did many pre-service teachers struggle with the saliency of the message (i.e., that discrimination is counterproductive), but they also, to a degree, resisted the messenger—the high school student researchers. For example, many pre-service teachers struggled with the physical dispositions of the students—dispositions that were different from their own. For instance, as the student researchers were high school students in a large urban city, many of their identities reflected various forms of urban youth culture— baggy jeans, long t-shirts, head wear, the use of non-standard English, and physical expression. Over the course of the semester, it became clear that most of the pre-service teachers were unfamiliar with urban youth culture as evident by their lack of familiarity with many urban cultural mediums I shared over the course of the semester (art, graffiti, spoken word, music, youth-created media, etc.). Thus, there seemed to be a correlation between the ways in which the pre-service teachers received the youth researchers and their own degree of awareness, consciousness, and political and ideological clarity about issues of race, class, gender, and social inequality (Bartolomé, 2002). Conversely, those without this consciousness or clarity had a much more difficult time receiving the youth presentations.

Angela, for instance, a middle-class Latina and one of the pre-service teachers made it clear earlier in the semester that she was not "urban" as stated in her reflection after the presentation: "in the future, these students should work on their body language and eye contact...[so that] ... the common stereotypes may not affect them and they can be taken seriously." Upon review of the videotape, some student researchers slouched in their seats or sat perpendicular to the audience. However, Angela's admission that these dispositions reinforce "common stereotypes" about the student researchers insinuates her deflection of the substance of their presentation. She later admitted this when referencing the pervasiveness of teacher discrimination in school: "I do think that every story has two or more sides to it as well and sometimes a group, when they have issues like these, should be talked about together with a mediator of some sorts." Because the student researchers spoke about their lived experiences in school, some pre-service teachers had a difficult time placing value on this knowledge, such as Angela, who needed to hear the other side of the argument. Angela would not legitimize the youths' experiences, especially when it is widely known that youth, especially youth of color, are rarely given an opportunity to speak about their "side of the story." While the dialogue revealed much of the thinking among the pre-service teachers, much more learning is required to build political clarity among teachers like Angela (Bartolomé, 2002).

Like Angela, Camilla also struggled with the content of the presentations, but also noted the youth's physical appearance. Camilla, a middle-upper-class "Hispanic" (self-identified) critiqued their physical disposition: "they [student researchers] were a little intimidated while talking. They should have been sure of themselves and had confidence." It is unclear what "sure of themselves" should look like, but upon review of the videotape the student researchers spoke with confidence and clarity about their experiences in school. For each claim, the youth researchers provided videotaped interviews to support their arguments. Camilla's critique of the students' physical presence reveals her limited exposure and understanding of students from urban youth culture and seemed to frame her critique based on her preconceived social stereotypes of the students. That is, sporting baggy pants, caps, or slouching in their chairs while giving their presentations was translated into the notion that the youth lacked confidence.

Camilla also struggled with the content of the presentation. Camilla actually questioned the sources of the knowledge the student researchers presented. Because the student researchers presented interviews and personal narratives as data, Camilla stated, "I think they did it [presented research] more or less based on how they feel and their opinions," and "if they wanted to change something I feel they should have had more statistics." Camilla needed more "facts" to be convinced that the student researchers were telling the truth about teacher discrimination. Thus, she discredited their experiences as opinions, not facts. As future teachers, Angela and Camilla must understand their power and privilege in dismissing other people's experiences, particularly in schools where teachers hold positional authority over students and specifically in urban schools where there is a pervasive cultural divide between students and teachers.

Respect During Dialogues

Another theme that arose during the dialogues revolved around the issue of respect and disrespect. I have written about this issue elsewhere, particularly in relation to low-income youth of color in U.S. schools (Conchas & Rodríguez, 2007; Rodríguez, 2005). To a large degree, respect mediates the communication and recognition between two different parties (individuals, groups, etc.). However, respect is also defined largely as a function of one's position in society (respect as a student, young person, teacher, parent, elder, etc.) and in relation to the "other" (Valenzuela, 1999). Unsurprisingly, the pre-service teachers had significantly different perspectives on what constitutes respect and disrespect as compared to the student researchers. Below is a discussion of three pre-service teachers' reflections on the dialogues.

After the presentation, Magdalena, a middle-class Latina, found the dialogues invaluable. However, she had a difficult time understanding the student researchers' reactions to some of the pre-service teachers' comments and feedback. For instance:

> I understand they [high school students] are sick and tired of living inequity everyday of their lives but they need to be a little wiser.... For example when

they were asked if they knew what they were getting themselves into [summer research project], they took...offense.... I believe that their voice would be heard if they were first given a communications class so that they learn to take criticism well, not personal[ly].

Although Magdalena recognizes the challenges of inequity the students' face, she does not seem to acknowledge that the pre-service teacher's comment may have indeed been offensive to the student researchers. Rather than trying to understand the significance of their reaction, she disregards this possibility, an obvious exertion of power. If Magdalena is unable to recognize her role in mediating the power of knowledge, she will struggle to engage students, especially those whose life and educational experiences that may be starkly different from her own.

Another student, Luis, a middle-class Latino, also found merit in the student presentations, but quickly criticized their "disrespect" toward the pre-service teachers. Said Luis:

> Their presentations were well put together and brought up great points.... To be honest, when we were giving them feedback...they did not take the feedback very well...I think they should have shown more respect.... These reactions that they made are what teachers see in the classroom, which can lead to teachers getting upset.

Like Magdalena, Luis also believed that the student researchers were disrespectful to the pre-service teachers because of the way they responded to the verbal feedback during the dialogues. Upon reviewing the videotapes of the dialogues, there was no more disrespect by the youth than by the pre-service teachers. The pre-service teachers felt like they were asking legitimate questions, whereas the youth interpreted some questions as disrespectful. Yet, for Luis, a pre-service teacher, the student researchers were the perpetrators of disrespect, not the pre-service teachers. Luis seemed to uncritically accept the pre-service teachers' feedback as appropriate and acceptable. It is as if any comment originating from the pre-service teachers should have been accepted because the pre-service teachers were the presumed authority figures as adults in the classroom. Because the student researchers took offense and were engaging in a dialogue where their experiences were an aspect of the data, they felt comfortable in sharing their discontent with what they deemed as offensive feedback. The youths' discontent was triggered by a White middle-class pre-service teacher who asked, "Did you know what you were getting yourselves into?" This was asked immediately after the author described the rigor of the summer program. An uncritical examination of this question seems harmless. However, the student researchers interpreted the question as a disguise of low expectations and a swipe at their perceived abilities, as if the student researchers would not have participated had they known about the rigor involved in the program.

However, not all pre-service teachers believed that the student researchers were disrespectful. In fact, Sean, a White middle-class male critically recognized the power of respect and the role of teachers in facilitating its presence or absence. In his reflection, Sean stated, "This [presentation] helped show how much simple respect comes into play for students related to their education in high school." Sean continued:

> The presentation affirmed my thoughts and views about the lack of values that some teachers in low-performing school emit towards their students.... it stems from the teachers and their perceptions and/or behaviors towards those students [and] can either compound those issues of respect or be the initial contributor.

Having grown up in a White middle-class community, but having attended racially integrated schools, Sean had a critical consciousness about his Whiteness and privilege, and had political clarity about the role that respect plays in student success in schools—particularly in low-performing urban schools. These dialogues essentially "confirmed" his already critical views toward schools and schooling. For the conscious teacher like Sean, or the developing teachers like Magdalena and Luis, these dialogues demonstrate the degree to which introspection, analysis, and reflection, triggered by opportunities to dialogue, are central to the development of all urban teachers.

Impact on Pre-Service Teachers

A critical mass of pre-service educators spoke about the impact that these dialogues had on their dispositions toward teaching, particularly in low-income urban schools in the city. For many, teaching in chronically low-performing urban schools was of no interest. After the dialogues, however, a significant number of pre-service teachers expressed interest in teaching at these low-performing schools. That is to say that at the beginning of the semester, the author asked, "Who wants to teach at the lowest performing schools in the district?" One pre-service teacher raised her hand. By the end of the semester, about 15 of the 45 pre-service teachers expressed interest in pursuing a job in a high-poverty school. Below are a series of reflections that revolve around the impact that these dialogues had on their own development as teachers, much to the credit of the high school student researchers.

Interestingly, the pre-service teachers and student researchers represent the race, class, and power dynamics that are emblematic of the larger social context—one that is driven by racism and classism. Because these dynamics are largely driven by ignorance and privilege, many stereotypes were challenged as a result of the dialogues. For instance, Jani, a middle-class Latina female, stated in her reflection, "Before I saw the presentations, I did not think students from [their school] would care about their education because of the school being a [chronically low performing school]." Prior to the dialogue, Jani admits her deficit orientation toward the student researchers, namely because of the reputation of the school, but the dialogues seemed to challenge her preconceived assumptions about the students and the school.

Another pre-service teacher also spoke about the impact that the dialogues had on her views toward the student researchers. Caty, a middle-class Latina, stated, "After listening to them [student researchers], I hope to one day be the teacher they described as 'the best teacher in the world.'" Kiki's comment about her school's need for the best teachers in the world had an obvious impact on her understanding the role that a great teacher can have on the lives of students, despite her experiences with discrimination and regardless of the teacher's race (her pledge to a group of pre-teachers who were racially and culturally different than the students at her school).

The dialogues also encouraged pre-service teachers to look at their individual agency. Viviana, a working-class Latina stated:

{sref}Sometimes teachers won't revolt...for fear of losing their job....I still can remember being a young teenager thinking the same way. What happened to that "stand up for your rights" attitude in all of us? I hope to re-gain it someday....I feel as though listening to these students' concerns and witnessing their bravery has empowered me.{\sref}

Viviana made significant personal, political, and intellectual strides over the course of the semester. At one point, she expressed a sense of anger about the oppressive education she had received as a working-class student. The student presentation helped her realize that she faced many of the same challenges in her own K–12 experiences and, as a result of the dialogues, she felt empowered to exercise her own agency as a classroom teacher.

Finally, and most enlightening, one student submitted a critical analysis of the dialogues. In her written reflection, Gina, a middle-class Latina, stated:

As the students presented...you could see in their eyes they spoke with passion, with knowledge, and with a desire for change....We were discussing how students get...frustrated with their teachers because their teachers don't listen to their voice...[because] [we] said that we don't want to teach in [low-performing schools] because they [student researchers] don't care for their education...After the presentation, I began to think differently about the students in [chronically low-performing] schools.... 'Why aren't these students being heard?'...The students have inspired me to work harder for them.

Gina has undoubtedly been moved by her experience with the dialogues. Not only did she recognize the significance of students conducting research on their own schools, but she also was quite insightful about the significance of the moment. Gina recognized that the ways in which pre-service teachers dismissed the data was in many ways analogous to the ways that teachers discriminated against students in their own high school. In fact, the same issues the student researchers were complaining about were to a degree being replicated during the dialogue. Gina recognized this reproduction of inequality and connected this reality to the silencing of students' voices that had been attempted during the dialogue. Gina's reflective analysis of the dialogue demonstrates the power that dialogues can have on pre-service teacher development.

IMPLICATIONS

In a climate of Test-Prep Pedagogy in urban schools and, to a degree, universities, pedagogical approaches must be revolutionary in order to see any significant changes in the ways in which we engage the most marginalized students in urban schools. Creative and courageous pedagogies must be driven by a love and a thirst for justice. Issues of race and racism, class, gender, privilege and power, and hope must guide the ways in which pre-service teachers are engaged, particularly in universities located in an urban context. Because urban schools are undeniably influenced by the social context in which they are situated (Noguera, 2003), universities must create opportunities for faculty and pre-service teachers to recognize how and why the socio-political context impacts what happens within schools (Trueba, 1999). This in part will lead to serious introspection and reflection about pre-service teachers' roles in resisting or perpetuating inequality. In order to do this, universities should prioritize pedagogies that raise consciousness (Freire, 1973), build political and ideological clarity (Bartolomé, 2002), and recognize the political role teachers play in U.S. society (Shor, 1993).

Marginalized youth can help lead the way for creative teacher development and engagement. Programs responsible for teacher development should require dialogues with youth, parents, and other community stakeholders. Dialoguing with youth is a critical yet introductory point into the significance of shifting and sharing power between youth, communities, pre-service teachers, and researchers. The possibilities associated with dialoguing are endless. Imagine the kinds of classrooms and schools that would develop if driven by dialoguing? Could/should pedagogical engagement bring an end to Test-Prep Pedagogy? Only future research and action can tell. Researchers, university administration, youth, and communities can lead the vanguard by engaging in pedagogies in which policies, practices, and processes are driven by individuals and collectives who are committed to serving the advancement of historically marginalized communities—low-income Black, Latino, Native American, many segments of the Asian-American community, English Language Learners, and immigrants in the U.S.

REFERENCES

Bartolomé, L. I. (1994). Beyond the methods fetish: Toward a humanizing pedagogy. *Harvard Educational Review, 64*(2), 173–194.

Bartolomé, L. I. (2002). Creating an equal playing field: Teachers as advocates, border crossers, and cultural brokers. In Z. F. Beykont (Ed.), *The power of culture: Teaching across language difference* (pp. 167–191). Cambridge, MA: Harvard Educational Publishing Group.

Bartolomé, L. I, & Balderrama, M. (2001). The need for educators with political and ideological clarity. In M. de la Luz Reyes & J. Halcon (Eds.) *The best for our children: Critical perspectives on literacy for Latino students* (pp. 48–64). New York: Teachers College Press.

Conchas, G. Q., & Rodríguez, L. F. (2007). *Small schools and urban youth: Using the power of school culture to engage students.* Thousand Oaks, CA: Corwin Press.

Córdova, T. (2004). Plugging the brain drain: Bringing our education back home. In J. Mora & D. R. Diaz (Eds.), *Latino social policy: A participatory research model* (pp. 25–53). New York: The Haworth Press.

Delpit, L. D. (1996). *Other people's children: Cultural conflict in the classroom.* New York: The New Press.

Emerson, R. M., Fretz, R. L., & Shaw, L. L. (1995). *Writing ethnographic fieldnotes.* Chicago: The University of Chicago Press.

Fine, M., Bloom, J., Burns, A., Chajet, L., Guishard, M., Payne, Y., Perkins-Munn, T., & Torre, M.E. (2005). Dear Zora: A letter to Zora Neale Hurston 15 years after Brown. *Teachers College Record, 107*(3), 496–528.

Flores, B., Cousin, P. T., & Diaz, E. (1991). Critiquing and transforming the deficit myths about learning, language and culture. *Language Arts, 68*(5), 369–379.

Freire, P. (1970). Pedagogy of the oppressed. New York: Continuum.

Freire, P. (1973). *Education for critical consciousness.* New York: Continuum.

Lauria, M. & Mirón, L. F. (2005). Urban schools: The new social spaces of resistance. New York: Peter Lang Publishing, Inc.

Meier, D., & Wood, G. (2004). *Many children left behind: How the no child left behind act is damaging our children and schools.* Boston, MA: Beacon Press.

Nieto, S. (1994). Lessons from students on creating a chance to dream. *Harvard Educational Review, 64*(4), 392–426.

Noguera, P. A. (2003). *City schools and the American dream. Reclaiming the promise of public education.* New York: Teachers College Press.

Noguera, P. A. (2005). It takes more than pressure to improve failing high schools. Retrieved September 7, 2007, from http://www.inmotionmagazine.com/er/pn_pressure.html

Rodríguez, L. F. (2004). Latinos and school reform: Voice, action, and agency. *Re-Vista: Harvard Review of Latin America, 3*(2), 38–39.

Rodríguez, L. F. (2005). Yo, mister! An alternative urban high school offers lessons on respect. *Educational Leadership, 62*(7), 78–80.

Shor, I. (1993). Education is politics: Paulo Freire's critical pedagogy. In P. McLaren, & P. Leonard (Eds.), *Paulo Freire: A critical encounter* (pp. 25–35). London: Routledge.

Solorzano, D. F. (1989). Teaching and social change: Reflections on a Freirian approach in a college classroom. *Teaching Sociology, 17,* 218–225.

Solorzano, D. & Yosso, T. J. (2001). From racial stereotyping and deficit discourse toward a critical race theory in teacher education. *Multicultural Education, 9*(1), 2–8.

Strauss, A., & Corbin, J. (1998). *Basics of qualitative research: Techniques and procedures for developing grounded theory.* Thousand Oaks, CA: SAGE Publications.

Trueba, E. T. (1999). *Latinos unidos: From cultural diversity to the politics of solidarity.* New York: Rowman & Littlefield Publishers, Inc.

Valencia, R., & Solorzano, D. (1997). Contemporary deficit thinking. In R. Valencia (Ed.), *The evolution of deficit thinking in educational thought and practice* (pp. 160–210). New York: Falmer Press.

Valenzuela, A. (1999). *Subtractive schooling: U.S. –Mexican youth and the politics of caring.* Albany: State University of New York Press.

Yosso, T. J. (2005). Whose culture has capital? A critical race theory discussion of community cultural wealth. *Race Ethnicity and Education, 8*(1), 69–91.

CHAPTER 12

INTERLUDE

FROM *PROSPECTUS* *FOR A SUMMER FREEDOM* *SCHOOL PROGRAM*

Submitted by Charles Cobb
Student Non-Violent Coordinating Committee (SNCC)

December 1963[1]

It is, I think, just about universally recognized that Mississippi education, for black or white, is grossly inadequate in comparison with education around the country. Negro education in Mississippi is the most inadequate and inferior in the state. Mississippi's impoverished educational system is also burdened with virtually a complete absence of academic freedom, and students are forced to live in an environment that is geared to squash intellectual curiosity, and different thinking. University of Mississippi Professor James Silver, in a recent speech, talked of "social paralysis...where nonconformity is forbidden, where the white man is not free, where he does not dare express a deviating opinion without looking over his shoulder." This "social

Listening to and Learning from Students, pages 101–113
Copyright © 2011 by Information Age Publishing
All rights of reproduction in any form reserved.

paralysis" is not limited to the white community, however. There are Negro students who have been thrown out of classes for asking about the freedom rides, or voting. Negro teachers have been fired for saying the wrong thing. The State of Mississippi destroys "smart niggers" and its classrooms remain intellectual waste lands.

In our work, we have several concerns oriented around Mississippi Negro students:

1. The need to get into the schools around the state and organize the students, with the possibility of a statewide coordinated student movement developing.
2. A student force to work with us in our efforts around the state.
3. The responsibility to fill an intellectual and creative vacuum in the lives of young Negro Mississippians, and to get them to articulate their own desires, demands and questions. More students need to stand up in classrooms around the state, and ask their teachers a real question.

As the summer program for Mississippi now shapes up, it seems as if hundreds of students as well as professional educators from some of the best universities and colleges in the North will be coming to Mississippi to lend themselves to the movement. These are some of the best minds in the country, and their academic value ought to be recognized, and taken advantage of.

I would like to propose summer Freedom Schools during the months of July and August, for tenth and eleventh-grade high school students, in order to:

1. Supplement what they aren't learning in high schools around the state.
2. Give them a broad intellectual and academic experience during the summer to bring back to fellow students in classrooms in the state, and
3. Form the basis for statewide student action such as school boycotts, based on their increased awareness.

I emphasize tenth and eleventh-grade students, because of the need to be assured of having a working force that remains in the state high schools putting to use what it has learned.

The curriculum of this school would fall into several groupings:

1. Supplementary education, such as basic grammar, reading, math, typing, history, etc. Some of the already-developed programmed educational materials might be used experimentally.

2. Cultural programs such as art and music appreciation, dance (both folk and modern), music (both folk and classical), drama, possibly creative writing workshops, for it is important that the art of effective communication through the written word be developed in Mississippi students.
3. Political and social science, relating their studies to their society. This should be a prominent part of the curriculum.
4. Literature.
5. Film programs.

Special projects, such as a student newspaper, voicing student opinion, or the laying of plans for a statewide student conference, could play a vital role in the program. Special attention should be given to the development of a close student–teacher relationship. Four or five students to one teacher might be good, as it offers a chance of dialogue. The overall theme of the school would be the student as a force for social change in Mississippi.

If we are concerned with breaking the power structure, then we have to be concerned with building up our own institutions to replace the old, unjust, decadent ones which make up the existing power structure. Education in Mississippi is an institution which can be validly replaced, as much of the educational institutions in the state are not recognized around the country anyway.

The Program
1. *General Description:* About 25 Freedom Schools are planned, of two varieties: day schools in about 20 to 25 towns (commitment still pending) and one or two boarding, or residential, schools on college campuses. Although the local communities can provide schools buildings and staff housing, all equipment, supplies and staff will have to come from the outside. Students should have an opportunity to work with the staff in other areas of the project, so that the additional experience will enrich their contribution to the Freedom School sessions.
2. *Curriculum:* On the weekend of March 21 and 22, the National Council of Churches sponsored a conference in N.Y.C. to develop a curriculum for the Freedom Schools. This conference brought together a group of well-qualified educators and many of the more perceptive minds presently engaged in studying our society. The conference participants worked from a preliminary outline which laid out the basic skills which the students need to improve, divided into four areas:

I. Leadership development
   a. To give students the perspective of being in a long line of protest and pressure for social and economic justice (i.e., to teach Negro history and the history of the movement.)
   b. To educate students in the general goals of the movement, give them wider perspectives (enlarged social objectives, nonviolence, etc.)
   c. To train students in the specific organizational skills that they need to develop Southern Negro communities:
      1. public speaking
      2. handling of press and publicity
      3. getting other people to work
      4. organizing mass meetings and workshops, getting speakers, etc.
      5. keeping financial records, affidavits, reports, etc.
      6. developing skill in dealing with people in the community
      7. canvassing
      8. duplicating techniques, typing, etc.
   d. To plan with each other further action of the student movement.
II. Remedial Academic Program
   a. To improve comprehension in reading, fluency and expressiveness in writing.
   b. To improve mathematical skill (general arithmetic and basic algebra and geometry.)
   c. To fill the gaps in knowledge of basic history and sociology, especially American.
   d. To give a general picture of the American economic and political system.
   e. To introduce students to art, music and literature of various classical periods, emphasizing distinctive features of each style.
   f. To generate knowledge of and ability to use the scientific method.
III. Contemporary Issues
   a. To give students more sophisticated views of some current issues.
   b. To introduce students to thinking of local difficulties in a context of national problems.
   c. To acquaint students with procedures of investigating a problem-rudimentary research.

IV. Non-academic Curriculum
   a. To allow students to meet each other as completely as possible, in order to form a network of student leaders who know each other.
   b. To give students experience in organization and leadership.
      1. field work—voter registration
      2. student publications
      3. student government
   c. To improve their ability to express themselves formally (through creative writing, drama, talent shows, semi-spontaneous discussions, etc.).

As a result of the curriculum conference, the curriculum planning took the following direction:

The aim of the Freedom School curriculum will be to challenge the student's curiosity about the world, introduce him to his particularly "Negro" cultural background, and teach him basic literacy skills in one integrated program. That is, the students will study problem areas in their world, such as the administration of justice, or the relation between state and federal authority. Each problem area will be built around a specific episode which is close to the experience of the students. The whole question of the court systems, and the place of law in our lives, with many relevant ramifications, can be dealt with in connection with the study of how one civil rights case went trough the courts and was ultimately decided in favor of the defendant. The campaign of a Negro for Congress provides a basis for studying all the forces that which are against the Negro candidate, and which have worked against a Negro's even attempting to run for Congress. The challenge of the regular Mississippi delegation at the Democratic National Convention provides the starting-point for a study of the whole presidential nomination and the election procedure. These and other "case studies" which can be used to explore larger problem areas in the society will be offered to students. The Negro history outline, as presently planned, will be divided into sections to be coordinated with the problem area presentation. In this context, students will be given practice activities to improve their skill with reading and writing. Writing press releases, leaflets, etc. for the political campaign is one example. Writing affidavits and reports of arrests, demonstrations, and trials, etc. which occur during the summer in their towns will be another. Using the telephone as a campaign tool will both help the political candidates and help students to improve their technique in speaking effectively in a somewhat formal situation. By using the multi-dimensional, integrated program, the curriculum can be more easily absorbed into the direct experience of the student, and thus overcome some of the academic problems of concentration and retention.

MISSISSIPPI FREEDOM SCHOOL CURRICULUM—1964

A Note to the Teacher

As you know, you will be teaching in a non-academic sort of setting; probably the basement of a church. Your students will be involved in voter registration activity after school. They may not come to school regularly. We will be able to provide some books, hopefully, some films, certainly some interesting guest speakers—yet other than these things you will have few materials apart from those you and your fellow teachers have brought.

In such a setting a "curriculum" must necessarily be flexible. We cannot provide lesson plans. All we can do is give you some models and suggestions which you can fall back on when you wish. You, your colleagues, and your students are urged to shape your own curriculum in the light of the teachers' skills, the students' interests, and the resources of the particular community in which your school is located.

The curriculum suggestions which follow fall into three parts, corresponding to three blocks of time into which you may wish to divide your school day. First come some ideas about the presentation of conventional academic subjects: English, mathematics, and the like.

We think such instruction is likely to be most fruitful at the beginning of the school day, when students are fresh. But we urge you, whenever possible, to use as materials for instruction in these subjects the actual problems of communication and analysis which the student encounters in his daily life, e.g. how to write a leaflet, how to calculate the number of eligible voters in a community.

Most of the material in this curriculum belongs to the citizenship curriculum, which you may want to present during the second half of the morning on a typical day. We assume that in this, as in all other phases of your teaching, you will use an informal, question-and-answer method. Hence, you will find that the material on citizenship is divided into seven units, each of which springs from a question, and each of which leads on to another question, which forms the next unit.

A large number of case studies have been provided to help you make the citizenship curriculum as concrete and vivid as possible. Many people, in many organizations, have taken part in preparing these case studies. If you disagree with the viewpoint of a particular case study, or of some part of the citizenship curriculum, please feel free to approach the problem in your own way.

Finally, we have some suggestions about the artistic, recreational and cultural activities which we think you may want to schedule in the afternoon, when it's hot. Don't neglect this phase of the curriculum. The comradeship formed on the ball field or in the group singing may be the basis of your relationship with a student.

PART I: ACADEMIC CURRICULUM

Introduction

It would seem advisable that, considering the special conditions under which the Freedom Schools will operate, some form of the team approach be adopted, to divide responsibility, yet retain an integrated educational approach to the student. The teachers should plan the activities together, so that each subject area correlates and reinforces the others. If, for example, the group of students plan to canvass, the language arts phase of the program could concentrate on an appropriate verbal skill, the social studies area could be devoted to the study of the population to be canvassed in terms of economic, social, religious factors and the implications of those factors, the math area could be given over to statistical breakdowns, charts, etc. (This example is a little advanced.) Or, if the students were to publicize a mass meeting, the language arts phase could study the considerations involved in writing persuasive material, the arts and crafts programs could make posters and leaflets, etc. One other advantage of the team approach is that, since students are first of all individuals, a group of teachers working in concert can serve their separate, special needs better. It is not likely that there will be sufficient time or variety of personnel to organize the staff in a detailed manner, but some version of the team concept could probably be implemented.

It is very important that there be cohesiveness and cooperation among the Freedom School personnel. Hopefully, before the opening of each school (there will probably be a week to prepare), the staff can make plans and agree on overall aims and apportion individual responsibilities. Frequent planning conferences after school begins are essential.

The value of the Freedom Schools will derive mainly from what the teachers are able to elicit from the students in terms of comprehension and expression of their experience. The curriculum should derive from the students' background, and all aspects of classroom activity should be an outgrowth of their experiences. The classroom groups will be small; the social interaction between teacher and students will be as important as academic instruction. The following list of procedures is designed to serve as a guideline, not proposed as any rigid formula. The formal classroom approach is to be avoided; the teacher is encouraged to use all the resources of his imagination. . . .

PART II: CITIZEN CURRICULUM

Introduction

One of the purposes of the Freedom Schools is to train people to be active agents in bringing about social change. We have attempted to design a developmental curriculum that begins on the level of the students' everyday lives and those things in their environment that they have either already experienced or can readily perceive, and builds up to a more realistic perception of American society, themselves, the conditions of their oppression, and alternatives offered by the Freedom Movement.

It is not our purpose to impose a particularly set of conclusions. Our purpose is to encourage the asking of questions, and hope that society can be improved.

The curriculum is divided into seven units:

1. Comparison of student's reality with others (the way the students live and the way others live)
2. North to Freedom? (the Negro in the North)
3. Examining the apparent reality (the "better lives" that whites live)
4. Introducing the power structure
5. The poor Negro and the poor white
6. Material things versus soul things
7. The movement

Each unit develops concepts that are needed for those that follow.

Physically, the content (suggested questions and concepts) is on the right side of each page with suggested case studies and visual aid material listed opposite. The suggested questions and concepts in the content portion of each page constitute the teaching guide. It should be emphasized that these are only suggestions, and that individual teachers may interpret the concepts in different ways or substitute other methods. There is probably more in each unit than it will be possible to use, but it was included so that each teacher would have a range of material to choose from, and extra material if necessary.

There are two additional sets of questions THAT ARE TO BE REINTRODUCED PERIODICALLY, both permit an on-going evaluation of the effectiveness of the curriculum, and to provide students with recurring opportunities for perceiving their own growth in sophistication.

The BASIC SET OF QUESTIONS is:
1. Why are we (students and teachers) in Freedom Schools?
2. What is the freedom movement?
3. What alternatives does the freedom movement offer us?

The SECONDARY SET OF QUESTIONS is:
1. What does the majority culture have that we want?
2. What does the majority culture have that we don't want?
3. What do we have that we want to keep?

MISSISSIPPI FREEDOM SCHOOL CURRICULUM—1964 CONTENT EXCERPT FROM PART II—CITIZENSHIP CURRICULUM

Unit VI—Material Things and Soul Things

Purpose:

1. To develop insights about the inadequacies of pure materialism;
2. To develop some elementary concepts of a new society.

Summary:

Starting with a questioning of whether the material things have given the "power structure" satisfaction, to raise the question of whether achievement will bring the Negro and/or the poor white fulfillment. Then to explore whether the conditions of his oppression have given the Negro insights and values that contribute to the goal of a more human society. And finally to develop this relevance into some insights as to the characteristics of a new society.

Materials:

Statements of Discipline of Nonviolent Movements.

Introduction:

The last few days we have been exploring in another world—different than the one we live in everyday—the world of the "power structure," and we have made some interesting discoveries:

1. That the "power structure" has a lot of power to make things happen just as they want them to be.
2. That the "power structure" has a lot of money that buys—big, luxurious houses, expensive cars, expensive clothing, trips, and all the other things we see on TV and in the movies.

But we've also discovered that—

1. The "power structure" is afraid of losing its power and its money; and
2. The "power structure" is afraid of Negroes and poor whites find out the "truth" and getting together.

Ideas to be developed:

1. The possessions of men do not make them free. Negroes will not be freed by:
   a. Taking what the whites have.
   b. A movement directed at materialistic ends only.
2. The structure of society can be altered.
3. While a radically new social structure must be created in order to give man the room to grow in, it is not the changing of structure alone that produces a good life or a good world. It is also the ethical values of the individual.
4. There are many kinds of power we could use to build a new society.

Concept:

That just taking the "power structure's" money and power would not make us happy either.

We have seen that having money and power does not make the "power structure" happy. We have seen that they have to pay a price for it.

Questions:

Would just taking their money and power away and keeping it ourselves make us happy? Wouldn't we have to be afraid and distrust people too? Wouldn't we have to make up lies to convince ourselves that we were right? Wouldn't we have to make up lies to convince other people that we were right? Wouldn't we, too, have to keep other people down in order to keep ourselves up?

Suppose you had a million dollars. You could buy a boat, a big car, a house, clothes, food, and many good things. But could you buy a friend? Could you buy a spring morning? Could you buy health? And how could we be happy without friends, health, and spring?

This is a freedom movement; suppose this movement could get a good house and job for all Negroes. Suppose Negroes had everything that the middle class of America has...everything that the rest of the country has...would it be enough? Why are there heart attacks and diseases and so much awful unhappiness in the middle class...which seems to be so free? Why the Bomb?

Concept:

That the structure of society can be changed. Discussion of a possible new society.

1. Money—should a few people have a lot of money, should everybody have the same, should everybody have what they need?
2. Jobs—should men be able to work at any job they can do and like, regardless of color, religion, nationality? Suppose a man were put out of a job by automation (like the mechanical picker?) What should happen to him? Should he just sit around? Should he be trained for a new job? Who can train him? When he is old, should he have to depend on his family or be poor? Should he be helped when he is old? Why? Should all workers join together if they wish? Should they share in the profits? Why?
3. Housing—Should every family be able to live where they wish to live, regardless of race or religion? Why? Should every family have a decent home? Should it have heat, a kitchen, a bathroom, hot water, nice furniture? Why does the kind of house a family has affect their family life? Suppose a family does not have enough money? Does a family have a basic right to good housing?
4. Health—should all people have a right to receive the same medical services regardless of religion or race or money? Should all people be able to receive whatever medical services they need regardless of how rich or poor they are? Why? From whom?
5. Education—Should all children be able to go to the same schools regardless of their race or religion? Should all children have the right to get as much education as they are capable of? Suppose they can't afford to go to special high schools or to college? Should they still be able to go? How? Who should pay?

   What should be taught in schools? Do we teach myths and lies? Why? Should we? Should we train people for jobs in schools? To be good citizens? What else should we train people for?—culture, resourcefulness, world citizenship, respect for other people and cultures, peace?

   What about teaching adults? Should they have a chance too? Should it be free? Should they be able to go to special schools if necessary?
6. Legal—Should the laws and the courts treat all people the same? Should the laws be more concerned with protecting the property a man has or the man himself? Why?
7. Political system—should every man have the right to vote? What if he cannot read? Should he still have the right to vote and choose his representatives? Should politicians have a right to give out favors?

Can they be honest in this system? Suppose people can get good housing, jobs, health services, etc., in other ways . . . will they need political favors?

8. Mass media—should newspapers, TV, magazines tell the truth? Should that be their basic job? Should they have to support themselves by advertising? How else could they get enough money?

9. International relations—how should we want to treat other countries? Should we help them if we have more than they do? Should we work for peace? Can we have peace if we keep building bigger bombs and faster planes? (What does fear do, threats? What about children fighting?)

10. Cultural life—are artists, actors, musicians, and writers important? Why? Should art and acting and music and writing be considered work? Should there be free concerts and free plays for everyone to see? Why?

Concept:

It is not simply the changing of the structure of society that will make a good world, but the ethical values of the individual.

What if men were just naturally bad to each other—if they didn't care about each other? Would it matter about the structure of society? Are men good to each other because of laws? What is an ethical value? Would it matter about the structure of society? Are men good to each other because of law? What is an ethical value?

Discuss "do unto others as you would have them do unto you." Do you have a set of values? Are society's laws enough? Are your own personal "laws" important, too? Are they even more important that society's laws?

Case Study: Statements of Discipline of Nonviolent Movements.

Is the movement the germ of a new society? How do people act toward each other in the movement? How do people act toward each other in Freedom School? How does this way of life differ from the way of life of the larger society? We must keep these good ethical and spiritual values in the new society which we build.

Concept:

That there are many kinds of power we could use to build a better society. What is power? (Power is the ability to move things.) What kinds of power are there? Discuss.

Mississippi		Freedom Movement
<u>Police state</u>	<u>Physical Power</u>	Federal intervention
Intimidation	(Power to coerce or frighten)	
One party	<u>Political Power</u>	Vote
No vote	(Power to influence)	Convention Challenge
Unjust laws		Negro candidates
Citizen Council	<u>Economic Power</u>	Boycott,
control, banks, jobs, etc.	(Power to buy)	Strikes

Do these "powers" balance each other? Do they succeed in bringing the two sides together or do they tend to pull apart? Are there other kinds of power?

Truth Power
(Power to Convince or Persuade)

Does persuasion pull people apart? Is it a different kind of power? Can we use truth to reveal the lies and myths? What happens once they are revealed? Once someone is convinced or persuaded, can they join with us? Is the better world for them too?

Soul Power
(The Power to Love)

Can you love everyone like you love your family or your friends? What does compassion mean? Is that a kind of love? Is there something in other people that is like what is in you? Can soul power change things? How?

NOTE

1. The Mississippi Freedom School Curriculum is not here in its entirety; this is an unedited, yet abridged version. As the editor of this collection, I have captured the introduction, framings, and curriculum content overviews from the first two of three parts to reflect the ideas of how/why teachers need to think about listening to and learning from students. I have excerpted one section of content from Part II—Citizenship Curriculum here as an example. The original documents, including the suggested case studies, activities, and addenda, can be found in their entirety in the SNCC, The Student Nonviolent Coordinating Committee Papers, 1959–1972 located at the King Library and Archives, The Martin Luther King Jr. Center for Nonviolent Social Change, Atlanta, GA.

CHAPTER 13

LESSONS FROM THE JOURNEY

Exploring Citizenship through Active Civic Involvement

Jennifer Ponder
California State University–Fullerton

Michelle Vander Veldt
California State University–Fullerton

Genell Lewis-Ferrell
Birmingham Southern College

January 25, 2008

Dear Senator Hillary Clinton,

Here at Good Citizens Elementary School, the fourth and fifth grade combination class has been given a chance to write to a candidate. I picked you
because you have many excellent ideas to help us and our world. I love your
ideas about Universal Healthcare. Our class has been trying to raise money

Listening to and Learning from Students, pages 115–130
Copyright © 2011 by Information Age Publishing
All rights of reproduction in any form reserved.

for a little girl's operation; she has a rare disease called Moebius Syndrome. This disease affects the sixth and seventh cranial nerves, which means she cannot smile or make any other facial expressions. She is only 3 years old and her insurance company thinks of this surgery as plastic surgery, so they won't cover the operation fee. Some countries cover the payment when you go to the hospital, so maybe you can change it and make sure everyone has health insurance at a reasonable price. We would really appreciate it if you would come to our school.

Sincerely,

Ayana

HOW IT ALL STARTED

An elementary student from a combination fourth- and fifth-grade classroom wrote the above letter while her class was immersed in an active citizenship project that encouraged students to critically examine issues in their community and beyond. The idea for the active citizenship project was born out of an assignment from a graduate social studies class that the student's classroom teacher was taking while working on her master's degree. The classroom teacher was challenged by an assignment in the course to create a democratic classroom that fostered opportunities for students to engage in participatory and justice-oriented citizenship (Westheimer & Kahne, 2004), while using emergent curriculum as the vehicle to facilitate the project (Epstein & Oyler, 2008; Schultz, 2008; Schultz & Oyler, 2006).

The following goals were the focus of the assignment for the graduate course: (1) elementary students will recognize their rights and responsibilities as citizens in a global, interdependent world; (2) elementary students will view themselves as change agents and realize that their voices can make a difference; and (3) elementary students will use civic skills to design a plan of action that will address an issue and work towards making change. The purpose of the project was to encourage classroom teachers enrolled in the graduate course to consider how to provide their elementary students with the opportunity to make an impact in the world outside of the confines of the classroom, while negotiating a meaningful curriculum with their students as the project developed.

THEORETICAL FRAMEWORK:
CIVICS FROM A WORLD PERSPECTIVE

As U.S. citizens, our civic competency has been tested in the last decade. When the twin towers fell on September 11, 2001, a major shift occurred in how Americans viewed their country (Westheimer, 2007). Similarly, the world seemed like a much smaller place in 2004 when a Tsunami killed thousands of people in Southeast Asia. Again in 2005, mortal reality struck close to home when Hurricane Katrina destroyed much of New Orleans, and many Americans were left homeless.

How people responded to these events tested civic character and has direct bearing on the kind of civic education we provide in schools. Did citizens have the skills necessary to critically examine the evidence presented in these situations? Were they able to piece together acceptable solutions from the information provided by the media? Could they collaborate and problem-solve for positive outcomes? Did they step beyond themselves and look at the larger societal picture? Did they attempt to take action? If Americans had been held accountable for these tests on our civic competency, how would they have fared? We are afraid that many of us would have failed. It was from such observations that we began to ask, "Is it the responsibility of schools to prepare citizens to effectively respond to situations like these? If so, how should classroom teachers navigate through the complex and often messy process of helping students define and understand citizenship?"

If school is where children acquire their civic knowledge, skills, and dispositions, we agreed that it is crucial for teacher educators to help teachers become knowledgeable, civic-minded citizens, echoing Mason and Silva's (2001) declaration:

> In both explicit and implicit ways, the curriculum of the elementary school provides a foundation for civic responsibility. For this reason, it is imperative that elementary school teachers be well prepared to guide their students toward an understanding of the roles and responsibilities that citizens of a democratic society must assume. (p. 65)

Similarly, Patrick and Vontz (2001) suggest that "aspiring teachers need to develop, through civics-centered methods courses, the capacity for teaching components of education for citizenship in a democracy" (p. 49). Unfortunately, many teachers initially reject the idea of a civics-centered curriculum because it does not support their district's curriculum goals. Since the implementation of the No Child Left Behind Act (2001), our teachers often report that their curriculum has been sharply narrowed to focus on mathematics and language arts. Real-world experiences and meaningful curriculum projects are obsolete because their format does not support the test-preparation regimen mandated by their school districts. As a result, any request to deviate from the script is often met with resistance from the administration.

In an attempt to revive civic education in the curriculum and reaffirm its role in the preparation of citizens, we determined that teachers must first experience the complex task of integrating a meaningful civics curriculum into their everyday curriculum. To facilitate this experience, the teachers in our courses are required to conduct an action research project to document, reflect, and analyze the process of allowing the curriculum to develop, as their students identify and examine social issues. The classroom teachers are encouraged to follow the teachable moments that are born out of their classroom discussions and research, and ultimately to allow students' interests to guide the direction of the project. The teachers are encouraged to allow the curriculum to emerge as students are immersed in a social action curriculum that encourages active citizenship and decision making through thoughtful deliberations (Epstein & Oyler, 2008; Schultz & Oyler, 2006).

CIVICS CURRICULUM

A worthy definition of education for citizenship in a democracy must be congruent with credible and practical definitions of democracy and democratic citizenship.

—Patrick, 2002, p. 6

Since civic competence is the goal of social studies (National Council for the Social Studies, 1994) and citizenship is usually mentioned in most school mission statements, then the next topic of discussion should be to explore what democracy looks like when translated into a common curriculum. It is essential that teacher educators find curricula to help students understand that civic education is not a list of mechanical skills for a test, but knowledge for "creating a public" (Postman, 1995, p. 18). Patrick (2002) developed a framework that defines components of common education for citizenship in a democracy. For the present study, we used Patrick's framework to create the following three categories of civic education as related to civic curriculum: (1) civic knowledge, (2) civic dispositions, and (3) civic skills. These three components guided the development of our civics-infused social studies methods course and this research study.

Civic Knowledge, Dispositions, and Skills

If active civic involvement is necessary to promote civic competence, it is crucial that citizens are knowledgeable, for "when participants possess a rich storehouse of knowledge about democracy and social life near and far, their discussions and decisions are more intelligent and their service projects more effective" (Parker, 2005, p. 92). With any discussion about knowledge, it is inevitable that the issue of what knowledge should be deemed important will arise. We believe this will depend on the nature of the project and the meaningful connections the students will find as they examine the issue. We argue that natural connections related to the knowledge of the concepts, principles, practices, contexts, and history of democracy and institutions of representative democratic government (Patrick & Vontz, 2001) will emerge through the curricular experience. If this is true, then teachers should attempt to use the context of a social action project to expand students' civic knowledge, both past and present.

The second aspect of civic education critical to quality civic curriculum is the development of attitudes and values regarding the roles and responsibilities of citizenship. These civic dispositions are the elements of civic education concerned with the habits and inclinations that summarize an individual's behaviors and values in relation to democracy. According to Parker (2005), these virtues include responsibility, civility, honesty, courage, fairness, and lawfulness. Wynne (1986) emphasizes the importance of civic dispositions by stating that "the transmission of moral values has been the dominant educational concern of most cultures throughout history" (p. 4). This transmission of civic dispositions continues through the current filtering of character education through public school domains (Lickona, 1991). According to Patrick and Vontz (2001), qualities such as promoting the common good, recognizing and supporting equality for all people, and responsible civic participation are all traits necessary to sustain a representative democracy. By perpetuating and promoting these dispositions through a social action curriculum, educators can begin to help students move beyond citizenship that focuses on good deeds, and develop the participatory civic skills of deliberation and policy analysis necessary in order to maintain democracy.

Civic skills, or the skills necessary to "empower citizens to influence public policy decisions and to hold accountable their representatives in government," are a crucial piece to civics curriculum (Patrick & Vontz, 2001, p. 42). Through social action projects, teachers can provide students with opportunities to identify, describe, evaluate, analyze, and think critically about issues related to civic life. More specifically, students should be actively engaged in thoughtful deliberations that encourage the consideration of multiple perspectives before decisions are made. Creating and implementing a plan of action to inform and influence social change will allow students to use valuable civic skills and participate in civic life beyond the four walls of their classroom (Patrick & Vontz, 2001).

Types of Citizenship

Civic participation can be examined through different levels of involvement. Westheimer and Kahne (2004) identify three categories of citizenship: personally responsible, participatory, and justice-oriented. Personally responsible citizenship requires individuals to act responsibly in the community. Such action involves the individual: working, paying taxes, obeying laws, recycling, and volunteering. Participatory citizenship centers on organizing community outreach for those in need. These citizens are active members of community organizations and work to accomplish collective tasks. Finally, justice-oriented citizenship focuses on critically assessing the social, political, and economic circumstances surrounding the surface conditions. These types of citizens seek to identify areas of injustice in the world. They have knowledge of democratic social movements, which informs how these citizens effect systemic change.

While all three types of citizens are necessary to sustain a democracy, we challenged our teachers to engage their students in activities that would require active civic involvement on a participatory or justice-oriented level. We wanted our teachers to move beyond projects with a narrow focus such as a charity donation or a one-time volunteering event. Instead, we encouraged them to provide opportunities for their students to critically examine the root causes of specific problems in society and to develop their own plan of action to inform or to influence others. One classroom teacher and her fourth- and fifth-grade students rose to the challenge and developed an active citizenship project that led them to think and act as participatory and justice-oriented citizens.

METHODOLOGY AND RESEARCH DESIGN

The inception of this research began with a call to action that stemmed from an assignment in a classroom teacher's graduate social studies methods class. The project lasted for two years and became the focus of our research. We use narrative inquiry to tell the story of how the project developed. Connelly and Clandinin (1988) define narrative inquiry as "the making of meaning from personal experience via a process of reflection in which storytelling is the key element and in which metaphors and folk knowledge take their place" (p. 16). A variety of known methods were employed to collect data for this study. In an attempt to reconstruct our experiences and to tell the story about the development of this project, we used the classroom teacher's reflections from her graduate class project, our reflections after teaching our weekly graduate classes, and transcriptions articulated from the students' perspective via a video documentary. Within the naturalistic setting of the classroom, which was a qualitative component of the study (Bogdan & Biklen, 2007), the collection of data included interviews, observations, and field notes. Data analysis involved the constant comparative method (Merriam, 1998) in an attempt to identify recurring themes.

Participants

During the first year of the project, Morgan, a fourth- and fifth-grade combination-classroom teacher, launched an active citizenship project with 30 students. The following year, 14 fourth-grade students who were a part of the project during the first year remained in Morgan's combination classroom for fifth grade. Due to the structure of a combination classroom, 12 new fourth-grade students joined the fifth graders, and the project continued for a second year.

Data collection consisted of Morgan's field notes and reflections from her action research project during the first year along with our weekly reflections after the graduate class. During the second year, data collection took place in Morgan's classroom from September to April. Classroom observations took place four times a month for approximately two hours each visit. We recorded field notes documenting students' responses to the teacher's lessons, as well as student interactions during these lessons. Eleven students also participated in individual interviews that lasted approximately 30 minutes.

THE STORY BEGINS

Accepting the Challenge: Promoting Active Citizenship in the Classroom

Morgan, a bright-eyed, energetic elementary teacher enrolled in our social studies methods course as part of her master's degree requirements. She reported on the first night of class that her students were not motivated and she was willing to try anything to capture their interest. To spark a discussion about active civic involvement and emergent curriculum in class, we used a clip from the movie *Pay it Forward* (Leder, 2000). The scene we used showed the first day of school in a seventh-grade social studies class. The teacher in this movie, played by Kevin Spacey, asked the children to think about the world and their responsibility as citizens. He encouraged them to become global thinkers and step outside of their egocentric ways to change the world. After a very passionate speech and some humorous yet typical responses from students about their role in society, he flips up a world map to display a year-long assignment on the chalkboard: *Think of a way to change the world and put it into action.* Based on this video clip, we asked Morgan, along with her classmates, to consider how they could implement an active citizenship project that would address social issues in their classrooms. Discussions about emergent curriculum and meaningful integration were central to the conversation.

After discussing the types of citizenship presented by Westheimer and Kahne (2004) and components of democratic classrooms (Parker, 2005) during the second week of class, Morgan reported in her post-assignment reflections that she was intrigued by the possibilities of the project and decided to design an active citizenship project with her students. Morgan went back to her classroom the next day and started to put a plan into action.

Morgan kicked off the project with her students by sharing examples of the different types of citizenship in children's literature that exemplified each type by making connections to active civic participation throughout history. Next, she asked the students if they could pick one problem to solve in their community, what would they choose? After several brainstorming sessions, one of the students in the class brought up the idea that a toddler in their community needed money for a very expensive surgery. The students discovered that the toddler has a disorder called Moebius Syndrome. Upon further research, they learned that Moebius Syndrome is a nerve disorder that affects a person's ability to talk, chew their food, or smile, but could be corrected with a simple surgical procedure. As they continued investigating, they came to understand that the family's health insurance denied surgery because it claimed the procedure was cosmetic. This outraged the students and prompted them to take action to help the family raise money. This is how the "Mobilize for Moebius" project was born.

Over the next six months, the students worked on an action plan that led to the development of a school-wide recycling program that encouraged students, teachers, and members of the community to get involved and to raise money for their cause. The students conducted research and discovered that aluminum cans, plastic bottles, and glass could be recycled for money. The students decided to place recycling bins in each classroom and ask members of the school community to recycle these materials. Each week the students collected, sorted, and coordinated a drop-off service to the local recycling center to redeem cash for their recyclables. This project raised funds to help pay for the toddler's much-needed surgery. Furthermore, the students made posters and hung them up around the school, and they wrote letters to local businesses, government officials, and organizations to ask for their support in the recycling campaign. They even spoke at the local City Council meeting to share their understanding of a citizen's responsibility in society and to thank everyone in their community for their support. The students' efforts also attracted media attention from local newspapers and television. This coverage encouraged more people to get involved and to donate their recyclables and cash to the cause. By the end of the second school year, the students had raised about $10,000 to help pay for the surgery.

Beyond Recycling and Raising Money

From the onset of this project, the students were determined to raise a large amount of money to support the toddler's surgery. However, during the second year of the project, Morgan pushed the boundaries of the initial project by incorporating environmental issues, connecting civic knowledge related to the history of democracy and the functions of government, and examining social inequity as a challenge to citizenship. Throughout the entire project, the students were involved in thoughtful deliberations that led to important decisions for the project. Students were also required to conduct research regarding issues associated with the project to become experts. The students asked questions about how they could effect change beyond their school site and community.

The students were eager to extend their work on the project during the second year, so curricular themes and meaningful connections emerged naturally out of the project. The students were no longer satisfied with simply raising money for the surgery. They wanted to know how they could get more "powerful" people, such as politicians and other community members, involved in their project. They wanted to see changes beyond raising money for the surgery. Through these discussions, questions about democracy were raised and the students were interested in how people could get involved. Specifically, the students wanted to know if and how *they* could get involved with changing issues they did not like. As a result of this conversation, the students wanted to know more about the history of our government and the rights and responsibilities of all citizens. Morgan used the Constitution and resources such as *We the People*, to help the children learn more about the different levels of government, and their roles and responsibilities as citizens of the United States (Center for Civic Education, 1988).

The students were fascinated by the Constitution. At first, Morgan brought in replicas of the document to create interest. It was interesting to watch the students try to read the information on the replicas with magnifying glasses and process the meaning of the difficult language in the document. Since the students were so interested in what the Constitution said, we were able to obtain a pocket-sized copy of the Constitution for each student. In fact, we were in the classroom the day the copies arrived. The students cheered wildly and immediately began flipping through the reader-friendly text as soon as each received a copy. Eventually, the students deconstructed the text in the Constitution and rewrote it in kid-friendly language to help them understand the ideas presented. The students also conducted inquiry through the exploration of primary documents, and deliberated on the difference between individual rights and the common good. The students learned about which government official or agency they should contact if they wanted to propose a change or to address an issue in their community or state. This knowledge was meaningful to the students because it confirmed that the students' voices could make a difference.

After gaining new knowledge about the government and their rights as citizens, the students were eager to take action at the state level. After learning about the Bill of Rights and how a bill becomes a law, they decided to propose an idea for a bill to their California representatives. At first, the students wanted to propose a bill related to healthcare using the toddler they had been raising money for as an example of social injustice. The students were even interested in challenging the health insurance company that denied the initial claim. However, the students had to shift gears after the toddler's family asked the students not to get involved with the legal aspect of the issue. As a result, the students had to reconsider the focus of the project.

During a brainstorming session about other issues related to the project that could be addressed through public policy, several students brought up issues related to the environmental knowledge they had gained from recycling to raise money for the toddler's surgery. After weeks of discussion, the students agreed to propose a bill related to recycling. The students' proposal suggested that all California schools should be designated as community recycling drop-off centers. Their rationale for this proposal was to make it more convenient for people in every community to recycle while also raising money for each school from the California Redemption Value, a deposit paid on certain recyclable materials at the time of purchase.

Once informed, they wrote letters and spoke publicly to elicit support from local and state government officials as well as other members of the community. A small group of students spoke at a local city council meeting, while the entire class wrote a letter to the California representative from their district. Students also contacted the local media and worked to build a partnership with the local waste management. All of these activities emerged from the students' work on their project, which also led the students to construct their own definition of citizenship.

EMERGING KNOWLEDGE, SKILLS, AND DISPOSITIONS

More important than whether or not the students succeeded in persuading a representative to sponsor their bill, the students learned that they have the power to propose a change in their community and elicit support for their concerns by writing letters, making phone calls, and sending emails to government officials from their district and state. The students also learned they can use their voices to start a grassroots movement that can make a difference in the lives of others.

As evidenced in the letter at the beginning of the chapter, involvement in the project also pushed the students to think beyond recycling and raising money for the toddler. This is a great example of emergent curriculum (Beane, 2005; Schultz, 2008). Questions regarding injustices related to our current healthcare system became more prevalent in informal conversations and emails initiated by the students. One of the fifth-grade students sent us the following email one weekend after watching *Sicko* (Moore, 2007), a documentary that examines problems with the healthcare system in the United States:

> I just want to tell you about a movie that I just watched. The movie is called *Sicko*. Michel Moore is in the movie. The movie is about people and their heath insurance companies. These people have cancer and other sicknesses, but their health insurance rejects them. In the middle of the movie, Michel Moore goes to Canada and finds out that you don't have to pay to go to the doctor. I think you should watch this film so you can see how the toddler's family feels. I felt it too. Thank you!
>
> Your Friend,
> Kya

The activities connected to the project also allowed students to practice skills necessary for active civic involvement. To probe for more in-depth answers, eleven of the students were interviewed individually to determine how they would respond to a hypothetical scenario that would require skills for civic action. For example, the students were asked what they would do if they noticed that drivers were speeding in their neighborhood. Common responses from students included actions such as: recruiting other people to help, conducting research about the issue, talking about the problems with other people to see if they might have other ideas before making a decision (deliberation), and contacting the mayor or speaking to the city council to elicit support.

During the interviews, students were also asked to discuss how their work with the project had impacted their beliefs and knowledge about active citizenship. When we asked the students what they had learned from participating in this project, a few themes were consistent throughout their responses: recycling saves the planet, children have a voice, there are different types of citizenship, and children can make a big difference in this world. The following quotes summarize students' responses:

Christian: Our responsibility is the same as adults. We have a voice and we can make a change in our environment and our community too. I have learned how to stop global warming and all the ways to recycle. I have learned about the Constitution and the three branches in our government. And most im-

> portantly, kids have a voice and they can make a difference in this world.
>
> **Amari:** Just a little can make a big difference!
>
> **Lex:** I have learned about the levels of citizenship. We can make a difference in this world. We, the people, have a voice to make a change in this world.
>
> **Scarlett:** I have learned that kids can make a big difference in their community.
>
> **Lily:** We have the right to speak up!

One Step Further

By February of the second year, the students were thrilled with the results of the project because, according to them: (1) they had reached their monetary goal, (2) they were doing their part to protect the environment, and (3) they had proposed a bill to state government officials. However, they did not want the project to end. Their enthusiasm was contagious. During a brainstorming session to determine the direction of the project, one of the students suggested that they should try to spread the word and encourage other kids in the school to be good citizens. This student's suggestion resulted in yet another expansion of the project.

The students immediately began brainstorming ways they could spread the word and encourage others to do something great in their community. Some of the ideas included developing a class website to explain their project to show other people how they can address issues in their own community, creating a video documentary about their project to inspire other kids and teachers around the world to become active citizens, and a letter-writing campaign to the media, celebrities, and government officials that would attract attention to their cause and inspire others to get involved.

After a few months of intense work, the students published a website and finished shooting the live footage for their documentary. After editing the documentary, the students were able to produce 100 copies to share. The children used maps and the Internet to research and select one elementary school in each state to receive their video documentary. Each school site was selected using different criteria. Some sites were selected because students had friends or relatives at a particular school. Other sites were selected after they researched state tourism or discussed current or historical events in a specific area. Students would often Google elementary schools in an area of interest and then select a site after perusing school websites. A large map was posted on the wall to track locations of each site. Each time a school was selected, the students would place a marker on the map and give a brief overview explaining their rationale for site selection.

They also decided to send the video to influential people such as government officials, celebrities, and talk-show hosts in an attempt to convince them to support the project and help spread the word. The kids were hopeful that this movement would inspire people everywhere to stand up for those who are in need of help and to oppose situations that lead to inequity. In late April of the second year, the students mailed out 75 copies of their DVD and promoted their website. The students made business cards with their website address and distributed them to students at other schools. As a result, the class was featured in the local newspaper (Petix, 2008), as well as in an online university magazine (Cano Ramos, 2008). Many people visited their website and posted messages of support. Unfortunately, the school year ended before the students could get feedback from any of the schools that received their documentary. However, the students' sense of accomplishment and pride was certainly not diminished.

Although this project started as an assignment for Morgan's graduate class, she stated in her post-assignment reflections that it quickly grew into something much larger than she ever expected. This teacher and her students' take-action project encapsulates how posing a simple question and providing students with the opportunity to become actively involved in their curriculum can turn into a life lesson in citizenship, the common good, and student involvement beyond the four walls of the classroom.

CONCLUSIONS

Findings from the study suggest that projects that are situated in a real-world context focusing on community needs and student interest can impact students' level of involvement and sense of agency. These results are consistent with previous research (Schultz & Oyler, 2006; Wade, 2001; Werner, Voce, Gaufin, & Simmons, 2002). The data from this study suggest the students in Morgan's classroom gained valuable civic knowledge, skills, and dispositions as a result of their engagement in this project. This growth was demonstrated in the students' successful efforts to raise the money, their developing interest in issues outside the immediacy of the project, as well as their responses during class discussions and interviews.

Active citizenship projects may have a catalytic ability to motivate students into using active democratic skills to better their surrounding community. In regards to the use of active citizenship projects, we concur with Westheimer and Kahne (2004), and support their claim that teachers can develop "civic commitment by exposing students to problems in society and by creating opportunities for students to have positive experiences while working toward solutions" (p. 265). Through this project, students came to realize that civic engagement is not a private endeavor. They learned how to initiate and develop projects that are informed by their civic ideas, skills, and strategies.

The nature of student-led projects allows the curriculum to evolve and transform beyond its original intent. As a result, students are deeply connected to the material and are key partners in the development of curriculum that is meaningful. The process of working toward a solution for a meaningful cause often creates opportunities for students to delve into more complex issues that would otherwise be hard for students to understand with a relatable context. The letter to Senator Clinton and the email about the healthcare documentary shared earlier are both excellent examples of how the students connected the toddler's personal healthcare struggle with the broader issue of inadequate healthcare in our country. This move toward a discussion of healthcare happened organically, and was generated through the project as it was happening.

The attainment of civic knowledge, skills, and dispositions is influenced by a variety of factors (Schugurensky & Myers, 2003). Our findings parallel Schugurensky and Myers' (2003) ideas: "From a lifelong citizenship perspective, it is possible to suggest that we build our understanding and assumptions about the political world from a hodgepodge of ideas and learning experiences" (p. 325).

The transfer of civic knowledge, skills, and dispositions may be more likely to transfer into adulthood if authentic civic experiences were consistent throughout schooling. While this study cannot generalize or make suggestions regarding the effectiveness of projects such as this for all classrooms or groups of students, it does suggest that further research in this area would be beneficial. Based on our work with this particular classroom teacher and her students, along with numerous other teachers who have facilitated active citizenship projects as part of the requirements for our courses, we strongly encourage teacher educators to include experiences that will help teachers explore civic knowledge, skills, and dispositions through social action projects and emergent curriculum. Clearly, we have witnessed the positive effects that opportunities for active civic involvement can have on the classroom teachers and their young pupils. Ultimately, the process for defining and understanding citizenship is messy and complex; however, we wholeheartedly believe that the journey is the reward.

REFERENCES

Beane, J. A. (2005). *A reason to teach: Creating classrooms of dignity and hope.* Portsmouth, NH: Heinemann.

Bogdan, R., & Biklen, S. (2007). *Qualitative research for education: An introduction to theories and methods* (5th ed.). Boston: Allyn and Bacon.

Cano Ramos, D. (2008, April). Class assignment turns into real world lesson for graduate and her young pupils. *Inside Online.* Retrieved April 28, 2008, from http://campusapps.fullerton.edu/news/Inside/2008/ponder_assignment. html

Center for Civic Education. (1988). *We the people . . . The citizen and the Constitution.* Calabasas, CA: Center for Civic Education.

Connelly, M. F., & Clandinin, J. D. (1988). Narrative meaning: Focus on teacher education. *Elements, 19*(2), 15–18.

Epstein, S. E., & Oyler, C. (2008). An inescapable network of mutuality: Building relationships of solidarity in a first grade classroom. *Equity and Excellence in Education, 41*(4), 405–416.

Leder, M. (Director). Abrams, P., Carson, P., Levy, R.L., McLaglen, M., Reuther, S., Treisman, J. (Producers). (2000). *Pay it forward* [DVD]. Warner Bros. Pictures.

Lickona, T. (1991). *Educating for character.* New York: Bantam Books.

Mason, T., & Silva, D. (2001). Beyond the methods course: Civics as the program core in elementary teacher education. In J. Patrick, & R. Leming (Eds.), *Principles and practices of democracy in the education of social studies teachers: Civic learning in teacher education* (Vol. 1, pp. 65–86). Bloomington, IN: ERIC.

Merriam, S. B. (1998). *Qualitative research and case study application in education.* San Francisco, CA: Jossey-Bass.

Moore, M. (Producer & Director), & Glynn, K., O'Hara, M., Weinstein, B., Weinstein, H. (Producers). (2007). *Sicko* [DVD]. The Weinstein Company.

National Council for the Social Studies. (1994). *Expectations of excellence: Curriculum standards for social studies.* Retrieved January 18, 2009, from http://www.social-studies.org/standards

Parker, W. (2005). *Social studies in the elementary school.* Upper Saddle River, NJ: Merrill Prentice Hall.

Patrick, J. (2002). Defining, delivering, and defending a common education for citizenship in a democracy. In J. Patrick, G. Hamot, & R. Leming (Eds.), *Principles and practices of democracy in the education of social studies teachers: Civic learning in teacher education* (Vol. 2, pp. 5–21). Bloomington, IN: ERIC.

Patrick, J., & Vontz, T. (2001). Components of education for democratic citizenship in the preparation of social studies teachers. In J. Patrick, & R. Leming (Eds.), *Principles and practices of democracy in the education of social studies teachers: Civic learning in teacher education* (Vol.1, pp. 39–64). Bloomington, IN: ERIC.

Petix, M. (2008, March 23). Class recycles to put a smile on girl's face. *Inland Valley Daily Bulletin,* p. A1

Postman, N. (1995). *The end of education: Redefining the value of school.* New York: Alfred A. Knopf.

Schugurensky, D., & Myers, J. (2003). A framework to explore lifelong learning: The case of the civic education of civics teachers. *International Journal of Lifelong Education, 22*(4), 325–352.

Schultz, B. D. (2008). *Spectacular things happen along the way: Lessons from an urban classroom.* New York: Teachers College Press.

Schultz, B. D., & Oyler, C. (2006). We make this road as we walk together: Sharing teacher authority in a social action curriculum. *Curriculum Inquiry, 36*(4), 423–451.

Wade, R. (2001). Social action in the social studies: From the ideal to the real. *Theory Into Practice, 40*, 23–29.

Werner, C., Voce, R., Gaufin, K., & Simmons, M. (2002). Designing service learning to empower citizens and community: Jackson elementary builds a nature study center. *Journal of Social Issues, 58*(3), 557–559.

Westheimer, J. (2007). *Pledging allegiance: The politics of patriotism in America's schools.* New York: Teachers College Press.

Westheimer, J., & Kahne, J. (2004). What kind of citizen? The politics of educating for democracy. *American Educational Research Journal, 41*(2), 237–269.

Wynne, E. (1986). The great tradition in education: Transmitting moral values. *Educational Leadership, 43*(4), 4–9.

CHAPTER 14

INTERLUDE

A.D.D.

Rafael Casal

I'm watching 6 kids
standing around a play structure
that just abruptly stopped shooting out the water they were playing with.

My nephew, Sean, years and feet behind his insta-friends at Cedar Rose
    park
stands among the cluster of kids trying to summon the water back.

The other parents and I watch and chuckle as the cluster of kids try varia-
    tions of "Open sesame!" at a non-responsive spout.

I'm afraid some day they're gonna tell him that he has Attention Deficit
a disorder that 1 in 4 men are infected with
the band aid on a mystery they wish to de-complicate
then medicate to accommodate the commonness of why he can't concen-
    trate.

Listening to and Learning from Students, pages 131–133

They'll say in class he seems lost
I'll say his mind has the free sight
but nowadays we raise young ones to be more machine-like
because big industry needs employees who are machines, right?
who don't make history just live on some . . . efficiency hype
march in submission, that's the mission, keep the seams tight
teach kids the repetition so they grow up industry types

now here's my nephew,
homework in one hand . . .
and a serious addiction to the '09 Tyco equivalent of Legos in the other.

in this corner . . .
an unbelievably blank white unanswered page of questions he could
not be less engaged in!

and in the other corner . . .
a 4-foot long working replica of the Star Wars millennium falcon he
      creatively constructed using pieces from 4 separate Lego sets with
      retractable landing gear and a working loading bay!

clearly it ain't trouble with payin attention
he'd just rather be playing invention
so as I investigate your motives for why you'd try to medicate him
I beg to question

let's do the equation:
$24 for 30 pills, or roughly a month, which is 10 milligrams
100 bottles for every one gram
which would be 2,400 dollars per every gram of ritalin in the country
1 kilo is a thousand grams
2,400,000 per kilo of ritalin
times the 17, 618 kilos that were brought in and sold in the pharmaceuti-
      cal business year of 2001,
. . . means it's a 42,283,200,000 dollar industry?
it's brilliant, tell kids they are inferior then have them buy back their ef-
      ficiency

and at first I thought attention deficit must be on some new epidemic sh•t
'til I found out the U.S. consumes globally 90 percent of it
diagnose you inferior so the privatized medics get
your money in the country where you go broke buyin' your benefits

and I don't want Sean to ever look up from his book and wonder why
    everyone else is on page 15 and he's still on page two
'cuz he's been off somewhere dreamin' about fighting dinosaurs, makin'
    Lego robots and drawing Spiderman 'til his fingers hurt
but had to snap out of his daydream just to satisfy you
don't tell Sean he learns wrong.
if minds didn't wander
we wouldn't have a Ghandi for your spiritual revolution
no black power fists shaking at a crumbling divide
no Vietnam soldiers on their way home
Hip-Hop came from kids who couldn't seem to pay attention
There's no Jazz, no Tap,
shoot, we'd still think the world was flat if not for straying attention

and as I watch
my now 3-year-old nephew's mind begin to wander...
while the rest of the kids continue to bark secret code words at a non-
    responsive tap
in hopes to bring the water back
Sean
much shorter and younger than the rest...
scans the playground
walks across the sand and presses a shiny silver-dollar-sized button on the
    red post
which restarts the spout and shoots water into the palms of eager young-
    sters.

He walks back to join the group.

right then he could have been Rosal, Monet, Marx, Malcolm, Neruda

the one to walk outside the box and do something powerful

They are afraid of you Sean
because you beg to question
because boys like you grow into men worth a mention
build a world with your blocks, draw in any direction
if they ever tell you you can't focus...

good.

Pay them no attention.

CHAPTER 15

LET MY SOUL SPIT

Young People Write for Reflection and Inspiration

Susan Wilcox
The Brotherhood/Sister Sol

How is it that young people's innate desire to learn, so fresh when they enter kindergarten, often wears away by middle and high school? How is it that youth who typically have an inherent sense of justice become apathetic teenagers? Adolescents are quick to recognize and challenge unfairness (perhaps particularly when it is aimed at them), and they have a desire for truth telling. Teens have acquired diverse knowledge and skills and are increasingly curious about who they are and their place within their family, peer group, school, and society. The Content, Perspective, Dialogue (CPD) Workshop Model (Wilcox, 2009) developed by The Brotherhood/Sister Sol (BHSS) assumes that these are qualities young people come bearing and that reflective writing (e.g., poetry, essays, journaling, spoken word, speeches) is an effective tool for exploring knowledge of self, developing a creative and ideological voice, and building community. CPD is centrally rooted in the Pan-African and Latino tradition of education for liberation.

Listening to and Learning from Students, pages 135–149
Copyright © 2011 by Information Age Publishing
All rights of reproduction in any form reserved.

Perry (2003) writes about the history in Black America of using reading and writing as an act of resistance, as a political act, and for uplifting the race. Kirkland (n.d.,) describes early 20th century Puerto Rican cigar makers who hired "readers" to read newspapers to them each morning. Each afternoon, the workers discussed the issues of the day. Black and Latino/a identity was tied to being educated, to being knowledgeable about current events and capable of engaging in critical dialogue, and, for Black Americans, something for which they risked their lives. Perceptions about the educational interests and acumen of Blacks and Latinos today, commonly conceptualized as the "achievement gap," are in stark contrast with this heritage, shaped as the perceptions are by subtle and blatant, though insufficiently examined, stereotypes about the inability of students of color to achieve educational success or to even have a desire to try. Many of the adults teaching Black and Latino/a youth, and sometimes the youth themselves, believe they are anti-intellectual and anti-school. BHSS, however, encounters young people who want to learn, but are frustrated that their schools are ineffective at helping them make connections to the curriculum or that teachers expect little from them. Their schools, it seems, have become anti-student (and it might be said that the overall tenor of American society is currently skewed toward a fondness for anti-intellectualism.) BHSS begins with youth's interests, culture, and history for content and inspiration.

> At Bro/Sis I was introduced to my ancestors. I began to be immersed in a history I never knew existed. Jacques and Silvia would give us research assignments and I was enthralled by the historical richness in each topic. For the first time in my life I was in a class where black was beautiful, smart, courageous, passionate, everything that I had been socialized to believe it wasn't. It is not so much that I faced overt racism in regular class (which at times I did) but omission and silence can sometimes have the same effect as blatant racism. Not having been sufficiently taught my people's history left me utterly confused and bitter. I was angry; angry because I was not white I did not know where I belonged. Since I was born I was bombarded with images of whiteness, purity, and goodness. Everyone important was white: Jesus, George Washington, Abraham Lincoln, Rockefeller, Bill Gates, Superman, Batman, Spiderman, my doctors, dentists, and teachers. The message was clear. If I wanted to be successful and important I had to be white. —Enmanuel

CPD was designed with belief in what Enmanuel so passionately expresses: When young people connect to information, ideas, and experiential activities, they develop deeper self-knowledge and self-love, as well as a love of learning. Learning about "beautiful, smart, courageous, passionate" and important Black people was transformative for Enmanuel. Previously "confused and bitter," his newly acquired knowledge instilled obvious pride in both his people and himself.

The CPD Workshop Model is an effective approach for bringing out young people's innate desire to learn and inherent sense of justice through reflective writing. This chapter describes the context in which CPD was created, the model's components, the assumptions necessary for utilizing the model, and the implementation steps. Since it is about young people's writing, their words are used throughout to illustrate the rationale and influence of this reflective writing model.

CONTENT, PERSPECTIVE, DIALOGUE WORKSHOP MODEL

BHSS is a Harlem-based, grassroots, youth development organization created to help young people develop into critical thinkers committed to personal and community change. I am former Co-Executive Director of the organization and in my current role am responsible for documenting our educational activities and facilitating internal and external professional development. Our members are predominately Black and Latino/a (Black American, Dominican, Puerto Rican, Haitian, Jamaican, Ghanaian). Some are straight A students and others struggle to pass their classes. Some come to us natural-born leaders, prone to making poor choices; others, reticent to assert their opinions. Through holistic, diverse, and long-term programming, youth gain knowledge of self, a belief that their contributions are significant, and a sense of solidarity with their peers and elders. The foundation of our work is the Rites of Passage Program—a multi-year process during which youth participate in weekly workshops based on our *10 Curriculum Focus Issues* (i.e., Pan-African & Latino History, Sexism & Misogyny, Political Education & Social Justice, Leadership Development, Educational Achievement, and Community Service & Responsibility). Youth organizing, after-school enrichment (including Writers Collective), international study, and job training and placement are other programs we offer teens.

The basis for CPD was created when BHSS was founded, but it has been honed over a decade of facilitating workshops for youth, ages 12–19, and documenting our practice. It is a dynamic educational approach that ignites youth, even those identified by their teachers as being un-teachable. For example, BHSS partners with public secondary schools to establish single-sex (Brotherhood or Sister Sol) Rites of Passage Program chapters. One of our chapter members was compared academically to other students in his school, and his participation in The Brotherhood was perceived as being the elemental difference between his achievements above that of his peers. CPD components are:

Content includes information, facts, and experiential activities. It is the common knowledge and experiences a class or group acquires for engaging in informed critique and dialogue. Facilitators carefully select socially salient, diverse, and challenging material that includes literature, essay, and poetry (such as by James Baldwin, Audre Lorde, or Sekou Sundiata), and mainstream media (e.g., *The New York Times*, music videos). They facilitate outings to museums and movies, ethnographic research and community mappings (e.g., young people research and analyze data about aspects of their own or other communities), and arts projects. Content draws young people in, exposes them to myriad ideas and ways of living, and builds on their knowledge, interest, and skills.

Perspective is the lens through which young people critique content. With the West African proverb, "Only when lions have historians, will hunters cease being heroes" in mind, CPD helps young people learn how to examine points of view (their own and others) and the influences from which they derive. Developing an immersed, coherent perspective comes from being exposed to and reflecting on rich content. It requires listening closely to viewpoints different from your own and realizing that learning is a process of exchange to which everyone has something to contribute. A *Framework for Analysis* (Wilcox, 2006) guides educators in developing individual or a series of workshops that bring out the relevancy of the topic to youth and examine it through multiple concepts including: knowledge of the world, unity, leadership, power, and transformation.

Dialogue brings in young people's voices in formal and informal discussion and through reflective writing. Dialogue connects and illuminates content and perspective. When Spike Lee's movie *Bamboozled* came to New York City several years ago, some of our members asked their Chapter Leaders when they would be going to see it. They knew it was the *type* of movie BHSS staff would choose because it was written and directed by a person of color and dealt with issues of race and gender that our young people confront each day and explore as part of our curriculum focus. Our members also knew and valued that the outing would begin with a workshop and end with a reflective discussion and/or writing assignment. Spoken and written dialogue helps young people deconstruct and analyze content and perspective.

CPD components are interdependent and non-linear. Facilitators could start a workshop with Dialogue (e.g., brainstorming, writing activity) that triggers young people's thinking and brings out their knowledge about the topic. This information can then guide facilitators in choosing materials and activities that will enhance young people's knowledge and experiences (Content) and Perspective. Alternatively, facilitators could approach a topic by taking youth to a movie (Content) and then facilitate a workshop that gives greater detail about its focus. For example, a Brotherhood chapter went to see *Hotel Rwanda* and were so moved by the depicted atrocities of the civil war that they wanted to learn more about the internecine conflicts in Africa. They were therefore inspired to read lengthy articles and hear a presentation on the issue. CPD components are synergistic, but what BHSS has found to be most important is that educators think and act intentionally about their role and the context in which learning takes place.

NINE CORE ASSUMPTIONS OF CPD

Whether our members live in public housing or in private homes their families own, their route to the BHSS brownstone is fraught with negative distractions. But enter our building and you will see by their shoeless feet or easy exchange of affection how at home our young people feel. You will see youth working together on an organizing campaign, a young person finalizing her college essay, or a group of teens in an intense discussion with a staff member about the merits of a popular song. Our walls display imagery and words meaningful to and/or created by our members, not signs of vandalism. The contrast between our brownstone and the public schools our members attend is striking.

After traveling from their homes through a gauntlet of violence, drug dealing, litter, and the presence of underemployed adults, they enter their school, perhaps through a metal detector, and are likely met with a punitive greeting (e.g., "Tuck in your shirt." "Be quiet." "Get in line."). Even before they take a seat in a crowded and under-resourced classroom, they have absorbed a phenomenon of neglect and hopelessness, but must somehow quickly shift their attention to learning. The debilitating social factors in which youth like our members live can make it difficult for them to concentrate on their education and undermine any sense of respect and possibility (Noguera, 2003). BHSS seeks to counteract this reality by creating a literally safe space and by fostering cohesion between young people and adults. A culture equal parts order, authenticity, respect, and empathy provides the context in which written and oral dialogue can flourish. This is the culture from which the Workshop Model's nine core assumptions derive:

1. Teachers and youth workers serve as facilitators, providing information and fostering critical inquiry so young people can discover answers and identify questions for themselves. Facilitators are not required to have all the answers, but to promote critical exploration. They must also cultivate respect between and among youth and adults so that the learning environment becomes one of shared trust.
2. Affirming young people's skills and knowledge instills confidence and courage. To have their thoughts heard and see their words in print

is to recognize that their knowledge and perspectives are meaning-ful. Facilitators need to encourage participation of all young people, whether by contributing to discussion or reading a piece of their writing, so that their unique voice can be heard and can inform others.

3. Two facilitators enhance educational and enrichment activities and group building. When educators collaborate with each other to develop and facilitate workshops and programs, they bring increased creativity and diverse perspectives, as well as can be more able to better manage the multiple needs of their group. They also provide each other with mutual support.

4. Young people's experiences and backgrounds are essential assets in the learning process. They are not empty vessels waiting to be filled, but can inform lessons and facilitate learning. Youth become educators when they can share their stories and connect their personal experiences to larger social issues. With guidance, they can also facilitate workshops. Their approach will no doubt reveal activities that are especially appealing to young people.

5. The learning environment matters. It needs to be inclusive of young people's interests and values, and safe for them to express their opinions, fears, and aspirations. Their writing or work should hang on the walls; learning content should represent their culture and history; and the space should be one for which they feel responsible for maintaining.

6. Workshop topics and materials need to resonate with young people. In order to be intellectually and socially well rounded it is necessary for young people to explore a vast variety of issues. They are, however, naturally engaged by reading and learning about the experiences of people like themselves and/or about realities similar to their lives, and this is where facilitators can begin.

7. Young people need positive alternatives. Rather than having their negative choices and behaviors pointed out, they mature by being pushed to articulate what they stand for and by placing decision making in their hands.

8. Youth desire what many adults forget is so essential: fun. Learning needs to engage young people's minds, bodies, and spirits. Energize youth with activities that make them think and move. Also, be attuned to their mood and immediate needs and be flexible to modify activities if necessary.

9. Youth excel when held to high expectations. Choose intellectually demanding content, develop challenging activities, help young people make decisions, and hold them accountable to their self-defined beliefs and commitments. These strategies will help them take responsibility for shaping their life paths.

In the process of documenting the CPD Workshop Model, I asked Lyrical Circle (the award-winning founding poetry group of the Writers Collective) for their perspectives on our writing approach. One member shared these thoughts:

> I was writing for about 7 years prior to LC's creation, but my focus was on myself (and whatever pain I was dealing with at the time). Working with Jacques, I learned how to improvise writing a piece. He was always random in selecting assignments which manifested in my ability to write a thematic piece at the drop of a dime. Now with Silvia, she always allowed the space for the most conversation at LC, the topic at the time would become the next assignment, and the convo was always deep, even if it was a lighthearted discussion. Her nurturing demeanor and desire to help us with whatever we needed and to hook us up with opportunities to spit has been surpassed by none. DaMond brought out the performer in a few of us. He definitely brought me to a place where I could channel my innermost pain, and translate it to the stage. Working with Bro/Sis has turned our potential talent into control over our artistic futures. —Frantz

It was important to Frantz that he highlight the specific influence of each BHSS facilitator he worked with, and in so doing, he underscores how having access to multiple adults enriches young people's learning. When Frantz writes about Silvia's "nurturing demeanor," he is showing appreciation for receiving affirmation that instills confidence. And though he says he initially only focused on "whatever pain I was dealing with at the time," the opportunity to bring his personal experiences into Lyrical Circle was an essential precursor to developing and strengthening his writing.

CPD IN ACTION

Daddy keeps
saying that my private parts are just not so to him.
He says that it's ok to touch cuz he helped to make 'em.
Mommy says that's it not right to but … I hate him.
Daddy keeps
peeking at me from behind the TV.
Winking cuz he's sworn me to secrecy.
No one knows the games we play at our midnight slumber parties.
    —Cheyenne

This excerpt is a powerful example of the synergy of Content (incest), Perspective (a personal story), Dialogue (a poem describing an experience for the purpose of bringing it to light for personal and public contemplation), and of how CPD enables youth to unburden themselves and think critically about what weighs so heavily on them. Cheyenne's willingness to publicly explore a deeply painful topic demonstrates the level of emotional security created by her peers and program facilitators. Through writing with truth she began to recognize the personal in the universal and vice versa, that issues she faces are not uncommon and as such there is opportunity for solidarity building. Any sense of apathy she may have felt is now challenged from having gained new insight and formed authentic bonds.

Implementing CPD has four main steps: (1) setting the tone, (2) creating and facilitating learning experiences, (3) nurturing reflection, and (4) helping young people revise their writing.

1. Setting the Tone

Setting the tone is the beginning and an ongoing aspect of implementing the CPD. Because knowing and caring about each other draws out the group's opinions, beliefs, and personal stories as a consequence of feeling supported and safe (see Cushman, 2003), young people and adults intentionally and continually co-create a learning environment that nurtures respect and relationship building. Together, they achieve consensus on a Rules of Conduct (or create a Mission Statement) that become the tenets which everyone agrees to uphold. "One person speaks at a time" (one mic), "attack the idea not the person," and "anything said in the circle should stay in the circle" are common rules. A Mission Statement is more in depth, expressing the group's collective values and goals. The power of words—the idea that a person's word is a bond—is emphasized by carefully articulating group values and reinforcing them through regular reference. Setting the tone also includes facilitating *Check-in* during which each person shares what is on his or her mind so they can center themselves for the group's activities. *Check-in* is when the group develops common knowledge and inside jokes, as well as practices good listening skills.

Embodying shared values is no small challenge because, as Payne writes (2008), "maintaining a sense of comradeship, may be particularly difficult for African Americans now, many of whom are growing up in communities that don't exhibit the level of internal solidarity that once characterized Black communities" (p. 9). Again, gaining inspiration from Pan-African and Latino traditions (here, a sense of responsibility for others in the community as transcending blood ties), a member of Writers Collective explains how our Workshop Model nurtures camaraderie.

> This group means an opportunity to
> let angst, anger, hope, dismay
> & all else come out.

It is a means of surviving
in a time when I feel no one else is listening.
It is a cadre of young people
who subject the ears, hearts and minds
of others to listening to their
poetic bliss for only
a few moments.
Our minds are open to new ideas,
hot lines, fresh phrases.
Our hearts are opened to witnessing
the experience of others &
the occasional realization that
others are going through the same thing.
The group provides the aura in which
I feel free to express.
Express my mind, my soul, my world.
This group shares stories of the country/city/world
in the fast lane moving too quickly to see its downfall . . .
This group is my release
where I feel free to pull the trigger
& let my soul spit.

> —Marsha

Marsha's poem expresses the personal, collective, and educational meaning of Writers Collective and its power to engender solidarity through empathy. She describes it as being a space of "poetic bliss" where she can reveal her deepest feelings to people who listen with open minds and hearts when no one else is. These are allies whom she relates to because they are "going through the same thing," while also offering "stories of the country/city/world" that no doubt broaden her knowledge. Marsha suggests that writing collectively is simultaneously edifying and liberating.

2. Creating and Facilitating Learning Experiences

Although CPD components do not necessarily precede one another in the implementation of this model, identifying curriculum issues and specific topics provides a roadmap for workshop or activity planning. Topics come from young people's interests (e.g., images of women in the media, police brutality) and from issues that facilitators think are important for youth to explore (e.g., military recruitment, the history of youth leaders). Exploration of critical social issues enables youth to deconstruct societal, familial, and personal perspectives about gender, race, sexuality, class, and power. Facilitators choose salient and challenging materials (e.g., literary excerpts, editorials, memoir), expose our members to new experiences (e.g., trips outside their neighborhood, outings to cultural events, wilderness retreats), ask good questions (a combination of the open-ended, clarifying, and explanatory), and provide significant time for our members to process information and experiences in both oral and written dialogue.

A Brotherhood chapter, for example, read two articles describing issues facing Black men in urban America. The two-hour session included a range of educational materials (e.g., relevant quotes, statistics) and techniques (e.g., reading the articles out loud and stopping at unfamiliar words, highlighting the author's main points, discussing the young men's personal experiences). The meaningfulness of young people's personal experiences should not be underestimated. They provoke immediate connection to the topic (e.g., What does it have to do with me?), are the initial lens of analysis (e.g., How does it affect my community or society?), and are the impetus for further inquiry (e.g., What are the roots of this issue?).

The Chapter Leader also explained that the reason for the workshop was not to leave the young men depressed or disillusioned, but to provide information and identify common experiences that would ultimately help everyone feel empowered. By knowing the realities, youth would also learn the obstacles that must be overcome. By knowing how pervasive the struggles are, they would learn not to internalize the poverty, mis-education, and racism they face. A 20-minute free write at the end of the workshop gave the youth an outlet for their feelings that included a resolute desire for achieving individual success and social change because both, they learned, are in fact linked.

> The idea of being seen and treated as an equal dwells in my mind. Police brutality is a reality I never wanted to accept because I aspired to become an officer. I can no longer close my eyes and pretend nothing has happened because racism still plagues our justice system and the first initiative I must take to improve the system is to acknowledge the problem. Through my fellow members, brothers and Chapter Leaders' anecdotes I have seen the atrocities that drain the spirit of the young black male. Random stops by the police and an abuse of their power has scarred many and weakened others. I do not understand why we as black males and black people should fear those who vowed to protect us. Justice cannot be allowed to wander around blindfolded in black communities violating people's personal space and state of being. The lesson I have learned today does not hinder me but instead prepares me for what is to come. A white man leaves his son riches in a novel, but a black male leaves his son with a torn mother, police who target him for simply being black and a lacking of knowledge of self. I feel as though the world has used color and material possessions to define an individual—the idea is that most accept this, and that is why there is no change. Many argue that capitalism is all about moving up in the world, but understand how few become millionaires and

billionaires. Also, consider how this race started and all the obstacles and devious traps that have been implemented to place the black and Hispanic communities behind the starting line. People speak as though slavery was not a crime to humanity, when in actually it was constructed to destroy the beams of our humanity and drive. We cannot assume that we all started on the same level and had one common goal. —Sequan

Sequan used the free write to try to make sense of devastating facts that "drain the spirit of the young black male." Summarizing what he learned helped him process facts with feelings. He moves back and forth from the past to present, from himself to others, and from acknowledging the problem to encouraging a solution. Sequan is in Dialogue with the workshop Content and his own Perspective, troubling through the contradiction he feels as a result of wanting to be a police officer with awareness of the brutality they have rained on his community. Very simply, he yearns to be "treated as equal" to white men. Sequan's words nearly bounce off the page, so active is his thinking. Critiquing the work of Lyrical Circle, Sundiata (Lazarre-White, 2006, p. 9) writes that their poems "remind[s] me of the link between philosophy and poetry in the sense that they inevitably gravitate towards big questions, towards making meaning out of the human experience" with "a sense of urgency and re-discovery." He could just as easily be speaking of Sequan's piece.

3. Nurturing Reflection

Reflective writing is a journey of critical exploration. Young people need opportunity and a safe, comfortable space for thinking about what they are learning, seeing, or experiencing. As opposed to any literary outcome, reflective writing helps young people tap into their feelings, articulate a point of view, or practice creative expression. Each activity may not lead to a polished piece, but it will help youth make the content their own through finding personal connections to it and through being critical of and inspired by what they are learning.

To nurture reflection we make sure young people feel physically comfortable (they can sit anywhere they like in the room) and are not distracted (they cannot sit close together). We do not rush discussion. Getting through a learning activity is less important than having our members acquire new understandings. We do not clock watch, and as our members mature, neither do they. When we have a finite amount of time, we return to the topic the next time we meet and/or continue the discussion informally. Nurturing reflection is also a group process. While participating in our International Study Program, our members collaborate on a group journal. More than recording the day's events, they reflect on what the experience means to them. Group journaling can happen during local activities, such as in conjunction with a workshop series or over the course of a semester.

Nurturing reflection does not necessarily infuse new Content, but it can bear out new Perspectives as a result of fostering internal or shared Dialogue. During a Sister Sol wilderness retreat we asked each member to find "her spot." A few stayed nearby. Others sought solitude atop a large boulder under an overhanging branch, or beside a rolling creek. When the group came back together several sisters volunteered to share their words. The voices that streamed forth from having been quiet were honest, insightful, and poignant.

> Sisterhood isn't just a word it is a state of mind. It is a true blessing. It is a crown that is earned and must be worn proud. You have to rock it right. Every single one of my sisters here are doing more than giving it justice. And not only are our Chapter Leaders teaching us the numerous, countless ways to be a sister but they are teaching us how to spread and share sisterhood. I only hope that I am learning how to rock it and that I will be able to share it. I am truly and deeply in love with Sister Sol. Ashé. —Written anonymously on evaluation survey

Perhaps the young woman who wrote this suddenly realized that her Chapter Leaders were "teaching [her] the numerous, countless ways to be a sister." More likely, having time to pause helped her articulate their intent. Appreciating her Sister Sol experience anew, she also saw where her responsibility lay in supporting sisterhood. Nurturing reflection, it seems, provokes awareness and response.

4. Help Young People Revise Their Writing

By exposing youth to a range of thought-provoking literary forms and providing opportunity for them to think critically through writing, they begin to see that quality writing engages readers' minds and spirits. They learn that good writers choose their words intentionally; that each writer has a unique focus, perspective, and rhythm (or voice). Finally, youth recognize that writing can be a force for personal and social change through its expression of ideas that evoke personal meaning and inspire response. When it is time for our members to develop their work, they understand revisions are essential to creating a well-crafted essay, poem, story, paper, or article.

Sequan reworked his reflections on the state of Black men into a college essay about his coming of age (see excerpt below). His Chapter Leader helped him work through a series of drafts, first by acknowledging the essay's strengths (overall and specific sections) and focusing on the big ideas (clarity of focus, point of view), before giving feedback on grammar and format. Our members also read their work to each other or have it read out loud to them. These group exchanges provide constructive critique that is supported by a culture of mutual respect and purpose. It is also meaningful that they know each other well and are familiar with each other's voices.

> When I walk out of my house each day I cannot help but feel I am in a battlefield. Missiles are flying over my head and carnivorous bullets originating from advertisements and stereotypes are harming anyone with traces of individuality. My only weapons are my words, ideas, and thirst for knowledge. I have been born not only to win the battle, but also the war. I do this while focusing on the words of Fredrick Douglass as if they were the solution to all that is wrong: "Without struggle there is no progress." I will struggle to succeed.... Throughout my life, I have faced an endless amount of hardships. Born into a single parent household setting, my mother had to provide for the two of us, and many of her own problems were taken out on me. The biggest change came in my junior year when my living environment transformed from a safe haven to a place I detested; my mother continuously dealt with abusive men and too often forgot she had a 16-year-old son. The pain from being put aside, as though I was a toy no longer desired by its owner, took a toll on my motivation. During my junior year I had to take a leave of absence due to family stress.... This led to an excessive amount of absences that though excused, created a difficult environment. The experience was disabling, preventing me from learning and participating to the fullest of my abilities while leaving me vulnerable to the razor sharp questioning of my peers. I was embarrassed by my situation and unable to fully interact with most peers, except for the members of Bro/Sis.... I moved out of my mother's house in November of 2006. The stress of having to provide for myself was exhausting and made me consider pursuing a General Equivalency Diploma. Luckily, my brothers would not allow it, and said, "You have too much potential." With these strong, positive people all around me there is no way I can ever fall and not have the strength to regain balance.... I see life as an obstacle course now. I will face challenges, but I can look back on what I have overcome and be ready for anything... I do not see myself as a victim. I am the victor because I still stand strong. —Sequan

Where the free write enabled Sequan to begin working through his understanding of the issues facing Black men in America, his college essay coalesced into a fusion of those ideas with his knowledge of history and his personal story. His Chapter Leader helped him preserve the active thinking of his visceral response to the workshop topic as a building block for expressing more polished, complex ideas. Part of the facilitator's role was to make sure Sequan felt comfortable with his candidness and maintained his unique focus, perspective, and rhythm (or voice).

SUMMARY

I wrote because the people in the circle were really good and I wanted to be as good. I wrote because I was expected to have at least one assignment weekly, and it was enjoyable homework. I wrote because the discussions made me want to put everything I felt, and thought, and saw into words. I wrote because people listened, people told me I was good, and because I was told it mattered. I would have been a writer despite The Brotherhood/Sister Sol, but they taught me discipline and they set up an environment that made me grow. —Elizabeth

Listening to our members "spit"—read their poetry or other work aloud—BHSS staff are usually in awe. Taking no claim for their lyrical skills, we know we have provided a context and nurture from which youth can hone their inherent inquisitiveness, intellectualism, and sense of justice. The challenge for educators working with youth "like BHSS members" is to engage them such that they feel safe and proactively seek to be transformed by knowledge. Facilitators need to not shut down young people's words because they are not well spoken or written, or because the issues they raise are painful or uncomfortable. Young people have a real desire to explore ideas that will help them process hardships, foster mutual empathy, and strengthen their character and commitments. Using the Workshop Model, BHSS staff seek a balance between providing our members with a safe context, challenging Content, varied Perspectives, and critical Dialogue, while getting out of their way so their authentic voices can emerge. To paraphrase a letter Elizabeth wrote to BHSS, through CPD writing becomes a way for young people to negotiate with the world.

REFERENCES

Cushman, K. (2003). *Fires in the bathroom: Advice for teachers from high school students.* New York: The New Press.

Kirkland, H. (n.d.). Cultural history of cigar workers in late 19th and early 20th century American history. Retrieved January 15, 2009, from http://pages. prodigy.net/gramsci7/_import/pages.prodigy.net/gramsci7/index2.html

Lazarre-White, K. (2006). *Off the subject: The words of Lyrical Circle of the Brotherhood/ Sister Sol.* New York: The Brotherhood/Sister Sol.

Noguera, P. (2003). *City schools and the American dream: Reclaiming the promise of public education.* New York: Teachers College Press.

Payne, C. (2008). Introduction. In C. Payne & C. Sills Strickland (Eds.), *Teach freedom: Education for liberation in the African-American tradition* (pp. 1–11). New York: Teachers College Press.

Perry, T. (2003). Freedom for literacy and literacy for freedom: The African-American philosophy of education. In T. Perry, C. Steele, & A. Hilliard III (Eds.),

Young, gifted and black: Promoting high achievement among African-American students (pp. 117–129). Boston: Beacon Press.

Wilcox, S. (2006). *Brother, sister, leader: The official curriculum of the Brotherhood/Sister Sol.* New York: The Brotherhood/Sister Sol.

Wilcox, S. (2009). *Why did this happen? Content, perspective dialogue: A workshop model for developing young people's reflective writing.* New York: The Brotherhood/Sister Sol.

CHAPTER 16

INTERLUDE

THINGS I WISH I TOLD
MY GRANDMA

kahlil almustafa
Urban Word NYC

Things I wish I told my Grandma instead of "Aight" when she asked me, "how was school today?"

NO, I did not have a good day today, Grandma. Today we learned about slavery. I am not sure why, but I felt embarrassed by it. I felt like when the book said slave, it was talking about me. Not me specifically, but I knew Black people got here from slavery and that somebody in my family at some time was a slave.

Also, Grandma, remember that birthday cake I made for my fifth-grade teacher, Mr. Oresky. Well, yeah, his fiancé Miss Wesson—she's the librari-an—she asked me if I washed my hands before I made the cake. And I do not know if she thought I was usually dirty, but somehow I felt like it was because I was Black.

Grandma, I hate school. I wish I could have gone to a school closer to home, but they are so dangerous. There is so much violence that I have to

Listening to and Learning from Students, pages 151–153
Copyright © 2011 by Information Age Publishing
151

go so far away. It takes me at least an hour and forty-five minutes to get to and from school each day.

It is like going to a foreign world. There are so many White and Asian people there and I am not really used to being around them. In every single one of my honors classes, I am the only Black male, and sometimes the only Black student. I feel like I am an outsider. These students are different from me. They speak different and care about different things. There are so many girls in the class. And they generally sit with one another. All the guys are so nerdy. Nothing that interests me interests them.

I hate my English honors class teacher, Mrs. Steinberg. She always embarrasses me in front of the class "Well, maybe you do not belong in the honors classes. Maybe you want to be in another class with the rest of the dumbies." All I hear is her telling me I do not belong in the honors class because I am Black and the other Black boys are in the dumb classes. I do not say anything in return to her. The whole class is silent with me. Possibly, they are as embarrassed for me because sometimes one of them walks up to me after class and asks me if I need help or if things are going alright in my life. I stay silent with them too. Their pity disgusts me.

There was this one girl in my class I like. Her name was Lorena. She is a short white girl with big glasses and really curly hair. I like her a lot, a whole lot. I used to look forward to sitting next to her each day. This was last year. I am not sure why, but now when we see one another in the hallways, we do not say hello. We do not look into one another's eyes or acknowledge one another in any way.

There is only one teacher I hate more than Mrs. Steinberg, and *that* is Mr. Scharfman, Dr. Scharfman. I think he must hate his entire life and the fact that he has to babysit a bunch of teenagers all day. He makes racial jokes about us everyday, about how we talk, about our music, about how we dress. He imitates the way we talk. Sometimes he throws the eraser at us if we are not listening. We laugh, especially me and Hakim. We laugh. I am not sure why we laugh, but we do. I do know that I feel real uncomfortable laughing. It is kind of double-sided. One part of me laughs. And another part wants to tell Dr. Scharfman that he is a racist and he is an unfit teacher. I used to be able to tolerate him until what he did that one day. One day this Asian girl was trying to pronounce this word and she could not pronounce it. He would say the word to her, and she would say it wrong. They went back and forth, and each time he got closer to her, and said it louder, until finally he was right in her face screaming. And she finally broke out in tears. And it was not until she started crying that I even realized where I was. And I don't know if I am more mad at Dr. Scharfman or myself for not getting up and screaming "this is wrong." Either way, I left that class hating Dr. Scharfman, and I've hated him ever since.

During lunch today, I went to my Guidance Counselor, Mrs. Baumbach. She must get a commission each time she sends a student to a state school because no matter what school I tell her I want to go to, she kept telling me to go to a state university. She made it seem like it was some prized promise land that I should be grateful for going to. No matter what she said all I heard was, "kahlil you are not good enough to do that."

Actually, Grandma, I did not go to school today. I went to the park and wrote poetry. I cut school and go there sometimes to write and to figure things out that no one is talking about in school. I go there to think about where AIDS came from, and why all the young black boys are dying in our neighborhood, and all the drugs there are where we live, and why are we told to pray and, if our prayers do not come true, it was God's will anyway. None of these things are spoken about in my classes, and so I hate school, grandma. I hate school.

How was your day?

CHAPTER 17

CONSTRUCTING AND CONSTRICTING TEACHERS

RateMyTeachers.com as a Knotted Space of the Educational Imaginary

Jake Burdick
Arizona State University

Colleges of education, and the scholars and research they produce, largely fixate on schools, school people, and the institutionalized process of schooling as the epicenter of educational activity, often to the exclusion of all other sites of learning and teaching. Whereas this emphasis finds its ground in the historical emergence of education as an academic field (Spring, 2005), it manufactures a synecdochical reduction of education as a broad human activity to a specialized, institutional form. Further, and more germane to this chapter's argument, the bracketing off of schools from other cultural sites of education obscures the complicated structural reciprocity between schools and the culture in which they are embedded. That is, looking at schools as closed institutional systems ignores the ways in which dominant, extra-institutional cultural notions of schooling and teaching work to re/create

Listening to and Learning from Students, pages 155–167
Copyright © 2011 by Information Age Publishing
All rights of reproduction in any form reserved.

expectations, performances, and evaluations of school life, particularly from our students' perspectives. From the Hollywood curricula of savior-teachers and savvy-slacker, miscreant students (Carpenter, Milam, & Lovett, 2006; Dalton, 2006, 2004; McCarthy, 1998; Trier, 2001) to the ubiquitous derision of post-Reagan educational policy discourse (Pinar, 2004; Spring, 2005), schools and their inhabitants are largely (over)determined for students via complex, often contradictory, public pedagogies. And, in ironic fashion, it is these very pedagogies that delimit teaching and learning to the activities found within a school, and even there, to a fixed range of acceptable performances and practices.

In the contemporary landscape of schools and schooling, historical, cultural, and political pedagogies find teachers and teaching a common object of interest, be it for the sake of vilification or valorization (Dalton, 2006). More importantly, I argue that these cultural constructs of teachers serve to prefigure students' very images, expectations, and evaluations of their teachers, often in problematic, perhaps impossible ways. Hollywood and other mass media have taken a particular interest in the depiction of teaching as a heroic act, producing images of teachers as idiosyncratic, rebellious, and even reckless in their passion (Dalton, 2004, 2006). Conversely, the portrayal of teachers as inept, unprofessional, and ultimately damaging has entered into American political rhetoric with increased vehemence since the *A Nation at Risk* legislation at the core of President Reagan's educational politics (Spring, 2005). These attacks have exercised their influence beyond debates and posturing to produce a profound material effect on teachers' practices and lives, including tremendous funding cuts, increased licensure requirements, the obdurate move toward *teacher-proof* curricula, and the now ubiquitous top-down mandate of standards and measurement in teaching and learning—what Pinar (2004) collectively labels "the nightmare that is the present" (see pp. 15–34). Despite their incongruity, these images and the representative continuum on which they fall work to create shared, commonsensical cultural meanings around the institution of schooling, meanings that shape the expectations of the public that schools are intended to serve. As Pinar notes, "we teachers are conceived by others, by the expectations and fantasies of our students and by the demands of parents, administrators, policymakers, and politicians, to all of whom we are sometimes the 'other'" (p. 30).

In an attempt to illustrate how this complex array of expectations, beliefs, and stories converges and interbraids, I use the space of this chapter to explore RateMyTeachers.com, a Web site that offers middle and secondary school students a forum for evaluating their teachers as well as publishing these ratings for public consumption. The site, a companion to ratemyprofessors. com, pickaprof.com, ratingsonline.com, and whototake.com (all of which focus on *post*-secondary instructors), emanates from a zeitgeist of ratings/

evaluation-oriented Web sites and memes that manifested in the early part of the 21st century. Ranging from the ability to rate others' physical appearance (AmIHotOrNot.com) to one's interactions with police officers (RateMyCop.com), these sites all afford the ability for users to instantaneously communicate their perceptions of people, objects, and phenomena via instrumentation that closely resembles consumer-satisfaction surveys or movie reviews. To carve their own niche within this surfeit, the creators of RateMyTeachers.com offer the following explication of the central purposes:

> Several of the original founders of this site have an interest in education (two of us are teachers) and asked: "who is accountable to whom?" Are teachers accountable to the school administrators? Are the administrators accountable to the school board? Are school boards accountable to the state or federal governments? Where do the student and the parent enter this equation? At the end of the day, we concluded that teachers have to be accountable to their students. We decided that a site like RateMyTeachers.com would be an effective tool, which could be used to elevate the student voice in the public discourse on quality education. (Davis, 2004, n.p.)

Beyond the clear nod towards standards- and evidence-based schooling that is made in this paragraph, I contend that the site itself, especially the student-produced ratings therein, can be engaged as a microcosmic view of what Barone and Lash (2006) call the *educational imaginary*, "a set of broadly disseminated images about what schools and school people within a nation are supposedly like" (p. 22) that exists inter-psychically throughout the culture and is reinforced via a complex array of public pedagogies centered on schools and schooling. To this effect, the site acts as a *knot* in the cultural discourses and public pedagogies of teaching and teachers—a space in which these countervailing, complementary, or disparate discourses weave into a cohesive whole, all under the problematic guise of evaluative criteria for *good* teaching. Further, and as a guiding element to this chapter, it is crucial to note that, collectively, the knotted discursive space of RateMyTeachers.com is undergirded itself by yet another, seemingly ubiquitous public pedagogy—the reduction of democratic activity to consumptive choice, in this instance, the transformation of education from a public good to a private commodity. The site overwhelmingly posits the metaphors of education as commodity and students as consumers, a signpost of the collapse of this public space into private discourse and interests and of the impoverishment of education's democratic potential (see Dewey, 1909; Molnar, 2004). Education, under this metaphor, loses its capacity as a servitor of the public good and becomes (yet) another site for the fulfillment of private want.

Other researchers (e.g., Bonds-Raacke & Raacke, 2007; Felton, Mitchell, & Stinson, 2004a, 2004b; Kindred & Mohammed, 2005; Otto, Sanford,

& Ross, 2008; Wilhelm & Comegys, 2004) have utilized quantitative and qualitative approaches to inquire into students' perceptions and uses of teacher evaluation sites (largely RateMyProfessors.com). However, rather than addressing the internal efficacy of the RateMyTeachers.com, my desire in this chapter is to explore the ways in which the site both produces and is produced by this American imaginary of teachers (Barone & Lash, 2006) in the minds of students. Using an analysis of evaluative student comments taken from the five top-rated "Hall of Fame" (RateMyTeachers.com, 2008) teachers on the site, I construct a model of what these comments describe as a *good* teacher. From these findings, I examine the complicated relationship that exists between formal schooling and the public pedagogies that circumscribe the very ways Americans view and culturally valuate education, and I offer critiques of this construct that draw from psychoanalysis, cultural studies, and critical pedagogy scholarship, using these theoretical vantage points as a means to raise questions regarding the sociological and professional ramifications of these students' comments. In conclusion, I argue that educational researchers and practitioners need to attend to the myriad constructs of teachers, teaching, and schools that exist around and within their practice and that any attempt to revitalize the democratic vocation of schooling must work to counter *both* the institutional and the cultural commonsenses of education.

"MAD FUNNY": STUDENTS' PERCEPTIONS OF QUALITY ON RATEMYTEACHERS.COM

The RateMyTeachers.com Web site utilizes both a quantitative rating system, within which students rate teachers' *easiness, helpfulness,* and *clarity,* as well as a section for brief, qualitative commentary. For this inquiry, I focus exclusively on the comments section; however, the potential framing qualities of the site's qualitative ratings should not be ignored. The three categories, taken holistically, already presuppose a unidirectional student/teacher relationship, one that casts the teacher in a service capacity that has little to do with anything but the utmost exteriority of pedagogical (and curricular) practice. This construct, as my analysis will show, is prevalent throughout the site; however, rather than assume a linear trajectory of causation from these criteria to students' comments, it is more productive to view both as emanations of the imaginary (Barone & Lash, 2006), coherent to the overarching cultural logics at play on the site. In that regard, both criteria and the comments are mutually constitutive of and constituted by the dominant cultural perspective, rather than one another.

To pare down the wealth of student comments at RateMyTeachers.com, I limited my review to reading through only the comments sections for the top five[1] teachers listed in the site's "Hall of Fame" (a section that collects the highest-rated teachers who have been reviewed by a minimum of 75 students). From this process, I derived two overarching thematic groupings that spoke to students' espoused criteria for quality in teaching:

1. *Good* teachers are challenging for students, but they still manage to create a "fun" classroom environment.
2. *Good* teachers offer themselves to students beyond the classroom, the semester, and the confines of the professional relationship, even to the extent of taking on paternal (in the case of the data sources) qualities in their relationships with students.

I utilized this approach not to provide a comprehensive understanding of the ways in which students describe teachers, but rather to excavate the undergirding assumptions and cultural scripts used in the site reviews' language of *teacher quality*. It is my hope to begin to utilize this language in order to gain a greater understanding of how cultural pedagogies might re/create the "cumulative cultural text" (Weber, 2006) of teachers themselves. To accompany these findings, I also offer my review of the implicit and explicit pedagogical significance of these comments and the teacher identities they produce, drawing largely from the counternarrative of teaching and learning forwarded by cultural studies and critical pedagogy scholars.

Teacher As Entertainer: Pleasure and Stupidification

The first thematic category, a desire for both work and "fun" in the classroom, was highly prevalent in four of the five teachers' comment sections[2], with student comments emphasizing that, although the teacher assigned a great deal of homework or held high academic expectations, he or she also evidenced a charismatic demeanor within the classroom:

"by far the best teacher at […], makes class challenging but fun at the same time. i never wanted to miss his class"

"coolest teacher i've ever had, makes you want to learn, i wish Studies of War was a full year class. Uses cool movies in class, Saving Private Ryan, Blackhawk D[own]"

"lots of work, lots of studying and not an easy grader but an awesome guy none-the-less. you learn a lot in his class"

"my favorite teacher!!! lots of work but an awesome teacher. i had him for 3 years and hr. you WILL learn sooo much in his class. :-)"

"[he] gives hard work and expects us to learn it. i like the fact that he treats us with respect and he expects us to do good work. and he's mad funny"

"best teacher at [...] hands down. just finished doing worlds fair with mr h and it was totaly cool and awesome. he gives us a lot of work to do but it makes us smarter and he also makes it fun. i dont want the year to end with him."

What is primarily at play in these comments is the binary between "rigor" and pleasurable in the educational process, one that creates a mutual exclusivity between the content offered in the school and one's ability to enjoy the classroom experience. The official curriculum is not pleasure in and of itself; rather, the teacher is frequently called upon to "make" lectures and classes both fun and compelling, placing a powerful requirement on the teachers' classroom *performance* rather than his or her professionalism. To better understand students' equivocation of fun and learning within the classroom, I suggest that we first locate the development and widespread normalization of the "edutainment" model of pedagogy within the larger educational imaginary—in this case, in its portrayal in film. The teacher-as-entertainer metaphor emanates most clearly in the film *Dead Poet's Society* (Haft & Weir, 1989), in which the teacher, John Keating (played by Robin Williams), enacts a radically performative and unorthodox approach to a literature classroom. Throughout the course of the film, the same dualism of rigor and pleasure is enacted; however, it is crucial to note that, on screen, Keating rarely invites his students to engage in anything but a pleasurable exchange with course content, most clearly represented in the film's early scene of students emphatically ripping pages from their literature texts. Still, whether by standing on their desks to gain perspective or reading verse while kicking rubber balls, his students undergo profound changes to their very identity, reinforcing the notion that the experience of pleasure is somehow crucial to or even analogous with educational development.

The commonsensical association of learning and fun does little to forward education's possibility as a site of critical intervention. As Marcuse (1992) argues, the psychoanalytical concept of *eros* has come to largely signify *comfort* in capitalist social orders: "the striving for pacification, for making pleasure eternal, indicates an instinctual resistance... to giving up a pleasurable equilibrium once reached. This resistance, if not hostile to life, is nevertheless static and 'resistant to progress'" (p. 225). In concert with this perspective, Žižek (1989) suggests that there is an underlying awareness of the impoverished conditions of daily life, but an even more powerful psychic resistance to acknowledge this fundamental perception. For Žižek, questioning the available reality and its attendant structures (the Symbolic Order) jeopardizes the shelter that this configuration offers, even if that shelter is overtly repressive and alienating in its own right. Applied to educational practice, these theoretical perspectives suggest that any form of critical pedagogical intervention, despite its intellectual veracity or verisimilitude, would be met with strong resistance, thus condemning teachers to be *safe*, or at best *cathartic*, in their pedagogical address. An example of the sanitization of curriculum for the sake of comfort appears in one student's comments regarding his AP history class: "we learned that the Palace at Versailles had only two bathrooms for a palace the size of the school. When people had to use the bathroom, they pee on the wall or crap in the fireplace" (RateMyTeachers.com, 2008). Hailed as an example of the kind of pedagogy this "Hall of Fame" teacher employs in his classroom, this dehistoricizing of history itself harkens to what Donaldo Macedo (1994) laments as "stupidification," "illiteracy," and the "inability to link the reading of the word to the reading of the world" (p. 15). The Palace of Versailles is abstracted from its own history and historicity, and via reduction to trivia, it loses all possibility as a site for the exploration of power, war, or the economic disequilibrium this place symbolized in French consciousness. In essence, it becomes nothing at all—"everything is reduced to the same dead level" (Dewey, 1909, para. 35).

Whereas Macedo's argument condemns contemporary American cultural politics as the genesis for the fragmentation of curricular content into decontextualized and ultimately meaningless trivia, the same end is frequently achieved as teachers, at the behest of the media-driven educational imaginary, conflate education with pleasure. Critical educators like Macedo, Freire (1998), and Boler (1999) posit that for education to maintain any semblance of a democratizing endeavor, teachers must be willing and courageous enough to utilize a "pedagogy of discomfort" (Boler) that calls students' very sense of ease into question as a marker of privilege. Yet, positions of discomfort are rarely taken up in the current cultural milieu, either in the actual schools or within the imaginary that constitutes their functioning, and when teachers do engage students in this manner, they risk strong opposition, vilification, and potentially their livelihood. As I will argue in the final section of this chapter, a viable critical position towards education requires researchers and scholars to extend their scope beyond the classroom and towards "a 'traversal of fantasy,' a recognition of its powerful hold over the psyche, which then leads to a new beginning" (jagodzinski, 2004, p. 41), inclusive of the total educational imaginary (Barone & Lash, 2006). Doing so might allow, in whatever small way, for the reconceptualization of education beyond metaphors of pleasure and return some space for the disquieting project of democracy.

Teacher As Name-of-the-Father: Poverties of the Self in the Teacher Imaginary

The second thematic grouping of comments generally centered on the kind of interpersonal teacher relationship students preferred—one that transgresses the institutional roles ascribed to each position towards more personal, even familial, rapport. Student comments towards this theme centered exclusively on male teachers (4 of the 5 teachers reviewed were male), and frequently invoked a sort of wish fulfillment regarding their perceptions of fatherhood:

"his work always meant something, his methods were amazing. no wonder he got teacher of the year twice. on top of that, he has taken kids to europe many times. i got to go. he is amazing"

"I'm a freshman in college, and i talk to him every day. He is like a father to me, and i know that i am like a son to him. I am still learning from him."

Mr. [...]—what isnt there to say about him? He has and still helps mold my mind into the impetus it stands to be and is my second father. God bless him."

"Mr. [...]...you are a great teacher, great man, great father, but most of all a great leader...god bless you"

"He's the roll model for all fathers...thank you..."

"Rock on Mr. [...]...Your the roll model students need..."The DAD everyone should have" Someone needs to make him teacher of the year!!"

"The DAD we all should have....With Love....You make us want to come to school....[T]hank you."

"I got to go to Italy with him and my brother went to Germany & Austria with him. how cool is that!?!"

Trier (2001) notes that, within the space of film, "good teachers, those with a special gift, are devoted solely to their profession, seemingly at the expense of having any kind of personal life" (p. 132). Films like *Dangerous Minds* (Bruckheimer & Smith, 1995) and *Dead Poet's Society* (Haft & Weir, 1989), as well as the increasing demands (without attendant compensation) placed on teachers via the accountability movement, (re)produce the cultural *fact* that the professional identity teachers embody is—to no small extent—encompassing of their lives (Carpenter, Milam, & Lovett, 2006; McCarthy, 1998). As a response to these constructs, students' expectations of teachers have come to extend far beyond what they offer within the institution, as evidenced in these comments.

Perhaps the most profound statements in this theme center on the paternal role these students have perceived in their relationships with the "Hall of Fame" teachers. Whereas some of these comments appear pedestrian in their relation of the teacher in question as a "second" father, others—namely, "the roll [sic] model for all fathers," "The DAD everyone should have," and "The DAD we all should have"—present an even more complicated and possibly illustrative situation. The students and/or former students making these comments have transcended any sort of mere ascription of their teacher to a paternal role and essentially cast these individuals in deific light—as the fathers of all fathers. To provide a possible interpretation of this powerful move and the factors that create its occasion, I suggest that we approach the notion of the construct *father* from the Lacanian psychoanalytical tradition: as the "name-of-the-father," the symbolic space of fatherhood within a social order that becomes synonymous with that order's efficacious functioning, its governing law (Lacan, 2006, p. 230). Operating from this foundational premise, jagodzinski (2004) reframes Freud's Oedipus within the sociological sphere to argue that an effect of postmodern/late capitalist/neoliberal ideology has been a death of the *symbolic* father, and with it, the sense of the social order's authority, efficacy, and stability. In this revision actual fathers serve as stand-ins or metonyms for this larger presence; however, up against the pervasive dominance of market imperialism, they, too, fail to restore meaning to social existence, leaving us with a traumatic lack that can only grow as we age and separate from our actual parents.

Perhaps then, given the tremendous anxiety youth (all of the comments for these sections were taken from junior high or high school teachers' reviews) face in the present, postmodern social order, emanating from the ongoing alienating functions of designer capitalism; the ubiquitously apocalyptic crises of global conflict, environmental destruction, and economic injustice; and the pervasive difficulty of identity-formation in an overly me-dia-ted world, we might reinterpret these students' identification of their teachers as occupying the space of the missing name-of-the-father. In jag-odzinski's (2004) terms, this "fantasmic [construction of the teacher] fills the lack (hole) so that the system . . . appears whole, so that it makes sense" (p. 38). Given teachers' position in institutional space, as well as their curricular and pedagogical mandate to craft cogent, linear teaching units for impossibly complex and ambiguous narratives, the association makes a fair amount of sense. What becomes problematic in this transference (beyond students' obvious misrecognition) is that the teacher him/herself must shoulder the additional psychic weight of serving as this stopgap for the anxieties and needs of students, and in occupying this impossible space, lose some access to his/her own sense of a meaningful personal life. In essence, the occupational role of *teacher* is mistaken for and transmogrified into the transcendent symbolic *father*, all at the expense of the individual human being who holds this occupation. Taubman (2008) argues that the teacher's primary responsibility is to him/herself, not the students, as the commonsense of the educational imaginary forwards:

> how seductive are the claims of those educators who tell us how central we are to students, how it's all about the students, and they are all about us—and

how easily we are led from there to a very different sacrifice—that of our very subjectivity as we disappear into the "best practices" that sustain our fantasies of omnipotence, provoke our sense of emptiness, and hystericize us as we turn more and more to student evaluations. (p. 102)

As this mandate of self-sacrifice is continually invoked in the public pedagogies of film and politics, as well as validated and reified in the comments on sites like RateMyTeachers.com, we might see new avenues for questioning ongoing problems in schools, such as teacher burnout and shortages.

PUBLIC PEDAGOGIES AND THE CONSTRU(I)CTION OF THE AMERICAN EDUCATIONAL IMAGINARY

From the critical perspective I take in this essay, the stupidification, demoralization, and de-professionalization evidenced on RateMyTeachers. com, as well as the underlying consumerist drive that characterizes the site, targets the very heart of education's purpose, deforming schools into training grounds and target markets with little regard for students or the social space they occupy. Teachers in this discourse are, at best, managerial-class workers and, at worst, ultimately superfluous to any educational function of schooling. Further exacerbating this point is the irony that the same alienating tide of market ideology that promotes these symptomatic (mis)identifications and subsequent deformations to the professional space of teaching also constructs the space within which many students have selected to voice *their* opinions of their teachers. My intention in performing these analyses is neither to deride students for their expectations of teachers and teaching nor to uncover some hidden truth underlying these expectations. Rather, my hope is to raise questions about the origins and nature of the seemingly impossible position teachers occupy in the American educational landscape and to forward ways in which other educational researchers might begin to ask these questions in their work.

As I stated in the introduction to this chapter, educational research has largely ignored the pedagogical spaces (Ellsworth, 2005) that exist beyond institutional walls, and in failing to address these spaces, allows them to define these very walls and the practices therein. To address schools effectively, there is a need to inquire into the entire corpus of the educational imaginary and the public pedagogies that comprise and sustain it. Perhaps more importantly, research of this kind needs to find its channel to educational practitioners – the very individuals who have been constructed and constricted by these pedagogies – and the publics that simultaneously consume and reproduce these well-worn stories. This call is addressed in part via practical interventions directed towards pre- and in-service teachers, such as the analysis of filmic teacher representations described by Trier (2001), as well as art that seeks to trouble the unambiguous narrative of teachers and teaching, such as Boden and Fleck's (2006) *Full Nelson* (as noted in Dalton, 2006). In his historical moment, Dewey (1909) cogently understood this relationship: "The teacher needs to understand public opinion and the social order, as much as the public needs to comprehend the nature of expert educational service" (para. 7). However, in this present moment, little attention has been paid to the public pedagogy of common-sensical educational imaginary writ large and the deformative effect that this greater discourse has had on American schools. If nothing else, the suggestions I make in this chapter and the situation they describe call for an enhanced perspective of what educational research *does* and *might do.*

NOTES

1. The same individual occupied the fourth and fifth places on the "Hall of Fame" list at the time of my review due to a site error in recognizing abbreviated names. As such, I combined this individual's entries and reviewed comments for individuals occupying places one through six on the list.
2. It should be noted that on the page dedicated to the teacher who did not receive similar comments, many students reported "easy 100%s" as the rationale behind their positive reviews.

REFERENCES

Barone, T., & Lash, M. (2006). What's behind the spotlight? Educational imaginaries from around the world. *Journal of Curriculum and Pedagogy, 3*(2), 22–28.

Boden, A. (Producer) & Fleck, R. (Director). (2006). *Half nelson* [Motion picture]. United States: Hunting Lane Films.

Boler, M. (1999). *Feeling power: Emotions and education.* New York: Routledge.

Bonds-Raacke, J., & Raacke, J. D. (2007). The relationship between physical attractiveness of professors and students' ratings of professors. *Journal of Psychiatry, Psychology, and Mental Health, 1*(2). Retrieved August 12, 2008, from http://www.scientificjournals.org/journals2007/articles/1227.pdf

Bruckheimer, J. (Producer), & Smith, J. N. (1995). *Dangerous minds.* [Motion picture]. United States: Buena Vista.

Carpenter, B. S., Milam, J., & Lovett, M. (2006, October). *White hopes and black subjects: Representations of race, power, and curriculum through film and television.* Paper presented at the 2006 Curriculum and Pedagogy Conference, Marble Falls, TX.

Dalton, M. M. (2004). *The Hollywood curriculum: Teachers in the movies.* New York: Peter Lang.

Dalton, M. M. (2006). Revising the Hollywood curriculum. *Journal of Curriculum and Pedagogy 3*(2), 29–33.

Davis, N. (2004). RateMyTeachers—A new approach to ratings of teachers by students. *Teachers College Record.* Retrieved August 31, 2008, from http://www.tcrecord.org/content.asp?contentid=11398

Dewey, J. (1909). *Moral principles in education.* New York: Houghton Mifflin Company. Retrieved July 21, 2009, from http://www.gutenberg.org/files/25172/25172-h/25172-h.htm

Ellsworth, E. (2005). *Places of learning: Media, architecture, pedagogy.* New York: RoutledgeFalmer.

Felton, J., Mitchell J., & Stinson, M. (2004a). Web-based student evaluations of professors: The relations between perceived quality, easiness, and sexiness, *Assessment & Evaluation in Higher Education, 29*(1), 91–108.

Felton, J., Mitchell J., & Stinson, M. (2004b). *Cultural differences in student evaluations of professors.* Academy of Business Education Conference Proceeding.

Freire, P. (1998). *Pedagogy of freedom.* Lanham, MD: Rowman & Littlefield.

Haft, S. (Producer), & Weir, P. (Director). (1989). *Dead poets' society* [Motion picture]. United States: Touchstone Pictures.

jagodzinski, j. (2004). *Youth fantasies: The perverse landscape of the media.* New York: Palgrave Macmillan.

Kindred, R., & Mohammed S. (2005). "He will crush you like an academic ninja!": Exploring teacher ratings on ratemyprofessors.com. *Journal of Computer-Mediated Communication, 10*(3). Retrieved from http://jcmc.indiana.edu/vol10/issue3/kindred.html

Lacan, J. (2006). *Écrits.* [Bruce Fink, trans.]. New York: Norton.

Macedo, D. (1994). *Literacies of power.* Boulder, CO: Westview.

Marcuse, H. (1992). Freedom and Freud's theory of instincts. In D. Ingram & J. Simon-Ingram (Eds.), *Critical theory: The essential readings* (pp. 221–238). St. Paul, MN: Paragon House.

McCarthy, C. (1998). Educating the American popular: Suburban resentment and the representation of the inner city in contemporary film and television. *Race, Ethnicity, and Education, 1*(3), 31–47.

Molnar, A. (2004). *School commercialism.* New York: Routledge.

Otto, J., Sanford Jr., D. A., & Ross, D. N. (2008). Does ratemyprofessor.com really rate my professor? *Assessment & Evaluation in Higher Education, 33*(4), 355–368.

Pinar, W. F. (2004). *What is curriculum theory?* Mahwah, NJ: Lawrence Erlbaum Associates.

RateMyTeachers.com. (2008). Retrieved January 27, 2009, from http://www.RateMyTeachers.com

Spring, J. (2005). *The American school 1642–2004* (6th ed.). Boston: McGraw-Hill.

Taubman, P. (2008). It's all about the kids! Or is it? In A. Fidyk, J. Wallin, & K. den Heyer, (Eds.), *Democratizing educational experience: Envisioning, embodying, enacting* (pp. 96–104). Troy, NY: Educator's International Press.

Trier, J. D. (2001, Summer). The cinematic representation of the personal and professional lives of teachers. *Teacher Education Quarterly, 28*(3), 127–142.

Weber, S. (2006). The public imaginary of education as cumulative cultural text. *Journal of Curriculum and Pedagogy, 3*(2), 72–76.

Wilhelm, W. B., & Comegys, C. (2004). Course selection decisions by students on campuses with and without published teaching evaluations. *Practical Assessment, Research & Evaluation, 9*(16). Retrieved August 31, 2008, from http://PAREonline.net/getvn.asp?v=9&n=16

Žižek, S. (1989). *The sublime object of ideology.* New York: Verso.

CHAPTER 18

INTERLUDE

THE MORAL TRAINING FROM METHODS OF INSTRUCTION

John Dewey
Teachers College, Columbia University

The principle of the social character of the school as the basic factor in the moral education given may be also applied to the question of methods of instruction,—not in their details, but their general spirit. The emphasis then falls upon construction and giving out, rather than upon absorption and mere learning. We fail to recognize how essentially individualistic the latter methods are, and how unconsciously, yet certainly and effectively, they react into the child's ways of judging and of acting. Imagine forty children all engaged in reading the same books, and in preparing and reciting the same lessons day after day. Suppose this process constitutes by far the larger part of their work, and that they are continually judged from the standpoint of what they are able to take in in a study hour and reproduce in a recitation hour. There is next to no opportunity for any social division of labor. There is no opportunity for each child to work out something specifically his own, which he may contribute to the common stock, while he, in turn,

Listening to and Learning from Students, pages 169–172
Copyright © 2011 by Information Age Publishing

participates in the productions of others. All are set to do exactly the same work and turn out the same products. The social spirit is not cultivated,—in fact, in so far as the purely individualistic method gets in its work, it atrophies for lack of use. One reason why reading aloud in school is poor is that the real motive for the use of language—the desire to communicate and to learn—is not utilized. The child knows perfectly well that the teacher and all his fellow pupils have exactly the same facts and ideas before them that he has; he is not giving them anything at all. And it may be questioned whether the moral lack is not as great as the intellectual. The child is born with a natural desire to give out, to do, to serve. When this tendency is not used, when conditions are such that other motives are substituted, the accumulation of an influence working against the social spirit is much larger than we have any idea of,—especially when the burden of work, week after week, and year after year, falls upon this side.

But lack of cultivation of the social spirit is not all. Positively individualistic motives and standards are inculcated. Some stimulus must be found to keep the child at his studies. At the best this will be his affection for his teacher, together with a feeling that he is not violating school rules, and thus negatively, if not positively, is contributing to the good of the school. I have nothing to say against these motives so far as they go, but they are inadequate. The relation between the piece of work to be done and affection for a third person is external, not intrinsic. It is therefore liable to break down whenever the external conditions are changed. Moreover, this attachment to a particular person, while in a way social, may become so isolated and exclusive as to be selfish in quality. In any case, the child should gradually grow out of this relatively external motive into an appreciation, for its own sake, of the social value of what he has to do, because of its larger relations to life, not pinned down to two or three persons.

But, unfortunately, the motive is not always at this relative best, but mixed with lower motives which are distinctly egoistic. Fear is a motive which is almost sure to enter in,—not necessarily physical fear, or fear of punishment, but fear of losing the approbation of others; or fear of failure, so extreme as to be morbid and paralyzing. On the other side, emulation and rivalry enter in. Just because all are doing the same work, and are judged (either in recitation or examination with reference to grading and to promotion) not from the standpoint of their personal contribution, but from that of comparative success, the feeling of superiority over others is unduly appealed to, while timid children are depressed. Children are judged with reference to their capacity to realize the same external standard. The weaker gradually lose their sense of power, and accept a position of continuous and persistent inferiority. The effect upon both self-respect and respect for work need not be dwelt upon. The strong learn to glory, not in their strength, but in the fact that they are stronger. The child is prematurely launched into the region of individualistic competition, and this in a direction where competition is least applicable, namely, in intellectual and artistic matters, whose law is coöperation and participation.

Next, perhaps, to the evils of passive absorption and of competition for external standing come, perhaps, those which result from the eternal emphasis upon preparation for a remote future. I do not refer here to the waste of energy and vitality that accrues when children, who live so largely in the immediate present, are appealed to in the name of a dim and uncertain future which means little or nothing to them. I have in mind rather the habitual procrastination that develops when the motive for work is future, not present; and the false standards of judgment that are created when work is estimated, not on the basis of present need and present responsibility, but by reference to an external result, like passing an examination, getting promoted, entering high school, getting into college, etc. Who can reckon up the loss of moral power that arises from the constant impression that nothing is worth doing in itself, but only as a preparation for something else, which in turn is only a getting ready for some genuinely serious end beyond? Moreover, as a rule, it will be found that remote success is an end which appeals most to those in whom egoistic desire to get ahead—to get ahead of others—is already only too strong a motive. Those in whom personal ambition is already so strong that it paints glowing pictures of future victories may be touched; others of a more generous nature do not respond.

I cannot stop to paint the other side. I can only say that the introduction of every method that appeals to the child's active powers, to his capacities in construction, production, and creation, marks an opportunity to shift the centre of ethical gravity from an absorption which is selfish to a service which is social. Manual training is more than manual; it is more than intellectual; in the hands of any good teacher it lends itself easily, and almost as a matter of course, to development of social habits. Ever since the philosophy of Kant, it has been a commonplace of æsthetic theory, that art is universal; that it is not the product of purely personal desire or appetite, or capable of merely individual appropriation, but has a value participated in by all who perceive it. Even in the schools where most conscious attention is paid to moral considerations, the methods of study and recitation may be such as to emphasize appreciation rather than power, an emotional readiness to assimilate the experiences of others, rather than enlightened and trained capacity to carry forward those values which in other conditions and past times made those experiences worth having. At all events, separation between instruction and character continues in our schools (in spite of the efforts of individual teachers) as a result of divorce between learning and doing. The attempt to attach genuine moral effectiveness to the mere processes of learning, and to the habits which go along with learning, can result only in a training infected with formality, arbitrariness, and an undue emphasis upon failure to conform. That there is as much accomplished as there is shows the possibilities involved in methods of school activity which afford opportunity for reciprocity, coöperation, and positive personal achievement.

CHAPTER 19

TEACHING JOHN DEWEY AS A UTOPIAN PRAGMATIST WHILE LEARNING FROM MY STUDENTS

William H. Schubert
University of Illinois at Chicago

When I speculate on the major contributions of John Dewey to education, I think of his integration of dualisms, his unification of theory and practice in principled action, and his utopian vision. As a professor in the area of curriculum studies, I try to teach these three dimensions of Dewey to graduate students.[1] Sometimes, to generate student interest in a lecture on Dewey, I semi-jokingly claim to have psychic powers that enable me to get in contact with the spirit of Dewey. After the blinking of classroom lights and asking the class members to chant Dewey's name several times, I find myself depicting Dewey's life and ideas as if his spirit has taken over my voice. While space here does not permit an elaborate rendition of this rather bizarre act of teaching, I will simply relate the three above-mentioned contributions. I do want to note, however, that on many occasions my students have taught me much about how to teach about (and to be, in the case of role-playing) John Dewey.

Listening to and Learning from Students, pages 173–178
Copyright © 2011 by Information Age Publishing
All rights of reproduction in any form reserved.

For each of Dewey's contributions that I want to mention below, I will show how a student has enlightened me about that dimension. To learn from one's students is clearly a hallmark of Dewey's philosophy of education. To listen to the strengths brought into class by students has, for me, been a dynamic source of ideas over the years. The inspiration of student insights illustrates the value of beginning with Dewey's psychological (i.e., the interests and concerns that students derive from experience) and its relation to Dewey's logical (i.e., organized knowledge, disciplinary, and personal-practical). Because of my own study and experience (Deweyan logical), I can often add to student interests and concerns (Deweyan psychological) to help an idea evolve through subsequent pedagogical relationships.

In the mid-1980s, a graduate student, Charles Smith, told me about an undergraduate philosophy class he had taken at another university. In that class the professor (whose name I do not know) suggested a strategy for understanding the significance of Dewey's contributions to education and philosophy. His message was to simply substitute the word *is* for the word *and* in Dewey's book titles. I tried it and thought it enlightening.

I thought of my long study of Dewey's life and work. Many of Dewey's book titles are, indeed, two key words or concepts joined by the conjunction *and*. Take, for instance, his educational magnum opus, *Democracy and Education* (1916), wherein the message becomes *democracy is education* and, conversely, *education is democracy*. Let us consider his earlier books, derived from the renowned laboratory school that he designed and developed at the University of Chicago from 1896 to 1904. Converting those titles, we have the *school is society* and *society is the school* from his classic 1900 book, *The School and Society*. From the 1902 companion book, *The Child and the Curriculum*, we are spurred to ponder meanings of *the child is the curriculum* (perhaps even read *as*) and *the curriculum is the child*. Much later, in his retrospective look (*Experience and Education*, 1938) at what happened in his name under the label of progressive education, Dewey argued that the issue runs deeper than a mere contention between advocates of progressive education and traditional education. He and philosopher of education Boyd H. Bode of Ohio State University separately were lone advocates who attempted to resolve the dualism that ultimately divided and broke the spirit of the progressive education movement and, with it, the Progressive Education Association (PEA). Some members of the PEA advocated child-centered (or child study) as the organizing center of their work, while others called for social reconstruction (see Bode, 1938). Again, using the is-for-and strategy in Dewey's 1938 call for unity, we should consider the deeper meanings of education as (or being) experience and, reciprocally, the question could become: What if we come to see that experience itself is education?

Broader ramifications of this is-for-and strategy can be traced in Dewey's corpus of philosophical works; consider for instance the idea that *charac-*

ter is event when reflecting on Dewey's essays from the New Republic and elsewhere, published under the title *Characters and Events* (1929). Think, too, of the ramifications of *experience being nature,* and *nature as experience,* in his *Experience and Nature* (1929), perhaps the closest he came to writing a metaphysical statement. Or consider his metaphysics of human beings (*Human Nature and Conduct,* 1922), which could inspire a discontinuance of the image that human nature is not merely the fount from which conduct flows, but that human nature is, in fact, conduct itself. Indeed, if pragmatist Dewey aligned firmly with pragmatist predecessor Charles Sanders Peirce's admonition that the meaning of a proposition resides in the consequences of acting on it, it would seem to clearly follow that conduct is the truth or meaning of human nature. What we do is what we are. The is-for-and strategy continues to challenge us along the same lines when we consider Dewey's *Liberalism and Social Action* (1935), as we observe that liberalism (to be more than shallow rhetoric) must be known by the instantiated social action that it is. Similarly, thinking of *The Public and Its Problems* (1927), it is not the public over here and the problems it faces over there; rather, it is the larger vision of public that creates and incorporates problems, must struggle with them, and tentatively strives to resolve them. Finally, Dewey's *Philosophy and Civilization* (1931) and *Freedom and Culture* (1939) stimulate similar integrations of potential dualisms. Can there be genuine culture that is not free? Can there be renditions of civilization that are not couched in philosophy? Can life be truly civilized only if it is philosophically reflective as it continues to re-create itself? Clearly, one could take the is-for-and strategy too far, but within proper balance it is a pedagogical heuristic that I think valuable for extending the spirit of Dewey.

In the early 1990s, Ann Lopez wrote her Ph.D. dissertation on an investigation of Deweyan progressive practices in three contexts of urban education: an inner city school, a dance school, and a home-based education project. As revealed in the above integration of dualisms, Lopez helped me understand more fully that theory and practice were one in the course of action. One must look at, even embody or take into oneself, the action in order to understand the theory implicit in it (Lopez, 1993). Again, we can return to Peirce's notion that the meaning of a proposition resides in the consequences of acting on it, and in Dewey's reconstructed titles: character is event, human nature is conduct, liberalism is social action, education is experience, democracy is education, the school is society, and the child is the curriculum. It may not be mere coincidence that George Dykhuizen's *The Life and Mind of John Dewey* (1973), a long-time definitive source for details of Dewey's life, also has *and* in the title. If this *and* were converted to *is,* it could imply the existence of mind that encompasses life and/or the existence of life that is only made alive by the mind embedded in it.

In any case, to understand the philosophy of John Dewey, we must see Dewey as a public intellectual who took difficult and controversial stances that illustrate (no, perhaps that *are*) his philosophy. When he created the Dewey School (lab school), his philosophy was to integrate philosophy, psychology, and pedagogy in practice. When he worked with the founder of social work, Jane Addams, at her settlement house (Hull House) in Chicago, his philosophy embodied the struggle of the poor and oppressed for a better life. When he left Chicago for New York and Columbia University in 1904, his philosophy was a statement of resistance against an inappropriate coupling of teacher training with the experimental derivation of educational ideas. By opening the door of his New York home to Maxim Gorky in 1906, he illustrated a courageous philosophical stance in the face of many American authorities, who saw Gorky as a radical socialist striving for support for causes deemed immoral and un-American. More of the political and economic strands of his philosophy were revealed as he helped to found the National Association for the Advancement of Colored People in 1909, the American Association of University Professors in 1915, and the American Federation of Teachers in 1916, and to promote the Women's Suffrage Movement from 1906 to 1919. In 1929, Dewey became president of the People's Lobby and chair of the League for Independent Political Action, and in 1937, he served as a member of the Commission of Inquiry into the Charges against Leon Trotsky, who was exiled in Mexico. He traveled widely to lecture and consult for extensive periods of time in other countries such as Mexico, Turkey, China, Japan, and Russia, as well as visits to several European countries. Frequently, Dewey defended the rights of both citizens and visitors to the United States to express ideas that even he disputed, such as those of Bertrand Russell on marriage and morals.

All of these actions, and many more, reveal deeply lived dimensions of Dewey's philosophy. I try to teach students that what his pragmatism or progressivism in education meant must be seen in actions he took as well as in books and articles he wrote. Sometimes, personal actions can be more revealing than political stances. Between the time Dewey left Chicago for Columbia, his family took an extended trip to Europe, where his eight-year-old son, Gordon, tragically died from typhoid fever; on the same trip they adopted an eight-year-old Italian boy, who became a full member of their family, and much later (in his seventies) a Vietnam War protestor. When Dewey was in his late eighties, he and his second wife were distressed at the plight of children orphaned in Europe during World War II, and they adopted two children, a brother and sister from Belgium. Again, Dewey's life is the story of his philosophical conviction, the theory embodied in his action.

Finally, I want to mention a little-known article that Dewey published in the *New York Times* in 1933.[2] The article is titled "Dewey Outlines Utopian Schools." It was introduced to me by a former doctoral student, Michael Klonsky, who has become director of the Small Schools Workshop in Chicago, a consultancy that helps schools in Chicago and throughout the United States to divide into small, more meaningful communities. Klonsky was intrigued by a point in the second paragraph of the piece wherein Dewey said that the educational environments he saw in his utopian vision housed "not much more than 200 people, this having been found to be about the limits of close, interpersonal acquaintance on the part of people who associate together." While Klonsky valued a source of legitimacy from a renowned philosopher for his small school efforts, I was more interested in other matters that Dewey found in his venture into educational utopia. There is much to build on in Dewey's short article, and I hope to do a much longer treatment of this document. However, I see the main idea behind it as a radical critique of the competitive economic system that sustains most state, private, and parochial schools as we know them throughout the world today. In essence, Dewey finds that the great culprit behind nondemocratic education is the acquisitive society. An attitude of acquisition—the capitalistic ethos, if you will—penetrates our being in ways we scarcely realize. It staunchly prevents the kind of education that Dewey proposes as most desirable.

I use the term *education* instead of *school,* because Dewey's utopian vision holds that the teaching–learning environments that would bring greatest growth are not schools as we know them. His first sentence of the article, in fact, is: "The most Utopian thing in Utopia is that there are no schools at all." He goes on to describe beautiful places where children and adults can grow together, where the very idea of purposes or objectives is not in the vocabulary, where instructional method is not necessary because learning is natural and needs to be nurtured rather than restricted, and where standardization and the surveillance of testing are anathema. The contemporary (then and now) form of education in the sorting machinery of schools (with its standards, goals, tests, and sordid comparisons) is a function of acquisitiveness. The remedy for this mis-educational state of affairs Dewey learned from the Utopians: "they said that the great educational liberation came about when the concept of external attainments was thrown away and when they started to find out what each individual person had in him from the beginning, and then devoted themselves to finding out the conditions of the environment and the kinds of activity in which the positive capacities of each young person could operate most effectually."[3]

In honor of the fiftieth year since John Dewey died, I advocate that we devote great energy to understanding why we are so far removed from his utopian vision, and much more importantly, how we can move toward it with courage and dedication.

NOTES

1. See Schubert (1986) and Schubert, Lopez-Schubert, Thomas, and Carroll (2002) for elaboration on how I have developed a Deweyan perspective in the teaching of curriculum studies.
2. First published in New York Times, April 23, 1933, Education Section, page 7 from an address on April 21, 1933 to the Conference on the Educational Status of the Four-and Five-Year-Old Child at Teachers College, Columbia University. Now available in Dewey, *The Later Works, 1925–53* (vol. 9, 1933–34), edited by J. A. Boydston (Carbondale, IL: Southern Illinois University Press, 1989).
3. Ibid., page 139.

REFERENCES

Bode, B. H. (1938). *Progressive education at the crossroads.* New York: Newson.

Dewey, J. (1900). *The school and society.* Chicago: University of Chicago Press.

Dewey, J. (1902). *The child and the curriculum.* Chicago: University of Chicago Press.

Dewey, J. (1916). *Democracy and education.* New York: Macmillan.

Dewey, J. (1922). *Human nature and conduct.* New York: Henry Holt.

Dewey, J. (1927). *The public and its problems.* New York: Henry Holt.

Dewey, J. (1929). *Characters and events.* New York: Henry Holt.

Dewey, J. (1929). *Experience and nature.* New York: W.W. Norton.

Dewey, J. (1931). *Philosophy and civilization.* New York: Minton, Balch & Co.

Dewey, J. (1933, April 23). Dewey outlines utopian schools. *New York Times*, p. E7.

Dewey, J. (1935). *Liberalism and social action.* New York: G.P. Putnam's Sons.

Dewey, J. (1938). *Experience and education.* New York: Macmillan.

Dewey, J. (1939). *Freedom and culture.* New York: G.P. Putnam's Sons.

Dykhuizen, G. (1973). *The life and mind of John Dewey.* Carbondale, IL: Southern Illinois University Press.

Lopez, A. L. (1993). Exploring possibilities for progressive curriculum and teaching in three urban contexts. Unpublished Ph.D. Dissertation, University of Illinois at Chicago.

Schubert, W. H. (1986). *Curriculum: Perspective, paradigm, and possibility.* New York: Macmillan.

Schubert, W. H., Lopez-Schubert, A. L., Thomas, T. P., & Carroll, W. M. (2002). *Curriculum books: The first hundred years.* New York: Peter Lang.

CHAPTER 20

INTERLUDE

DESIRABLE CONTENT FOR A CURRICULUM DEVELOPMENT SYLLABUS TODAY

The Tyler Rationale Reconsidered

Ralph W. Tyler
University of Chicago

When I was invited to speak on this subject at this conference, I assumed that the topic referred to the syllabus I prepared more that 25 years ago for a course I offered at the University of Chicago, and that I was being asked how such a syllabus would differ under the circumstances of today. Most of what I have to say is based on this assumption. [Note: The author's reference here to the "syllabus" and subsequently in this chapter to the "book" refer to his publication: Tyler, R. W. (1949). *Basic principals of curriculum and instruction.* Chicago: University of Chicago Press.]

Listening to and Learning from Students, pages 179–187
179

COMPREHENSIVE SYLLABUS

The term syllabus is applied to several kinds of guides for courses or programs. Some are in outline form without extended comments or explanations; others, like the one I prepared in 1949, are in the form of expository discourse. Whatever the form, a syllabus sufficiently complete to guide student learning might well include:

1. A statement of the reason for offering the course or program; for example, for whom it is intended, what values it is likely to have for these students, and how it is related to other courses or programs
2. What the educational objectives are; that is, what students will be helped to learn
3. For each division or unit of the course or program, a statement or listing of learning tasks that are provided
4. A suggestion of the time probably required to perform the tasks successfully
5. The means that will be used to evaluate the student's performance
6. Whatever else is necessary for the particular course or program to guide students utilizing effectively the resources available for their learning.

In brief, a syllabus should serve as a published guide to help students in selecting a course or program and in carrying on successfully the educational activities. The preparation of such a syllabus helps the instructional staff to identify unsettled issues regarding purposes and means, and requires thoughtful consideration and operational decisions to clarify learning goals and establish the student learning system.

As I reviewed the earlier syllabus, I found no reason to change the basic questions it raises. What should be the educational objectives of the curriculum? What learning experiences should be developed to enable the students to obtain the objectives? How should the learning experiences be organized to increase their cumulative effect? How should the effectiveness of the curriculum be evaluated? These are still basic and their importance has been reaffirmed by the experiences of the past quarter of a century. However, some changes of emphasis are necessary and I want to comment on two of them.

I would give much greater emphasis now to careful consideration of the implications curriculum development of the active role of the student in the learning process. I would also give much greater emphasis to a comprehensive examination of the nonschool areas of student learning in developing curriculum.

OVERLOOKING THE LEARNER'S ACTIVE ROLE

In the massive curriculum projects of the 1960s in the United States, the objectives were usually selected by subject matter specialists with little attention given to the needs and interests of the learners. Mention was most often made of the "educational delivery system" as though education could be delivered to students rather than their having to acquire it through their active learning. Educational technology was commonly treated as though it was the robot teacher rather than furnishing certain tools that teachers could employ as, for example, presenting material that could be used as part of a learning experience. Some of the projects actually sought to develop "teacher-proof materials." These terms and the attitudes they represent indicate that some leading curriculum builders are overlooking the fact that learning is a process in which the learner plays an active not a passive role. It is the behavior that the learner carries on with consistency that can become part of his or her repertoire of behavior and, in this way, will have been learned.

Human beings cannot be forced to learn intellectual and emotional behavior. Only under coercion or when offered tempting rewards will they even attempt a learning task which seems to them meaningless or distasteful, and even then if their experiences with the task are not rewarding, they will not continue the behavior and it is not learned. Furthermore, the behavior becomes a permanent part of their repertoire only if they continue to carry it on. This means that learners must see the way in which the things they learn can be used, and they must have the opportunity to continue to employ the learned behavior in the various situations they encounter.

IMPLICATIONS IN SELECTING OBJECTIVES

These conditions for learning have important implications to consider in selecting educational objectives. The curriculum objectives selected should not only be (a) important things for the students to learn in order to participate constructively in contemporary society, (b) sound in terms of the subject matter involved, and (c) in accord with the education philosophy of the institution, but also they should be of interest or be meaningful to the prospective learners, or capable of being made so in the process of instruction. This criterion is mentioned and briefly developed in the earlier book referred to, but is being overlooked even by some whose curriculum development rationale appears to be similar.

This does not imply that the interest of learners and their understanding of the meaningfulness of educational objectives at any given time are permanent and do not change. Quite the contrary, in a particular unit of study, although the initial objectives should be those that students at the time see are interesting and/or meaningful things for them to learn, as they go through the learning experiences they will broaden and deepen their interests. As they gain greater understanding of the relevance of what they are learning, they will see the meaning and develop interest in objectives that stimulate them to further study. For example, a child who has not been read to by parents and who has not seen others enjoying reading is not likely to participate actively in decoding exercises in a primary reading program nor is the child likely to see that they have any meaning for him or her. The appropriate initial objectives in reading may be those that help this child find fun in material that is read to him or her. Then, the child will want to read some of these materials, too. The objectives then can reflect these new interests the student has acquired.

IMPLICATIONS IN DESIGNING LEARNING EXPERIENCES

These conditions for learning are also important to keep in mind in the design of learning experiences. If students are to enter wholeheartedly into the learning, they should perceive what the behavior is that they are expected to learn and feel confident that they can successfully carry through the learning tasks. If they are uncertain about what they are expected to learn and lack confidence in their ability to carry on the learning task, they will balk, stumble, or openly avoid trying. They do not want to make fools of themselves or fail in their efforts. Hence, well-designed learning experiences will show learners clearly what they are expected to learn, and will employ learning tasks that are within their present abilities to carry through. As they succeed in their initial activities and gain satisfaction from their efforts, the learning tasks should be increasingly demanding in difficulty or in higher levels of attainment. This means that the sequential organization of learning experiences is developed in terms of the progress learners can make in undertaking successively more varied and more difficult learning tasks. Sequences that are designed solely in terms of the logic of the discipline are not likely to be effective in meeting these conditions for learning.

THE LEARNER'S ROLE IN TRANSFER OF TRAINING

The failure to transfer what is learned in school to situations outside of school is a problem that has long been central to educational psychologists. Schools are established help students to acquire behavior that is important for constructive out-of-school activities. If something is learned in school that is not used by the student in relevant situations outside of school, most of the value of the learning has been lost. This appears be happening in some of the current educational programs. For example, the National Assessment of Educational Progress in 1972–73 conducted an assessment of mathematical knowledge and skills. The 17-year-olds completed computations using integers, fractions, decimals, and percents. Over 90 percent correctly answered the addition, subtraction, and division problems involving whole numbers. The percentage was slightly lower (88 percent) for multiplication. Most 17-year-olds can compute correctly. However, the percents are much lower on exercises involving simple uses of mathematics. As an example, only 34 percent of the 17-year-olds answered correctly the following:

> "A housewife will pay the lower price per ounce for rice if she buys it at the store which offers
>
> > 12 ounces for 40 cents
> > 14 ounces for 45 cents
> > 1 pound 12 ounces for 85 cents
> > 2 pounds for 99 cents."

On other similar tasks involving other products, the results were about 46 percent incorrect responses. In contrasting this to the 90 percent correct responses on computation exercises, it seems probable that many students were following a curriculum that has been emphasizing drill on computation at the expense of practice in using mathematics in the situations common to contemporary life. Learning experiences can be designed that involve many situations like those outside of school, and students can be encouraged and asked to use what they are learning in school in relevant situations they encounter outside of school. The advice to schools now frequently heard, "Get back to basics," is being so narrowly interpreted that the importance of transfer of training is forgotten.

The results of the National Assessment are not the only indications that the objectives and learning experiences of some educational programs fail to interest and actively engage many students in learning and do not carry over beyond the school environment. Interviews with high school graduates and dropouts indicate that a majority cannot recall many subjects in which they learned things that would be helpful to them in later life. Clearly, the curriculum rationale should strongly emphasize giving serious attention in curriculum planning to the interests, activities, problems, and concerns of the students. Where possible and appropriate, the students themselves should participate in the planning and evaluation of the curriculum.

EXAMINING THE NON-SCHOOL AREAS
OF STUDENT LEARNING

Another needed change in the emphasis of the book is a greater recognition that the school curriculum is only part of the educational experiences needed by children and youth if they are to acquire the interests, attitudes, knowledge, skills, and habits that can enable them to participate constructively in a modern society and to use their talents fully in contributions both to society and to their own personal fulfillment. The total education system required today includes much more than the school. What young people experience in the home, in their social activities in the community, in the chores and jobs they carry on, in the religious institutions where they participate, in their reading, in their listening to radio and viewing of TV, and in the school, are all included in the actual educational system through which they acquire knowledge and ideas, skills and habits, attitudes and interests, and basic values. The school is an important part of this educational system in furnishing the opportunity to learn to read, write, and compute, and to discover and use the sources of facts, principles, and ideas that are more accurate, balanced, and comprehensive than are provided in most homes, work places, or other social institutions. The school also supplements and complements learning furnished by the other institutions, and is usually an environment which more nearly represents the American social ideals than the larger society. In most schools, each student is respected as a human being without discrimination, the transactions in the classroom are guided by an attempt to be fair and dispense justice, and the class morale is a reflection of the fact that the members care about the welfare of others.

In educational systems of the past, the several parts have certain interdependent features. The student's interest in learning what the school sought to teach was usually stimulated in other parts of the system, in the home, in the working place, and in the social life of the community so that the school did not need to develop particular motivation for learning on the part of the majority of students. Furthermore, as mentioned earlier, as skills in reading, writing, and arithmetic were developed in the school, the student found many opportunities for their use in his or her activities outside the school, particularly in work and in recreation. Skills quickly become inoperative when their use is infrequent. If the only reading required of youth is that assigned in school, reading skills do not reach a mature level. If writing is limited to an occasional note or letter, writing skills remain very primitive. If arithmetic is not used in such home activities as consumer buying, furniture construction, and budgeting, arithmetic skills and problem solving techniques are likely to be inadequate. Hence, the total educational system needs to be viewed as one in which practice as well as initial learning is provided.

The fact that an adequate educational system in a modern society must include experiences outside the school where young people spend most of their time, combined with the fact that, while the time available to the school has remained relatively constant, the time given to education by parents, community agencies, and work settings has been greatly reduced, has several implications for curriculum development.

EDUCATIONAL OBJECTIVES FOR THE SCHOOL

The school curriculum should give stronger focus to the important objectives that can be learned in school, making use of the specialized resources the school provides—teachers with training in the fields of scholarship; books and libraries; laboratories and shops; a humane tradition which encourages openness, trust, and a concern for others; and an environment where order and composure are possible. The contributions that can be made to young people by helping them learn to use these resources are not minor. A world beyond their direct experience can thus be opened to them and they can develop aspirations, styles of life, skills of accomplishment more varied and more individualized the typical limited patterns their own community affords.

THE OUT-OF-SCHOOL CURRICULUM

A second implication is that school leaders, particularly curriculum specialists, should work with the other community leaders to reestablish an effective educational at the community level. The public can be helped to recognize that an adequate education for their children and youth requires an effective educational system which includes the school but also depends on experiences provided outside the school. The community should be responsibly organized to provide comprehensive educational opportunities for young people. This means that some form of community council or board is necessary to assess educational needs, identify actual and potential resources (including the schools), and to develop the outline of educational programs to meet the needs identified. These community councils or boards should direct attention to the development of resources that will require little or no additional expenditures. It seems unlikely that a free society can levy the taxes required to furnish paid professionals to fill the gaps created by the erosion of our earlier educational system. The Soviet Union has been able to support the Young Pioneers and the Comsomol, which are part of school educational agencies, through compulsory levies. Doubling the tax rate for education in the free societies is unlikely to achieve public support. The curriculum for the comprehensive educational system will also need to be developed.

A third implication is that the school should help its students deal constructively with out-of-school environment. The school can help young people develop skill in evaluating mass media, particularly TV and the press, and in finding and choosing programs and publications that are helpful and satisfying. Since the viewing of television represents for many young people the major use of their waking hours, the development of knowledge, skills, attitudes, interests, and habits that will increase the value of the activity is very important. The school can also furnish opportunities both formal and informal for students to reflect upon the significant out-of-school experiences they are having and seek, through discussion, to clarify the consequences of their actions, and to formulate meaningful standards to guide them in these transactions.

THE COMMUNITY AS A RESOURCE

It is also possible, even where no community educational council exists, to work with other agencies in providing opportunity for what the National Association of Secondary School Principals (NASSP) calls "Action Learning." Action learning may be in paid form or in non-paid volunteer work with private, public, or community service agencies NASSP has published a report on 25 action-learning schools.[1]

A more extensive collection of concrete illustrations of existing programs that have enabled young people to participate in productive adult activities and to assume real responsibility for what they do is a book, *New Roles for Youth in School and Community*[2], prepared by the National Commission on Resources for Youth. These reports furnish evidence that some schools, at least, can develop a curriculum, that vitalizes and strengthens the educational experiences developed outside their walls.

IN SUMMARY

Many curriculum projects of the last two decades have overlooked the active role of students in learning and have assumed that they can be made to learn. They have given little or no attention to the interests, concerns, and perceptions of the students in developing the curriculum. Hence, it seems necessary to give special emphasis to the implications of the learner's active role when selecting objectives, developing learning experiences, and designing their sequences.

It is also clear that there is a great erosion taking place in the total educational system in America. The home, the working place, the religious institutions, and the educational milieu of the community are furnishing fewer constructive learning experiences for young people than was true in the past. It is particularly necessary now in curriculum development to give careful consideration to the non-school areas of student learning. In some cases, the school can help to establish a more constructive total educational system. It can always seek to maximize the effectiveness of the school curriculum in relating to the other learning experiences of the student.

NOTES

1. National Association of Secondary School Principals. *25 Action Learning Schools.* Reston, Virginia: NASSP, 1974.
2. National Commission on Resources for Youth. *New Roles for Youth in School and Community.* New York: Citation Press, 1974.

CHAPTER 21

STUDENT-LED SOLUTIONS TO THE DROPOUT CRISIS

Key Findings from a Report by Voices of Youth in Chicago Education

Voices of Youth in Chicago Education (VOYCE)

INTRODUCTION

Voices of Youth in Chicago Education (VOYCE) is a youth organizing collaborative led by students of color from seven community organizations and twelve public high schools throughout the city of Chicago. The organizations and schools that comprise VOYCE are:

- Albany Park Neighborhood Council | Roosevelt, Mather, and Von Steuben High Schools
- Brighton Park Neighborhood Council | Kelly High School
- Organization of the NorthEast | Senn High School and Uplift Community High School
- Kenwood Oakland Community Organization | Dyett High School and Kenwood Academy

Listening to and Learning from Students, pages 189–196
189

- Logan Square Neighborhood Association | North Grand and Kelvyn Park High Schools
- Target Area Development Corporation | Perspectives Calument High School
- Southwest Organizing Project | Gage Park High School

VOYCE builds on these community-based organizations' histories of organizing both parents and students around school reform issues such as creating a policy change granting in-state tuition for undocumented students, securing the construction of new schools to relieve overcrowding, developing schools as community learning centers, and more.

As student and parent leaders from these organizations continued to be impacted first-hand by the dropout rate, VOYCE was created with the goal of impacting teaching and learning at the high school level in order to keep students engaged in school and increase graduation and college enrollment rates.

The heart of VOYCE's work has been the development of a model of participatory action research in which young people examined the complex issues and multiple perspectives regarding students' desire and ability to graduate and continue on to college. Supported with funding from the Bill & Melinda Gates Foundation and Communities for Public Education Reform, student leaders undertook a year-long study of the dropout crisis and ways to address the problem.

On Thursday, November 13, 2008, VOYCE released a report on its findings and recommendations surrounding the dropout crisis. VOYCE is now working closely with Chicago Public Schools to implement its recommendations in pilot-project form at partner schools.

PARTICIPATORY ACTION RESEARCH

Utilizing a unique Participatory Action Research model, VOYCE students carefully examined their own lives and experiences in their schools and crafted two key learning questions to guide their research:

Learning Question #1

In the students' school curriculum, how does academic rigor, significant representation of the students' community and cultural heritage, and emphasis on critical thinking impact students' ability and willingness to develop into lifelong learners who can successfully compete in the 21st century?

Learning Question #2

How does the physical and emotional safety, the relationships among students and with teachers, parents/guardians, and school staff within the school environment impact the student's ability and desire to learn and graduate?

Youth used the questions to guide their research, which included a statistically significant survey of 1,325 CPS students; in-depth interviews with 208 additional students, 110 teachers, and 65 parents; and site visits to successful schools in six states.

During the research process, student leaders envisioned improved schools and learning environments, developed survey questions based on their own educational experiences, identified appropriate data collection methods, performed ethnographic mapping of school communities, made site visits to successful school in Illinois and across the country, reviewed relevant literature, and triangulated all data and responses to identify common themes and perspectives.

KEY RESEARCH THEMES AND FINDINGS

Reasons for Dropping Out

Through surveys and interviews, youth researchers explored the reasons why students drop out of school. Through the analysis of responses, two key findings emerged:

- *Finding #1:* Students in Chicago Public Schools have internalized the problem of the dropout rate and believe that they are the ones to blame for the failures of the school system. There is a difference between perception and reality when it comes to the reasons for the dropout rate, and it is only through a deeper critical analysis that students come to realize the systemic problems impacting public education.
- *Finding #2:* Dropping out is not something that students plan or anticipate. It is something that happens slowly over time.

What It Means to Be a Life-Long Learner

Youth prioritized the theme of life-long learning because it is their belief that learning is a life-long commitment that extends even after college. They also feel that students need to be challenged to take what they learn in their classes and expand on that knowledge outside of school. To the VOYCE student researchers, it is up to students to seek knowledge and take ownership of their education, and it is up to the school to encourage, develop, and support that desire. Much of the research was framed around what is needed for schools to develop life-long learners.

Rigor and Relevance of Curriculum

Student researchers explored the theme of relevance in curriculum because they felt a disconnect between the curriculum and the reality of their everyday lives, their culture, and community. Through their surveys and interviews, the researchers found that other students felt the same disconnect.

- *Finding #3:* While teachers, parents, and students agree that relevance in curriculum is critical to students' engagement in school, students feel that relevance is largely missing in their schools. Student researchers also explored the theme of rigor and college-going culture. Through surveys and interviews at their schools, the theme of college rarely surfaced. It was only through school site visits, conducted in Chicago, New York, New Jersey, California, Washington, and Texas, that the researchers came to understand the impact that rigor and college-going culture could have on a student's success.
- *Finding #4:* Through the national site visits, students came to understand that in addition to relating to students' culture and real-life situations, the curriculum needs to explicitly make the connection that school is a stepping stone to college and future careers.

Effective Teaching Techniques

VOYCE student researchers chose the theme of teaching techniques because they realized that even if they had a different curriculum, improved teaching techniques would create a stronger connection between teachers and students. Through their research, students came to the following conclusions regarding teaching techniques:

- *Finding #5:* Teaching techniques must accommodate many different styles of learning because different methods work for different students. Strong relationships, and the way that teachers connect with, motivate, and inspire students, are essential for effective teaching techniques to unfold.

SOLUTIONS

While VOYCE recognizes initiatives that are already underway to address the dropout rate through CPS departments such as Graduation Pathways, the Department of College and Career Preparation, and the Department of Teaching and Learning, it also recognizes that there is still a strong need for institutionalized and systemic student voice and perspective on issues of high school reform. In order to do this, there need to be strong partnerships between students and their teachers and administrators at local schools, and a strong relationship between those stakeholders and the district-level decision makers within CPS.

In order to accomplish this, based on the findings of its student-led major research project, VOYCE recommends improvements in the several key areas.

Rigor and Relevance of Curriculum

VOYCE recommends that CPS and its various curriculum vendors work with students to revisit curriculum and subject matter to make it more rigorous and relevant to students, create spaces for the combination of academic knowledge and community wisdom, and develop the critical thinking skills of young people.

In order to create a more relevant curriculum, VOYCE recommends:
- Connection to Life Experience and Real-World Issues: Relevance includes a connection between subject matter and students' real-life issues, and the historical struggles of their communities. Additionally, curriculum would work to broaden students' worldview, through analyzing local as well as international issues.
- Student-Led Research: Students should be encouraged to engage in high-level research projects of their choice that both build their academic skills and increase their understanding of the community around them.
- Connection to Career Opportunities: Courses should include a means to apply subject matter to real-world career and professional opportunities.

In order to create a more rigorous curriculum, VOYCE recommends:
- ACT and College Entry Requirements: The curriculum offered at every public high school is aligned with ACT standards and college entry requirements so that students will be able to attend the college of their choice.

- Avoiding Subject Matter Repetition: Curriculum is aligned across grade levels from 8th grade through the first year of college to maximize student learning and avoid unnecessary repetition of subject matter from one grade level to the next.
- College Level Coursework: Curriculum includes longer blocked classes with college-level coursework, time for student-driven learning, and interactive projects.

Teaching Techniques

- Community Orientations: VOYCE recommends that students have the opportunity to design and implement community orientations for teachers to build their understanding of the value of the communities in which they teach.
- Student/Teacher Partnerships: VOYCE recommends that students have the opportunity to partner with teachers, administrators, representatives from CPS, and institutions of higher education to discuss ways to broaden the range of teaching techniques that are used in the classrooms of Chicago's public high schools, keep teachers current with the most innovative teaching practices, and promote student-centered learning. VOYCE recommends that the training and professional development that teachers receive on these topics counts towards national board certification.
- Interdisciplinary Projects: Teachers need to have the space and time to communicate and collaborate with other teachers in order to share best practices and common challenges, and to develop interdisciplinary projects based on student interests.

Freshman Year

- Freshman Orientation: VOYCE recommends that students play a critical role in the design of freshman orientations. Freshman orientation should be led by dynamic teachers and students from different grades, experienced counselors, and in partnership with community-based organizations. Beyond freshman orientations that provide new students with inspiration and information about what to expect in high school, schools must ensure that freshmen have access to strong supports throughout the school year such as the VOYCE recommendations below.
- Personalized 4-Year Graduation Plans: VOYCE recommends that personalized plans be developed for students to determine what courses they will need in order to attend any college of their choice, begin

thinking about what careers they might be interested in, and courses and extra curricular activities that are based on their interests.

- Ongoing Relationship Building, Counseling and Motivation: VOYCE recommends that structures be put in place for the relationship building, counseling, and motivation that starts at the beginning of freshman year to continue throughout the four years of high school. This could happen during class time, through more effective use of homeroom and advisory time, the re-institution of student development days, learning circles around real-life issues facing students, meaningful coursework and/or extracurricular projects that connect freshman with upperclassmen, and more.
- Freshman Orientation Retreats: VOYCE recommends that CPS hold Freshman Orientation Retreats for a subset of every freshman class that targets students most at risk of dropping out. These students would be identified through existing data sources about on-track rates as well as student-developed processes.

Safety and Security

VOYCE believes that a positive learning environment creates the foundation for a safe and secure environment. In addition to the recommendations regarding the development of a positive learning environment, VOYCE has specific recommendations regarding how discipline is handled in the school, and how safe spaces can be created for all students.

- Regular Safety and Security Meetings: Have regular meetings with the principal, security staff, teachers, students, and parents to evaluate the safety of the school and to discuss and make decisions about how to improve safety. Through these meetings, students, teachers, and security guards would develop a better system of accountability and peer-to-peer influence.
- Prevention Versus Zero Tolerance: Change zero tolerance focus to one of prevention and increased support with non-punitive measures for non-criminal offenses. Instead of being suspended and falling so far behind that they can't catch up, the students would go through the following process:
  1. Warning for first offense.
  2. Being assigned to community service hours that are meaningful and not demeaning, providing the student a feeling of accomplishment and accountability to the community.
  3. Participating in a Peace Circle to talk about the problems they are facing and to create positive solutions.

4. Fourth offense would be suspension and a mandatory tutor to ensure that the student doesn't fall behind. In addition, there would be a mandatory meeting with the administration, parents, and student council (peer jury model) to discuss what is going on and how to help the student stay in school, and not be a negative influence within the school community.

Additional Recommendations

- Bringing Illinois up to national standards for equitable funding for public education. Illinois continues to have one of the worst records in the nation for providing adequate school funding, having the 49th lowest state share of school funding and the largest disparities in the nation in funding between its school districts.
- A longer school day for Chicago Public School students. In Illinois, poor-performing districts tend to have shorter school days and tend to have high concentrations of low-income, minority students. Wealthier districts with higher test scores tend to have longer school days.
- Increasing access to higher education for undocumented students. The State of Illinois passed in-state tuition for undocumented students in 2003; however, they are still unable to receive financial aid and loans for college, and it is difficult to receive scholarships.

CHAPTER 22

AFTERWORD

PRAYER FOR THE FIRST DAY OF CHICAGO PUBLIC SCHOOL

Kevin Coval
Louder Than A Bomb

May the twenty-seven students who lost their lives last academic year eat their grandmother's cooking in the afterlife, go to prom in the next world; their lives and deaths not be forgotten in vain.

May the bullets intended for the chests of children this year veer into Lake Michigan or fall from the air like dice. May the fingers on those triggers, rash or tickle before fire. May we humanize the gun holder, many of them kids who school didn't speak to, who were left behind, kicked out, dropped out, pushed out by our failure to educate. May the gangs that take them in, return to their political street organizing roots and give to the community more than they taketh away.

May the police who patrol the neighborhoods protect themselves, yes. But may they not harass and degrade, may they not brutalize and make false arrests and false judgments. May their nightsticks sock them into thinking

Listening to and Learning from Students, pages 197–199
Copyright © 2011 by Information Age Publishing
All rights of reproduction in any form reserved.

before use. Let sergeants not coerce confessions, let judges not convict the innocent, let our children not be criminalized.

Let the teachers teach this year. Let them teach to educate and inspire life learning not manipulate to standardized tests. Let them individualize their lesson plans based on the learner not on a bureaucrat's stat book in Springfield or Washington. Let the teachers dream and share what they love about learning, let them listen to the kids in their class, give them time to engage and disagree and come to school everyday not just to receive a check and a pension but to challenge and grow themselves, their students and their institutions.

Let the architects and engineers of the Chicago Public School system leave their offices and luncheons and travel in the same day to Northside College Prep or Walter Payton and then to Wells or Clemente or Kelvyn Park or the school formerly known as Orr or most public schools and the alternative schools like Prologue and EL Cuarto Ano or Bronzeville, which seek to serve the forgotten, and let all these suits swear they believe in equity, that this gross disparity is abhorrent and unjust, that kids on the West and South Side deserve what kids in Lincoln Park and Lakeview deserve.

Get Arne Duncan out the health club. Let him and the progenitors of Renaissance 2010 do more than revamp failed plans. May they consider the whole student body of CPS, not just those with clout and high tax bases. May they find the wisdom that the closing and redistricting of schools sends kids across gang lines they are not accustomed to crossing and that this might be one of the factors in the rise of deaths this past year. Let them admit this system is inadequate, that only fifty percent of CPS students who start high school will finish and of these only one-third will go to college and of these a small percentage will graduate. This is not the education they would want for their children. Even Obama's daughters go to private school.

This year may the parents of CPS students have sick days and health care, may they have job security and livable wages, may they take interest in their sons' and daughters' lives, ask them questions about what they learn, have time to take them to the library or Millennium Park or read with them for an hour a night while the TV rests, or cook with them and laugh with them and have time to attend their chess matches or swim meets. May the parents of CPS students get tax breaks and flex time during the summer and spring and winter break to spend more time with their kids. May they let their kids live their own lives and only demand they walk the world fairly, that they are loved and the future is more endless than CTA lines, the world, theirs to explore.

This year, on the first day of CPS, please let State Senator Meeks act just as hard and righteous when the cameras are off, let his crusade continue beyond week one. May the students he brings to Winnetka see the gigantic inequity in public education, and have the courage and communal counsel not to feel bad about where they come from, but to demand wrongs turned right. Perhaps they will not be turned away by fire hoses and German Shepards, but they will still return to a quarter of the public funding spent on some suburban schools, they will still return to racial profiling, a proliferation of prisons built to house their bodies and non-livable-wage service-sector jobs, they will return to the shackles of neighborhood segregation and canyons of disparity, which have not disappeared since Little Rock, but have grown and will not magically vanish when a democrat is in the White House.

May this year be about the students we seek to educate. May they be asked questions as much as and more than they are told answers. May their lives be made relevant and visible in the educational space. Let us ask them to become present in the classroom, by bringing their present circumstance into the learning process. May those who put on blue jeans and white tees, those whose uniforms look like training for a lifetime of institutional living (whether it be fast food or county jail), let them transcend the expectations this system has of them. Let them walk safe to school and home to their stoop or ball field or playground or mother's arms, let their interest in learning perk and peak, and lead them into the library or museum or oral histories of their families and communities, let them strengthen their language and critical thinking to prepare themselves for the wars waged against them on the (mayor) Daley.

Let them speak for themselves and may we listen. May they learn that Chicago/America is brutal and beautiful in the same moment, let them care deeply for their minds and bodies, may they know they are and can be great and extraordinary individuals and citizens, that the world is bigger than the block, that we live on a Great Lake and if they go to the shore and look to the east, and see the point where water and sky merge, that their imagination is bigger and wider and more beautiful than that, and that meeting of the heavens and earth is where they are from and where they are free to dream and realize the immensity of who they are and who they will become.

PERMISSIONS

Interlude 2

Excerpt from *Pedagogy of the Oppressed*, by Paulo Freire, copyright © 1970, 1993. Reprinted by permission of the Continuum International Publishing Group.

Interlude 6

This chapter first appeared as Hopkins, L. T. (1983). My first voyage. In M. R. Nelson (Ed.), *Papers of the Society for the Study of Curriculum History, 1980 and 1982* (pp. 2–6). University Park, PA: Society for the Study of Curriculum History. Reprinted by permission of the Society for the Study of Curriculum History.

Interlude 8

Chapter One: "What is a School?" (pp. 1–10) from *I Learn from Children* by Caroline Pratt. Copyright © 1948, 1970 by John G. Holzwarth. Reprinted by permission of HarperCollins Publishers.

Interludes 10 and 16

Permission to publish the poems and essays by kahlil almustafa, Miracle Graham, and Thomas Lloyd has been granted by kahlil almustafa.

Interlude 12

The author of the document, Charles E. Cobb, Jr., considers this and all "Movement" documents to be part of the public domain. Nevertheless, permission to include the document as a chapter was sought from the author. In correspondence with Mr. Cobb, he informed me of its public domain status, and encouraged its use within this edited collection.

Interlude 14

Permission to publish the poem has been granted by *Rafael Casal.*

Chapter 15

Susan Wilcox adapted this chapter from her previous publication: Wilcox, S. (2009). Why did this happen? Content, perspective dialogue: A Workshop model for developing young people's reflective writing. New York: The Brotherhood/Sister Sol.

Interlude 18

The chapter originally appeared as Chapter III in Dewey, J. (1909). *Moral principles in education.* Cambridge, MA: The Riverside Press. As noted in the *Moral Principles in Education,* Dewey drew freely upon his essay on "Ethical Principles Underlying Education," published in the Third Year-Book of The National Herbart Society for the Study of Education. This material is in the public domain.

Chapter 19

The chapter first appeared as Schubert, W. H. (2006). Teaching John Dewey as a utopian pragmatist while learning from my students. *Education and Culture 22*(1), 78–83. Copyright © 2006 Purdue University. All rights reserved. Permission to reprint granted by the publisher, Purdue University Press.

Interlude 20

Source: "Desirable content for a curriculum development syllabus today: The Tyler Rationale Reconsidered" (pp. 36–44), by Ralph W. Tyler, from *Curriculum Theory,* Alex Molnar and John Zahorik (Eds.). Alexandria, VA:

ASCD. © 1977 by ASCD. Reprinted with permission. Learn more about ASCD at www.ascd.org.

Chapter 21

Permission to excerpt from VOYCE's 2008 report, *Student Led Solutions to the Dropout Crisis: A Report by Voices of Youth in Chicago Education* is granted by VOYCE.

ABOUT THE CONTRIBUTORS

kahlil almustafa, the People's Poet, uses poetry to engage with communities in critical dialogue. almustafa is Nuyorican Grand Slam Champion (2002) and author of four books of poetry. His collection of 15 years of poetry, *Growing Up Hip-Hop*, is used in elementary to university classrooms. He has been was awarded a Hip-Hop Theater Festival grant from the Future Aesthetics Artist Re-grant (FAAR), funded by the Ford Foundation, and The Field's Economic Revitalization for Performing Artists (ERPA) grant, funded in part by The Rockefeller Foundation's Cultural Innovation Fund. almustafa recently completed "100 Poems For 100 Days" where he wrote 100 poems in the first 100 days of Barack Obama's presidency to be published in, *From Auction Block to Oval Office*. almustafa is completing an MFA in an interdisciplinary arts program. He serves as a Poet Mentor for Urban Word NYC.

William C. Ayers, Distinguished Professor of Education and Senior University Scholar at the University of Illinois at Chicago (UIC), and founder of the Small Schools Workshop and the Center for Youth and Society, teaches courses in interpretive and qualitative research, urban school change, and teaching and the modern predicament. Ayers has written extensively about social justice, democracy and education, the cultural contexts of schooling, and teaching as an intellectual, ethical, and political enterprise. He is Vice President of the curriculum division of the American Educational Research Association, and a member of the executive committee of the UIC Faculty Senate.

Paris Banks is a student at Prologue High School, an alternative Chicago Public School, on the west side the city. He grew up in the Cabrini Green

Listening to and Learning from Students, pages 205–210
Copyright © 2011 by Information Age Publishing
205

neighborhood and now lives on Chicago's South Side with his mom, dad, and six sisters. He recently recorded a CD with his rap group, *Cash Out Boys*. Paris is really interested in reading because he likes to challenge and push himself to learn new things. He hopes to someday get a record deal, but also has a backup plan to become a social worker because he likes working with people.

Tara M. Brown is Assistant Professor of Education at Brandeis University. She holds a doctorate in education from Harvard University and is the recipient of a Spencer Research Fellowship and a Jacobs Foundation Dissertation Fellowship. Tara is a former classroom teacher, having worked in alternative education, particularly around technological literacy. Tara's current research focuses on the sociopolitical contexts of schooling, educational equity, secondary education, dropout and disciplinary exclusion, and qualitative and participatory action research (PAR) methodologies. Her most recent research is a two-year PAR project focusing on the experiences of students excluded from mainstream educational environments.

Jake Burdick is a doctoral student in the Curriculum and Instruction program at Arizona State University, where his research focuses largely on public sites of pedagogy and curriculum. Jake has published in *The Mississippi Review* (creative non-fiction), *Qualitative Inquiry*, and the edited book *Democratizing Educational Experience: Envisioning Embodying, Enacting*. Jake is also a co-editor of the collections, the *Handbook of Public Pedagogy* and *Complicated Conversations and Confirmed Commitments: Revitalizing Education For Democracy*.

A 2003 graduate of Berkeley High/CAS, **Rafael Casal** is a writer, poet, recording artist, and educator. He is a two-time poetry slam finalist champion for Brave New Voices, has worked for Youth Speaks, and was featured numerous times on HBO's *Russell Simmons Presents Def Poetry*. He toured with his solo spoken word performance and his band The Getback Crew and co-wrote *The One Drop Rule*, a Hip Hop theater piece, with Jason Samuel Smith. He has taught in the public schools and is Creative Director for First Wave, a Hip Hop theatre-based performing arts program at the University of Wisconsin.

Charles E. Cobb, Jr. is a journalist and former member of *National Geographic Magazine*'s editorial staff. He is Senior Writer and Diplomatic Correspondent for AllAfrica.com, the leading online provider of news from and about Africa. He is also Visiting Professor of Africana Studies at Brown University. From 1962-1967 he served as a field secretary for the Student Nonviolent Coordinating Committee (SNCC) in Mississippi and was one of the conceptualizers of the 1964 Freedom Schools. He wrote *On the Freedom*

Road: A Guided Tour of Civil Rights Trails, and is co-author, with Robert P. Moses, of *Radical Equations: Civil Rights from Mississippi to the Algebra Project.*

Kevin Coval is the author of *everyday people* and *slingshots (a hip-hop poetica),* named Book of the Year finalist by The American Library Association. Coval writes for *The Huffington Post,* can be heard regularly on National Public Radio in Chicago, and has performed on four seasons of HBO's *Russell Simmons Presents Def Poetry.* Co-Founder of Louder Than A Bomb: The Chicago Teen Poetry Festival, the largest youth poetry festival in the world, Coval teaches at The School of the Art Institute in Chicago.

Cathy Coulter is Associate Professor at University of Alaska Anchorage. Her research interests include the experiences of English learners in public schools and narrative as a research methodology. Publications include a book, *Teaching English Learners and Immigrant Students in Secondary Schools* (co-authored with Dr. Christian Faltis), and articles in *Educational Researcher, Curriculum Inquiry,* and *Bilingual Research Journal.*

John Dewey (1859–1952) was an American philosopher, psychologist, and educational theorist. He wrote extensively about schools as spaces for developing democratic communities. His ideas about education, most notably that of progressive educational ideals, have had a profound effect on schooling in the United States and throughout the world. Dewey also wrote about experience, the arts, and nature and is considered a founder of the philosophical school called American Pragmatism.

Shira Eve Epstein is Assistant Professor in the School of Education at The City College of New York (CUNY). Her research agenda focuses on citizenship education and what happens when students and teachers work together to advocate for social change during the traditional school day.

Genell Ferrell is Assistant Professor at Birmingham Southern College. She has instructed on and researched numerous topics including most disciplines in education, special education, civic education, fine arts, and educational leadership.

Paulo Freire (1921–1997) was a Brazilian educator. His work has significantly influenced forms of progressive education, social justice educational work, and critical pedagogy in the United States and throughout the world. His book, *Pedagogy of the Oppressed,* is widely praised for its influence on emancipatory and liberatory practices in education and schooling.

Kevin Galeas is a researcher in the Action Research into School Exclusion (ARISE) project. He worked in the field for two years, conducting research and implementing professional-development workshops for teachers as the action component of the study. He graduated from high school in June 2008, valedictorian of his class. Kevin is also a poet and visual artist. He is now attending community college and plans to transfer to a college for arts and, eventually, work in the field of graphic design.

As a tenth grade student at Brooklyn Community Media and Arts (BCAM), **Miracle Graham** wrote the poem in this collection for a short video project during the "Break/s Beyond the Ballot" workshop series in partnership between BCAM, MAPP International, Hip-Hop Theater Festival, and Urban Word NYC.

L. Thomas Hopkins (1889-1982) was a progressive education theorist, professor, and a curriculum consultant. His work focused extensively on ideas of curriculum integration—most notably about how the organizing center for curriculum should be the individual or the student and not the subject matter. After a career at the University of Colorado, Boulder, he became professor of education and director of the laboratory school at Teachers College, Columbia University.

As a seventh grade student at PS 120 Queens, **Thomas Lloyd** wrote the poem included in this collection during a ten-week Virtual Poetry Slam in-class workshop facilitated by Poetry Mentor, kahlil almustafa, and classroom teacher, Vicky Antzoulis, in partnership between Queens Writes and Urban Word NYC.

Caroline Pratt (1867–1954) was an American progressive educator. She was frustrated by the way that "traditional" curricula was used with young children. In an effort to challenge what she deemed to be too rigid, Pratt founded the City and Country School in New York City in 1914 as an environment to put her ideas into practice with children. Her book, *I Learn From Children*, highlights her ideas in action.

Jennifer Ponder is Assistant Professor in the Department of Elementary and Bilingual Education at California State University, Fullerton. Her research interests focus on democratic and civic education, mentoring programs for beginning teachers, and infusing the arts into the curriculum.

Louie F. Rodríguez is Assistant Professor of Education at University of California, San Bernardino. Louie has published on educational-equity issues including school dropout, student engagement, creative pedagogy, educational policy, Latina/o education, and teacher development. Louie is also the co-author of *Small School and Urban Youth: Using the Power of School Culture to Engage Students* (Corwin Press, 2008). Louie is currently engaging in solution-oriented research initiatives. Louie earned a master's and doctorate from the Harvard Graduate School of Education.

William H. Schubert is Professor of Education and University Scholar at the University of Illinois at Chicago, where he coordinates the Ph.D. Program in Curriculum Studies and has been recognized with several awards for teaching, mentorship, and scholarship. A former elementary teacher and frequent lecturer, he has published 16 books and over 150 articles and chapters. Schubert is former president of the John Dewey Society, the Society of Professors of Education, and The Society for the Study of Curriculum History, and he is recipient of the 2004 American Educational Research Association Lifetime Achievement Award in Curriculum Studies. His most recent book is *Love, Justice, and Education: John Dewey and the Utopians.*

Brian D. Schultz is Associate Professor and Honors Faculty in the Department of Educational Inquiry & Curriculum Studies at Northeastern Illinois University in Chicago. His research focuses on students and teachers theorizing together, developing integrated curricula based on students' priority concerns, curricula as social action, and public pedagogy. His book, *Spectacular Things Happen Along the Way: Lessons from an Urban Classroom* (Teachers College Press, 2008) received the 2008 American Educational Studies Critics Choice Award and the 2009 American Educational Research Association Outstanding Book Award in Curriculum Studies. He also co-edited *Handbook of Public Pedagogy: Education and Learning Beyond Schooling* (Routledge, 2009) and *Curriculum and Pedagogy for a Just Society: Advocacy, Artistry, and Activism* (EIP, 2007). He is currently working on another co-edited collection, *Grow Your Own Teachers: Grassroots Change for Teacher Education* (Teachers College Press, forthcoming).

Ralph W. Tyler (1902-1994) was an American educator whose scholarly work focused on curriculum assessment and evaluation. He was the director of evaluation for the Eight Year Study while working at both The Ohio State University and University of Chicago. His book, *Basic Principles of Curriculum and Instruction* (1949), argued for a structural organization of curriculum and instruction in terms objectives, experiences, organization, and evaluation. His ideas in the book—commonly referred to as the Tyler Rationale—continue to influence how schools design, organize, deliver, and evaluate curricula even though the ideas are oftentimes misinterpreted or overly simplified.

Michelle Vander Veldt is Assistant Professor in the Department of Elementary and Bilingual Education at California State University, Fullerton. Her research interests focus on examining epistemological and ontological beliefs, exploring civics education through active-citizenship projects, and investigating effective mathematics instruction.

Voices of Youth in Chicago Education (VOYCE) is a youth organizing collaborative led by students of color from seven community organizations and 12 high schools throughout the city of Chicago. Through youth-led research and grassroots organizing, VOYCE works to create lasting, youth-led solutions to the high dropout rates and low college enrollment rates of Chicago Public Schools (CPS) students. To find out more information visit: http://www.voyceproject.org

Susan Wilcox is former Co-Executive Director of The Brotherhood/Sister Sol and currently facilitates Program and Professional Development. She launched and coordinates *Liberating Voices/Liberating Minds,* the organization's publications and professional-development initiative that since 2006 has trained hundreds of school and community-based educators around the country. Over the past 20 years Susan has done educational consulting with varied clients (program and curriculum development, research); coordinated education and development programs in Africa, Europe, Latin America and the Caribbean; and taught at Teachers College and The New School. Her work has appeared in journals and books including, *Teach Freedom: Education for Liberation in the African American Tradition* (Teachers College Press, 2008).